THE PENGUIN CLASSICS

FOUNDER EDITOR (1944-64): E.V. RIEU

PRESENT EDITORS:
BETTY RADICE AND ROBERT BALDICK

L 202

THE DISCOVERY AND CONQUEST OF PERU

A Translation of Books I to IV of Agustín de Zárate's *History* of these events, supplemented by eye-witness accounts of certain incidents by Francisco de Jerez, Miguel Estete, Juan Ruiz de Arce, Hernando Pizarre, Diege de Trujillo, and Alonso de Guzman, who took part in the conquest, and by Pedro Cieza de León, Garcilaso de la Vega 'the Inca', and José de Acesta, later historians who had first hand sources of information.

TRANSLATED WITH AN INTRODUCTION BY

J. M. COHEN

PENGUIN BOOKS

BALTIMORE · MARYLAND

Penguin Books Ltd, Harmondsworth, Middlesex, England
Penguin Books Inc., 3300 Clipper Mill Road, Baltimore Md 21211, U.S.A.
Penguin Books Australia Ltd, Ringwood, Victoria, Australia

—

This translation first published 1968

—

—

Made and printed in Great Britain
by Richard Clay (The Chaucer Press), Ltd,
Bungay, Suffolk
Set in Linotype Pilgrim

Contents

TO PAT AND TED PEACOCK

Introduction

ON completing my translation of Bernal Díaz, *The Conquest of New Spain*, I was inevitably faced with the problem of providing a similar account of the conquest of Peru. The immediate difficulty was that there is no full history written by an eyewitness and participator. Bernal Díaz was an exceptional man. In youth a soldier and adventurer, he turned historian in his extreme old age, and, with a memory that seldom failed him, described dramatically and at length the stirring events in which he had taken part almost fifty years before. But none of Francisco Pizarro's companions on the march to Cajamarca was more than barely literate. The best historian of the conquest and discovery of Peru, Agustín de Zárate, did not reach the country until 1544, eleven years after the destruction of the Inca empire. Remaining there as royal accountant during the turmoils of the civil war, he performed only one major public mission, the embassy to Gonzalo Pizarro's camp which he describes. For the rest he collected information from participants in the conquest, but was prevented by Gonzalo's violent second-in-command Francisco de Carvajal from beginning to write while still in the country. He composed his history only after his return to Europe.

Though Zárate drew first-hand information from Francisco Pizarro's comrades, of whom he mentions one, Rodrigo Lozano, then a settler in Trujillo, his account of the first landings and the march across the mountains to Cajamarca (1532), which ended in the seizure and execution – one might more justly say murder – of Atahuallpa, is brief; and he says very little about Hernando Pizarro's equally heroic march back across the mountains to the religious site of Pachacamac. Many of the most exciting events unaccountably failed to stir him. They were already eclipsed by the even more bloody dissensions among the conquerors themselves.

Fortunately there exist a number of briefer accounts of incidents from the conquest written by participants far less literate than Zárate, who tell their story clumsily perhaps, yet in arrestingly graphic detail. My problem was to construct a consecutive narrative of which Zárate's history would provide the skeleton, but to which – at any rate for those early years – these lesser chroniclers would add flesh. I have consequently interpolated much first-hand material, especially in Zárate's second book, which is by any reckoning unduly condensed. My principal source has been the 'true account' (*verdadera relación*), allegedly prepared for His Majesty the Emperor Charles V by Francisco de Jerez, a soldier who took part in the original march from the coast and describes himself as Francisco Pizarro's secretary. Francisco de Jerez set out for the Indies in 1519 at the age of 15, and presumably first joined Francisco Pizarro on the expedition of 1532–3, which began and completed the conquest. He gives a circumstantial picture of the landing at Tumbez and the march from the coast, is a little less satisfactory for the actual events at Cajamarca and Atahuallpa's imprisonment, and includes a description of Hernando Pizarro's march to Pachacamac in which he did not take part, written by a comrade Miguel Astete who did.

Two other contemporary witnesses fill out the story. The first is Juan Ruiz de Arce, who left for the Indies in his early twenties and followed after Pizarro in 1531, to join him when the Spaniards' fortunes were at their lowest, at the moment when they were suffering hunger and disease in the alligator-infested mango-swamps of what is now the coast of Ecuador. In his 'admonitions to his heirs' (*advertencias a sus sucesores*) he tells a tale which begins with hardships but ends, so far as his Peruvian adventures are concerned, in great prosperity. Juan Ruiz did not remain and settle, but took back to Spain his share in the two great divisions of the Inca spoils, made at Cajamarca and Cuzco. He returned to court a rich gentleman, and bought honours by contributing money to Charles V's African wars. He wrote his 'admonitions' in 1543, ten years after the events he described.

A third eye-witness, Diego de Trujillo, remained in his native town until the age of twenty-five. When its former citizen Francisco Pizarro came armed with his patent to recruit soldiers for his third and conquering expedition, Diego joined him. He shared the hardships and glories of the crossing of the Andes, accompanied Hernando Pizarro on his visit to Atahuallpa's camp on the day before the massacre, saw the Inca during his imprisonment, and took part in Hernando's march to Pachacamas, which is more fully described by Miguel Estete, who was the royal inspector. He returned to Spain in 1536 with his infantryman's share of Atahuallpa's treasure. Here he remained ten years, returning to Peru in 1546, when his old comrade Gonzalo Pizarro had defeated the viceroy Blasco Nuñez Vela and was master of the country. He did not commit himself too deeply to Gonzalo, however, and was able to change sides at the battle of Xaquixaguana, at which Gonzalo was defeated by the astute Pedro de la Gasca. Diego was again fortunate in not totally committing himself to another and later rebellion, that of his fellow Estremaduran, Francisco Hernández Girón, who almost succeeded in capturing the country in 1553–4. A conquistador of the old school, Diego no doubt resented the take-over by lawyers and officials of the rich empire conquered by penniless soldiers like himself. But with most of his fellows, he was loath to take up arms against his king. He wrote his brief 'relación' in 1571, the record of an obscure soldier who had made his fortune. In it he makes no reference to events after the conquest.

I have drawn brief excerpts from the chronicles of other soldiers, and have in addition quoted at some length from two later historians, who had access to the same authorities as Zárate, but whose interests differed from his. Of these Garcilaso de la Vega, 'the Inca', is the more picturesque. He has moreover a thesis: that the Incas far from being savages had a glorious history, and that their religion was only inferior to Christianity in its lack of an actual revelation. Garcilaso tends to exaggerate the scale of the drama, and also the number engaged and killed in any battle. He is a romantic historian, yet a careful citer of his sources. Though one of the prime inventors of the legend of the noble savage, he used his facts with care. Illegitimate son, by an Inca princess, of the conquistador Garcilaso de la Vega, whose name several times occurs in Zárate's *History*, Garcilaso was born at Cuzco in 1539, and brought up with Gonzalo Pizarro's son. Times changed however, and he and a comrade took a day off their lessons to witness the execution of Gonzalo and his lieutenant Carvajal. The boys picked up Carvajal's head after the beheading. Thanks to his father's capacity for adapting himself to new circumstances, Garcilaso received a good education in the Classics, history and Christian doctrine. Speaking the Quechua language as well as Spanish, he became familiar with the traditions of his mother's people also. He questioned survivors of the princely and priestly caste about the history of the Incas, and attended the illegal ceremonies of the old religion. On his father's death, however, which was quickly followed by his mother's, he found himself dispossessed in favour of his legitimate brothers and sisters. His mother's estate was confiscated. He then departed for Seville at the age of twenty-one to bury his father on Spanish soil and to seek redress for his own fortunes. He was unsuccessful. His father's friendship with the dead Gonzalo was held against him. So he took service in the royal armies, fighting under Don John of Austria. In 1587 he left the army, and two years later, at the age of fifty, settled in Córdoba, poor, lonely and disillusioned. For the rest of his life he wrote: first a translation of Leone Ebreo, then an account of the Spanish conquest of Florida, and finally the *Royal Commentaries* (*Comentarios reales*) of Peru (published in 1608). In these he recalled all that he knew of his ancestors' history, gathered from those long-ago conversations with his mother's relatives, of which he seems to have preserved notes. He had also read all the histories and chronicles of the conquest, including those written in Spain by official historiographers who had not crossed the ocean. Garcilaso's *Commentaries* were for a long time the best-known book about Peru. He told the whole story from the legendary beginnings of the Incas to the early years of the seventeenth century.

Pedro Cieza de León, though less biased in favour of the Peruvians than Garcilaso, gives a far more favourable account of them than the conquistadors or even Zárate. He appears to have come to the Indies, perhaps from Seville, in 1531 at the age of thirteen. He served as a soldier in Gasca's army against Gonzalo Pizarro, and in 1550 completed the first part of his *Chronicle of Peru* (*Crónica del Peru*), a topographical survey of the country distinguished by a broad interest in its history, archaeology, customs, crops, peoples and communications. I have allowed Cieza de Léon to put in the background with which the other historians are sparing. The second part of his book – mistakenly supposed in the nineteenth century, and by Prescott in particular, to be by Juan de Sarmiento – is devoted to the reigns of the last three Incas before the conquest and to the conquest itself. Though he holds the naïve belief that the Incas' religion was of Satanic inspiration, Cieza de León is at the same time critical of Spanish cruelty and the destruction of the old civilization. Garcilaso and Cieza try to reconstruct a past which was being only too rapidly forgotten, and both dwell on circumstances and details that failed to interest Zárate.

Agustín de Zárate, himself a treasury official seconded to Los Reyes (Lima) to make an overdue audit of the royal accounts, had the mind and something of the manner of the traditional historian. His introduction shows his familiarity with the Classical writers; and such splendid set-pieces as his accounts of the murder of Francisco Pizarro, the battle of Chupas, the mounting folly of Gonzalo Pizarro and the battle of Xaquixaguaya show his power of writing in their manner. Prescott, on one occasion in *The Conquest of Peru,* describes him as Thucydidian. Less romantic than Garcilaso and more dramatic than Cieza, he writes from the point of view of the second Peruvian generation, the officials who had come to clear up the anarchic disorders of the conquistadors. As for the Peruvians themselves, they were in his eyes not a people of ancient civilization but a serf population to be protected against undue spoliation by the *encomendervs* (estate-owners), and to provide generous tribute for the royal exchequer. His account of their ancient religion – cut by his nineteenth century editors – reduces their beliefs to crude superstition and stresses their unpleasant practice of ritual sodomy. Being no soldier, he makes too little of the passage of the Andes to Cajamarca, and is too blunt to explore in depth the mixture of motive – greed, fear, primitive religious fervour, and sheer duplicity – that led to the killing of Atahuallpa. He fails to note that many of the Spaniards themselves opposed Francisco Pizarro's ruthlessness. When he comes to describe Francisco Pizarro as a pioneer governor, however, in his last days at Los Reyes, Zárate draws a detailed and pleasing picture. He also presents the mingled rashness, obstinacy and primitive nobility of Gonzalo in a pleasing light. Zárate understands character, in the Plutarchian sense, and, though he came out as a follower of the unhappy viceroy Blasco Nuñez, does not show undue bias. On his recall from Peru, he was made superintendent of the royal finances in Flanders.

The drama of the conquest of Peru can best be understood in the light of knowledge gained by archaeologists in the last hundred years, which was largely hidden even from such patient inquirers as Garcilaso and Cieza. The Incas were, as these historians noted, themselves military conquerors, whose empire was not more than a hundred years old. They came from the uplands of Bolivia. Skilled in military organization, road-making and building in heavy masonry, they conquered groups of coastal peoples of higher culture than themselves. As weavers, metal-smiths and potters, the coastal peoples had enjoyed a series of cultures that went back to the ninth century B.C. The site of Pachacamac, for instance, with its step pyramid temple, was a religious centre long before the Inca conquest.

The Spaniards conquered a country racked by civil war and incapable of local resistance. By removing indigenous populations and substituting colonists or *mitimaes* from other places, the Incas built an empire that was bound to collapse on the removal of the central authority. Resistance to the Spaniards ultimately centred on Quito, which lay outside the borders of the Inca empire and on the Andean fastnesses in which groups of guerillas could take refuge. The capture of Atahuallpa, a deed modelled on Cortés' capture of Montezuma, twenty years earlier, was not premeditated for its political results. The Spaniards knew nothing of Inca organization; they thought of their enemy as like the Moors and even referred to Peruvian temples as 'mosques'. So little did they know of the Incas indeed that Francisco de Jerez was not alone in referring to Atahuallpa's brother Huascar and their father Huayna Capac as 'old and young Cuzco', confusing the city and the royal title. The march on Cajamarca was an undertaking of desperadoes eager for gold and emeralds. Only by chance did it prove an exploit of supreme political daring, which destroyed the Peruvian empire at a blow, since after the death of the emperor, no legitimate centre of resistance remained.

The unctuous piety of the clergy who accompanied the conquistadors must fill a modern reader – religious or otherwise – with horror. Fray Vicente de Valverde was probably more responsible for the massacre at Cajamarca than Pizarro himself. Nowhere was the cross so flagrantly used as a weapon of offence. Nowhere was charity so hideously divorced from faith.

As for the conquistadors themselves, Zárate affords us a close-up of Francisco and Gonzalo Pizarro, and a sufficient portrait of the more humane Hernando, who was so quickly removed to Spain, where, in prison, and involved in lengthy litigation, he more than atoned for his brothers' and partners' misdeeds. The comparatively humane Alonso de Alvarado and Hernando de Soto are more peripheral to the picture. The conquistador was a ruthless fighter and exploiter because his background was one of humiliating poverty. The frontier wars against the Moors had bred a race of gentlemen proud of their Christian blood but without a penny. Their one resource was to go to the wars. They were as remorseless with one another as with the Indians, and recklessly brave because they had literally only their lives to lose. The lawyers and civil servants who followed them to Peru recognized them for what they were: illiterate adventurers whose word was not to be trusted. The frequency with which they moved from one side to the other in the civil war shows their unprincipled devotion to their own interests. Many were butchered only because they were too stubborn or too slow to desert a losing cause in time. Their cruelty to one another, as to the Indians, was dictated by the law of the frontier, though on the Moorish frontiers with Castile gentlemen on both sides were spared for their ransom. But in Peru the goods and servants of the conquered fell automatically to the conqueror. To be defeated was to forfeit everything. Men hanged their former comrades, or their present friends if they suspected them, with complete indifference, and sometimes, as in the case of the priest who was hanged with an ink-bottle at his chest, they did not spare the cloth either. Some remained at the end of the story in possession of riches and estates. Their descendants still rule and own Peru. Far more died like Francisco and Gonzalo Pizarro without the money to cover their burial or support their bastards.

The book contains a translation of the first four books of Agustín Zárate's *Historia del descubrimiento y conquista del Peru,* which carries the story past the murder of Francisco Pizarro to the suppression of the Chile faction, who were responsible for it, at the battle of Chupas (1542). But the end was not yet. Vaca de Castro's pacification of the country was ineffective, and I have added the more dramatic parts of Zárate's last three books which give the history of the civil wars, cutting liberally and filling the gaps with my own brief account of the events omitted. For any history that stops short of Gonzalo's final defiance of President Gasca and his new men would end falsely. Not till the battle of Xaquixaguana (1548) was the spirit of the old conquistadors broken. Gonzalo went down like Macbeth, fighting for what he knew was irremediably lost. Peru then entered the colonial phase.

For my texts I have used with discretion the editions of Zárate, Francisco de Jerez, Garcilaso de la Vega and Cieza de León printed in the Rivadeneyra *Biblioteca de autores españoles.* For the first two, I have gone back on many occasions to the Barcia volumes of 1740, which have enabled me to replace cuts made out of prudishness or carelessness by the nineteenth century editor. For Juan Ruiz de Arce and Diego de Trujillo, I have used the Conde de Canilleros, *Tres Testigos de la conquista del Peru* (Espasa Calpe 1953), which reprints their brief chronicles together with Hernando Pizarro's letter to the judges of the Audiencia of Santo Domingo, written on his homeward journey to Spain in 1533. Other extracts come from MS notes quoted by W. H. Prescott in Spanish, in his justly famous *Conquest of Peru,* and in the case of Alonso de Guzmán only from the English translation of his Adventures, published by the Hakluyt Society in the mid nineteenth century.

Knappswood
July 1966

HISTORY OF THE DISCOVERY AND CONQUEST OF THE PROVINCE OF PERU

AND OF THE WARS AND OTHER EVENTS
WHICH TOOK PLACE THERE
UP TO THE DEFEAT OF GONZALO PIZARRO
AND HIS FOLLOWERS
WHO REBELLED AGAINST HIS MAJESTY

By Agustín de Zárate
AUDITOR OF ACCOUNTS
TO HIS IMPERIAL MAJESTY

To His Majesty the King of England,* our Lord and Prince, Don Philip II, Royal and Christian Majesty: In my capacity as secretary of the Royal Council of Castile, a post which I have occupied for fifteen years, I was commanded by His Majesty and Our Lord the King and Emperor and his Council of the Indies, at the end of the year 1543, to go to the provinces of Peru and Tierra Firme in order to examine the accounts of the officers of the Royal Treasury and bring back the proceeds of their stewardship. I therefore embarked in the fleet provided for me by the viceroy of Peru, Blasco Nuñez Vela, and on my arrival witnessed certain disturbances and dramatic events that seemed to me to demand record. When after my landing, however, I put these events on paper, I recognized that they would not be understood without the explanation of some previous matters. Such is the genesis of this book.

I went back, step by step till I came to the discovery of the country. For these events are so interdependent that if one is omitted the rest remain obscure. So I was compelled to begin, as they say, *ab ovo*. I could not compose an orderly account – and a perfect history must be ordered – while still in the country, for merely to begin writing would have put me in danger of my life. A lieutenant† of Gonzalo Pizarro threatened to murder anyone who recorded his master's deeds. For he realized that they deserved to be consigned to the law of oblivion (which the Athenians called *amnistia*), rather than be remembered and perpetuated. I had therefore to give up writing, and bring back such journals and notes as I had collected, in order to finish the book here. The account I have written is not so complete and detailed as to deserve the name of a history, or so brief and summary as merely to be a commentary.

* Philip claimed this title by right of his marriage to Mary Tudor in 1554, but was not acknowledged by the English. He did not become king of Spain until 1556, the year of the book's publication.

† Francisco de Carvajel.

Its division into books and chapters distinguishes it from the latter form. I should not have been bold enough to undertake either, had I not relied on that saying of Tully's which is repeated by G. Pliny, that though poetry and oratory have no virtue if they lack great eloquence, history is pleasant and entertaining, however written. For by histories men hear of unknown events, which are naturally interesting to them. Indeed they often enjoy hearing them described even by a peasant in his coarse and ill-ordered language. So, although the style of this writing is not as eloquent as it should be, it will serve to make known the truth of these matters. Anyone is welcome to use it as a basis for writing another more orderly history in better language; as has often been done not only by Greek and Roman historians but also in our own times. As for truth, which is the essence of history, I have endeavoured to put myself beyond reproach, by writing down the natural and historical events as I saw them, omitting and concealing nothing, and taking accounts of happenings at which I was not present from credible and unprejudiced persons – who are extremely difficult to find in that province. Almost everyone is attached either to the Almagro or the Pizarro party, as men were in Rome either to Pompey or Caesar and, a little before that, to Sulla or Marius. For there are few living or dead among the settlers in Peru who have not received either favours or disfavours from the two leaders or from their lieutenants. If anyone gives a different account of these affairs, it will differ under the last of the three heads under which history is habitually classified: that of cause and motive, about which authors habitually differ. Under the other two heads of deeds and events, I have done everything possible to avoid error.

On finishing this story I abandoned the opinion with which I had started, that historians are much to blame if they do not publish their works once they are completed. I used to believe that they wait for time to cover up their defects by removing the witnesses of events that they describe. But now I understand their real motives: they wait for the persons they have written of to die, and their family and descendants as well, since in telling a contemporary story there is risk of giving grave offence but no hope of gaining favour. A man whose actions have been reprehensible will always complain, however lightly they are mentioned, that the author has dwelt too long on his misdeeds and too cursorily on the excuses for them. On the other hand, anyone whose deeds are praiseworthy will always accuse the historian of being too brief. However full an account he may give of them, the doer will blame him for not describing them in even more copious detail. He would like a whole volume to be filled with his praises alone. So the historian is always reproached; those whom he blames find him too long, those whom he praises too short. He would be well advised therefore to keep his works not only for the nine years that Horace counsels for works of other kinds, but even for ninety, so that the descendants of the guilty may credibly deny their ancestry and the grandsons of the virtuous be content with whatever praise they receive. Risk of rebukes made me afraid to publish this book until Your Majesty did me the grace and favour of reading it during your happy voyage from Corunna to England, and of accepting the dedication, and ordering me to print and publish it. This I have done on reaching this city of Antwerp, making use of such leisure as I have had from the business of Your Majesty's treasury, which is my principal concern. I beg your Majesty to accept my labours in your service and this book also, which is yours, as is its author. This signal favour from Your Majesty will protect me from the slanders which works of this kind seldom escape. May Our Lord preserve your Royal Person, adding more kingdoms and dominions to your realms, as your servants desire.

Antwerp, 30 March 1555

ON THE DIFFICULTY OF UNDERSTANDING HOW THE ORIGINAL POPULATION OF PERU REACHED THE COUNTRY

THE general doubt concerning the way in which the inhabitants of Peru reached this province in ancient times can seemingly be resolved by a story told somewhat briefly by the divine Plato in his book entitled the *Timaeus* or *De natura*, and afterwards at greater length in another book or dialogue which immediately follows the *Timaeus* and is called *Atlanticus*. Here he recounts a story told by the Egyptians in praise of the Athenians, to the effect that in the past they had been so powerful as to conquer and destroy certain kings who came over the sea with large armies from a great island called Atlantis, which began at the Pillars of Hercules and was said to be more extensive than the whole of Asia and Africa. This island contained three kingdoms which Neptune divided among his three sons, the largest and finest going to his eldest, who was called Atlas.

Plato tells many most remarkable details about the customs and riches of this island, in particular about a temple standing in the principal city, the walls of which were covered with plates of gold, silver and brass. He says much else which it would be tedious to repeat, but which can be read at full length in his original works. Many of the customs and ceremonies which he there describes can be seen preserved to this day in the province of Peru. From Atlantis, men sailed to other great islands on its further side and near the continent beyond which lay the true sea. Plato's actual words, spoken by Socrates to the Athenians at the beginning of the *Timaeus*, are these: 'It is considered certain that in times past your city checked a large hostile army which had come from the Atlantic sea and seized and occupied almost the whole of Europe and Asia. For in those days that strait was navigable,* having at its mouth

* Presumably the Straits of Gibraltar. No modern critic would accept Zárate's interpretation.

and almost at its entrance an island which began close to the Pillars of Hercules and was said to have been larger than Africa and Asia combined. From here there was trade and passage to other islands, and from those islands communication with the continental mainland which faced them and was near to the true sea. For that sea can justly be called the true sea, and that land 'the continental mainland'.*

So far Plato, although he says a little later that nine thousand years before he wrote the power of the waters so increased in those seas that in a day and a night the island was submerged, drowning the lands and population, and leaving the sea so full of mud-banks and shallows, that it was never navigable again. No one could then travel to the other islands or to the mainland.

All commentators on Plato accept this history as true. The majority, Marsiglio Ficino and Plantin in particular, deny that it is an allegory, though some give it an allegorical sense, as Marsiglio himself mentions in his *Notes on the Timaeus*. Plato's computation of nine thousand years† is no argument that it is a fable; for according to Eudoxus these were not solar but lunar years, reckoned by the Egyptian calendar. The time was therefore nine thousand months or seven hundred and fifty years. Moreover it is almost a proof of this island's existence that all historians and cosmographers, ancient and modern, call the sea which submerged it the Atlantic, thus retaining its name from the time when it was land. Accepting this history as true, no one will deny that the island of Atlantis began from the straits of Gibraltar or a little beyond Cadiz, and extended across that great expanse which from north to south and from east to west is larger than Africa and Asia combined. The islands mentioned by Plato as visited by traders are surely Hispaniola, Puerto Rico, Cuba, Jamaica and others in that region; and the mainland facing them is what we know today

* Cf. The more exact translation by H. D. P. Lee (Penguin Books, 1965), p. 37. Zárate and those who share his opinion twist Plato a little to suit their geographical convenience.

† Which would have been longer than the existence of the world by accepted Biblical chronology.

as the Tierra Firme* and all its provinces, starting from the Magellan straits and running north to the land of Peru, the province of Popayan, Castilla de Oro, Veragua, Nicaragua, Guatemala, New Spain, the Seven Cities, Florida and the Cod islands, and running up from there to join Norway. Beyond all doubt, there is more land here than in all the populated earth known to us before its discovery. And it is not difficult to understand why it was not discovered before now by the Romans or other nations which at various times occupied Spain. For we must suppose that the seas remained so rough as to prevent navigation.

I believe it was Plato's authority that led to the discovery of these lands, and that they can certainly be identified with the mainland of which he speaks. For they show all the signs that he attributes to his continent, particularly that of being close to the true sea, which is what we now properly call the Southern Sea.† For so far as we have sailed it at present, the whole Mediterranean and so much as we know of the ocean vulgarly called the Northern Sea‡ are by comparison rivers.

Now if Plato's story is true – and all the evidences confirm him – I can see no difficulty in assuming that many peoples crossed by this route, both from the great island of Atlantis and from the other islands which were approached from it. They could have come to Peru either overland across the continent or, if this were too difficult, across the Southern Sea. For it is to be presumed that they had use and knowledge of navigation, learnt from their commerce with the great island where, according to Plato, there were many ships, and ports constructed to protect them where natural harbours were lacking.

So much can be gathered from the evidence; which is no small amount for so ancient and obscure a matter. This is especially remarkable because in Peru there is no writing to preserve memory of past events, nor even painting, which served for writing in New Spain. All the Peruvians had were knotted cords of different colours, with which they kept their accounts, recording them, though very inexactly, by means of

* The northern coast of South America, the 'Spanish Main' of the Elizabethans.

† The Pacific. ‡ The Atlantic.

the knots and the distance between them, as I shall explain at greater length in this history.

Therefore I will say with Horace

> Si quid novisti rectius istis,
> Candidus imperti, si non vis utere, mecum.*

And, regarding the discovery of this new land, I will quote some lines of Seneca in his tragedy *Medea* that seem prophetically apposite:

> Venient annis saecula seris
> Quibus Oceanus vincula rerum
> Laxet, novosque typhis detegat orbes,
> Atque ingens pateat tellus
> Nec sit terris ultima Thule.†

AUTHOR'S NOTE: *My chief information about the discovery of the country comes from Rodrigo Lozano of Trujillo in Peru and other eye-witnesses of events.*

* Should you have learnt anything more accurate about this, impart it to me if to no other.

† The age will come, in the ripeness of time, when Ocean will loosen the chain of things and bare new worlds to the storms. Then a huge country will be revealed and Thule will no longer be the last land.

BOOK ONE

THE LAND OF PERU

1. *The first news of Peru and how the discovery began*

IN the year of Our Lord 1525, three citizens of Panama, a port on the Southern Sea in the province of Tierra Firme called Castilla del Oro – Don Francisco Pizarro, a native of Trujillo, Don Diego Almagro of the city of Malagon (whose lineage could never be established, for it was said that he was abandoned at the church door) and a priest called Hernando de Luque – put all their capital together in order to increase it and serve His Majesty the Emperor Charles by exploring the eastern coast of the Southern Sea towards the lands which were afterwards known as Peru. These three were the wealthiest men in that province.

Having obtained a licence from Pedro Arias de Avila, then His Majesty's governor in Tierra Firme, Francisco Pizarro with some difficulty equipped a ship and sailed in it with a hundred and fourteen men. He discovered a small and poor province fifty leagues from Panama, which was called Peru; and this is why the whole land discovered along this coast for more than twelve thousand leagues was wrongly called by that name also. Passing on, he found another land which the Spaniards called Pueblo Quemado (the burnt town), where the Indians continually attacked him and killed so many of his people that he was forced to return, badly wounded, to the land of Chinchama, which is near Panama.

Meanwhile Don Diego de Almagro, who had remained behind, prepared another ship on which he embarked with seventy men to search for Don Francisco Pizarro. He sailed along the coast as far as a river, a hundred leagues from Panama, which he named the San Juan. Not finding Pizarro, he turned back and continued his search. Finally, he found traces of his partner's sojourn at Pueblo Quemado, where he landed. Having beaten Pizarro and driven him back to sea, the Indians defended themselves courageously against Almagro also, and did him much damage. The Spaniards took refuge in a fort, but one day, owing to the carelessness of the guards, the Indians broke in and routed them. Don Diego lost an eye and his men were so hard pressed that they were forced to put to sea. So they returned along the coast as far as Chinchama, where they found Don Francisco.

After this meeting, the two captains joined forces and sent for more men. Having built up an army of almost two hundred Spaniards, they sailed down the coast again with two ships and three newly made canoes. They suffered great hardships on this voyage, for the whole coast is thick with swamps, which lie at the mouths of the many rivers that enter the sea there. These are infested with many large lizards, called by the natives *caimanes* or alligators, which breed at the river-mouths and are commonly twenty or twenty-five feet long. If they scent a man or beast – especially a dog – in the water, they bite him and drag him to the bottom, where they eat him. They come out on the banks to lay their eggs, burying them in large numbers and hatching them on dry land. The young move rather clumsily down the beach and are then led to the water. In this and in other respects these beasts seem very like the crocodiles of the Nile.

The Spaniards also suffered greatly from hunger, for they found no food except the fruit of some trees called mangroves, of which there are great quantities on this coast. But these are very tough and tall and straight, and since they grow in salt water, their fruit is salt and bitter. But necessity compelled them to feed on this fruit and on the fish that they caught, and on shellfish and crabs, for maize does not grow anywhere on this coast. They rowed their canoes against the main sea current, which always runs north whereas their course was south. And all along the coast Indians came out against them, shouting and calling at them that they were 'banished men'. They taunted them with the hair on their faces, saying that they were the scum of the sea, and that they could have no other ancestry since the sea had thrown them up. 'Why do you wander the world?' they cried. 'You must be idle vagabonds since you stay nowhere to work and sow the earth.'

Since the captains had lost many men by hunger and in skirmishes with the Indians, it was agreed that Don Diego should return to Panama for reinforcements. He returned with eighty who, together with the survivors, were able to reach the land of Catamez, which lies beyond the mangrove-swamps: a country with much food and a considerable population. The warriors of this country had their cheeks pierced with holes in which they wore gold beads. They were so numerous that the Spaniards could advance no further until Don Diego had returned to Panama for still more men. Meanwhile Don Francisco Pizarro retired to wait for him to a small island not far from the coast, which they called Gallo island. Here he stayed, suffering great shortage of all necessities.

2. Don Francisco Pizarro's stay on Gorgona island, and his voyage with his small company across the Equator

ON returning to Panama for help, Don Diego de Almagro found that His Majesty had sent out as governor a gentleman of Cordoba, Pedro de los Rios by name, who prevented his return. For those who remained with Don Francisco Pizarro on Gallo island had sent him a secret message, begging him to allow no more men to go to their death in this dangerous and profitless expedition, in which many men had died already, and that they should themselves be recalled. Pedro de los Rios therefore sent a lieutenant with orders that all who wished should be free to return to Panama, and no one be forced to remain. On hearing this proclaimed, Pizarro's men immediately embarked with great joy, as if fleeing from the land of the Moors. Only a dozen elected to remain with Don Francisco, so few that he dared not stay there but went to an uninhabited island six leagues out to sea which they called Gorgona island, since it was full of springs and streams. Here they supported themselves on crabs, shellfish and large snakes, of which there are plenty, until the ship returned from Panama.* When it arrived, bringing food but no more men, he went aboard with his twelve companions whose courage and resolution led to the

* They spent seven months on this island.

discovery of the land of Peru. Among these were Nicolas de Ribera of Olvera, Pedro de Candia, from the Greek island of Crete, Juan de Torre, Alonso Birceño of Benavente, Cristobal de Peralta of Baeza, Alonso de Trujillo of that city, Francisco de Cuellar of that city, and Alonso de Mólina of Ubeda. The chief pilot was Bartolome Ruiz of Moguer.

They sailed with great difficulty and danger against the force of wind and currents till they arrived at a province called Motupe, which lies between two towns, afterwards settled by Christians and called by them Trujillo and San Miguel. Not daring to go further owing to his small numbers, Don Francisco turned back at this point, taking aboard at a river called the Puechos or Chira a number of the native sheep* and some Indians to serve as interpreters. Then putting out to sea again, he landed at the port of Tumbez, where, as he had heard, the lord of Peru had one of his chief palaces, together with a settlement of rich Indians, which was one of the finest sights in the country until the Indians of Puna island destroyed it, as will be described later. Here three Spanish deserters remained behind and, as afterwards transpired, were killed by the Indians.

Don Francisco returned to Panama with the knowledge he had collected, having spent three years on these expeditions and suffered great hardships and dangers, from lack of food and the attacks and resistance of the Indians, and from mutinies among his own men, most of whom did not believe that anything profitable would be discovered. With great courage and foresight, however, Don Francisco reassured them, confident that Don Diego de Almagro would diligently continue to supply him with provisions, soldiers, horses and arms. So, although he and his partners were to be the richest men in that country, at this time they remained not only poor but heavily in debt.

* These would be of the llama family.

3. Don Francisco Pizarro's visit to Spain to inform His Majesty of the discovery of Peru, and its results in Panama

HAVING made these discoveries, Don Francisco Pizarro came to Spain and, after informing His Majesty of his adventures, begged to be granted the governorship of that land as compensation for the hardships he had undergone, since he wished to return there in order to discover and make settlements. His Majesty agreed, making the same stipulations with him as he had with other captains to whom he had entrusted the discovery of provinces. Whereupon Don Francisco returned to Panama, taking with him his brothers Hernando Pizarro, Juan Pizarro, Gonzalo Pizarro and Francisco Martin de Alcantara. Of these only Hernando and Juan were legitimate and shared both parents, being sons of Gonzalo Pizarro the Tall, of Trujillo, formerly captain of infantry in the kingdom of Navarre. Don Francisco was his illegitimate son, as was Gonzalo Pizarro also, though by different mothers, and Francisco Martin was Don Francisco's brother, on his mother's side only. In addition Don Francisco took many others with him on his expedition, the majority of them inhabitants of Trujillo, Caceres and other towns in Estremadura.

And so, on arriving at Panama, they began to prepare the expedition in the name of the original company, which caused some dissension between Don Francisco and Don Diego. For Don Diego was very indignant that Don Francisco had negotiated with His Majesty business in which he, Don Diego, was equally concerned, and obtained for himself the title of governor and chief magistrate of Peru without mentioning the interest of his partner, who had made the larger contribution to the cost and labour of the exploration. Don Francisco consoled him by explaining that, despite his earnest pleas, His Majesty had declined to grant Don Diego anything for the present. But for himself he promised on oath to renounce the chief magistracy in Don Diego's favour, and to petition His

Majesty to confirm this transfer. Don Diego remained partially satisfied with this. And here we will leave them preparing men and material for the voyage of discovery, and describe the situation of the province of Peru, its notable features and the customs of its people.

4. *The Inhabitants below the Equator and other notable matters*

THE land of Peru, which is the subject of this book, begins at the Equator and extends southward. Its inhabitants below the line have a Jewish cast of feature, speak gutturally and are much given to unnatural vice. For this reason they neglect their wives and pay them little respect. The women wear their hair very short and go naked except for a small apron with which they cover their private parts. It is they who sow and grind the corn that is eaten throughout the province and is known in the language of the islands as maize, though in Peru it is called *zara*. The men wear short shirts down to the navel, leaving the private parts exposed. They wear tonsures rather like friars, though they have no hair before or behind, only at the sides. They delight in wearing golden jewels in their ears and nostrils, chiefly emeralds, which are found only in that region. Though the Indians would never reveal their mines, it is believed however that they originate here, since some have been found mixed with pebbles or attached to them – a sign that they were obtained from them. Round their legs and arms they tie strings of gold and silver and small turquoise beads, also little white and red ones, and shells: but they do not allow their women to wear any of these. It is a very hot country with much sickness. The inhabitants suffer especially from very painful warts,* which appear on the face and other parts and have very deep roots. They are worse than buboes.

In this province the doors of the temples face the east and are covered with cotton curtains; and in each temple there are

* This is *verruga*, a disease local to this part of Peru.

two massive figures of black goats, before which they burn the wood of a very sweet-smelling tree which grows in the country. When its bark is cut, a liquor flows that has so strong a smell as to induce nausea; and if they anoint a corpse with it and pour it down the throat that body never corrupts. They have also in their temples images of great serpents, which they worship. And besides these common images, each man has special images of his own, according to his trade and office, which he worships also; the fishermen images of sharks, and the hunters according to the game they pursue, and so on. And in some temples, especially in the villages they call Pasao, there were men and boys hanging on all the pillars. These may have been crucified. Their skins were so well tanned that they did not smell. They also had many heads of Indians nailed up which by some means known to them they shrank to the size of a fist.

The earth is very dry although it often rains, and there are few running streams of sweet water. Everyone drinks from wells or the water of pools, which they call *jagueyes*. They build their houses of the stout canes which grow there. The gold that is found there is of few carats; and there are not many sorts of fruit. Their navigation is in curved canoes, hollowed out of tree trunks, and balsa rafts. It is a great coast for fish, and there are many whales. In some villages in this province, they have over the doors of their temples figures of men wearing vestments cut like a deacon's dalmatic.

5. *The seams of pitch at the cape Santa Elena, the giants that lived there of old*

NEAR this province, on a promontory which the Spaniards called Santa Elena, are some veins from which there flows a bitumen which resembles pitch or tar and can be used for it. Near this point, according to the Indian inhabitants, there once lived giants so great that they were four times the height of an average man. They do not say where they came from, but that they lived on the same food as themselves, especially fish, for they were great fishermen. They fished from balsa rafts, each from his own; for though these rafts can carry three horses, they could take no more than one of these giants. They could wade into the sea to the depth of two and a half fathoms; and they greatly enjoyed catching shark or *bufoes* or other large fish, because these gave them more to eat. Each one of them ate more than thirty men today, and they went naked owing to the difficulty of making themselves clothes. They were so cruel that they would kill many Indians for no reason at all, and they were greatly feared.

The Spaniards saw two huge statues of these giants at Puerto Viejo, one male and one female, and an Indian tradition, passed from father to son, tells a great deal about them, in particular the story of their end. They say that a youth shining like the sun descended from the sky and fought against them, throwing flames of fire that pierced the rocks which they struck with holes that are still to be seen. And so the giants retreated to a valley, where they were all finally killed. These Indian tales about the giants were never entirely believed however, until Captain Juan de Olmos of Trujillo, lieutenant to the Governor of Puerto Viejo in the year 1543, who had heard them, commanded some men to dig in that valley. Here they found ribs and other bones so huge that, had it not been for the heads that lay beside them, no one would have believed that they were human. But with this confirmation and in view of the marks of thunderbolts in the rocks, the Indian tradition was accepted as true; and some of the teeth found there, each three fingers* wide and four fingers long, were sent to different parts of Peru. These tokens have convinced the Spaniards that, since this people was much given to unnatural vice, divine justice removed them from the earth, sending an angel for that purpose, as at Sodom and other places.

It must be realized that in this case, as in all others concerning antiquities discovered in Peru, confirmation is difficult. The natives neither know nor employ any kind of letters or writing, nor even painting, which takes the place of books in New Spain, but only memories which are passed from fathers to sons. Accounts are preserved by means of cotton cords, which

* A measure of 14 mm., a little more than ½ inch.

the Indians call *quipus*, numbers being denoted by knots of different kinds, spaced in ascending order from units to tens, and so on upwards, the colour of the cord conforming to the objects denoted. In each province there are persons entrusted with recording public matters on these cords, who are called *quipu-camayoc*; and governmental houses are found full of *quipus*, which are easily read by the person in charge even though they date from many years before his time.

6. People and things on the sea coast, south of the Equator

SOUTH of the Equator there is an island twelve leagues in perimeter very close to the mainland, which is called Puna and is rich in game and fish and has many sweet springs. It was once densely inhabited by a people who were at war with all their neighbours, especially with the men of Tumbez, twelve leagues away. They wore shirts and aprons, and owned many rafts, on which they put to sea. These rafts are made of long, light timbers, beneath which two other timbers are tied. These on top are usually odd in number, commonly five, but sometimes seven or nine, the middle one, on which the oarsman sits, being longer than the rest, like the pole of a cart. These rafts are made in the shape of an open hand, with the fingers diminishing from the middle, and they lay planks on top to save themselves from getting wet. Some rafts are capable of taking fifty men and three horses. The Indians are very skilful sailors, and navigate them with a sail and oars. On some occasions, when they had Spaniards aboard, they cunningly untied the timbers, which then drifted apart. Thus the Christians were drowned and the Indians saved themselves on the timbers, or even with no support at all, for they are great swimmers.

The people of this island fought with darts and slings, also with clubs and silver and copper axes. They have spears tipped with inferior gold. Both the men and women wear gold jewels and rings, and they use gold and silver vessels also. The ruler of the island is greatly feared by his subjects. He is so jealous that his house-servants and those who guard his women have their noses and genitals cut off.

On another small island close by, the model of an orchard was found, with trees and plants of silver and gold; and on the opposite mainland were some villages whose inhabitants had been punished for some insult to the lord of Peru by having the teeth extracted from their upper jaw. There are toothless men and women living there to this day.

Past Tumbez to the south for five hundred leagues down the coast and to the depth of ten leagues inland, there is no rain or thunder or lightning. But ten leagues, more or less, inland, the distance from the mountains to the sea, there is rain and thunder and summer and winter weather just as in Spain and at the same times of year. But when it is winter in the mountains, it is summer on the coast, and vice versa. The full extent of the land of Peru so far discovered, from the city of Pasto, where it begins, to the province of Chile, which is now being explored, is more than one thousand eight hundred leagues – which are longer than those of Spain. Along its full length runs a chain of very rugged mountains, that are sometimes fifteen or twenty leagues from the sea, though in other places spurs of these mountains encroach on the plain, making it rather less.

All Peru that has been discovered is described by two names; the parts between the mountains and the sea, whether broad or narrow, are known as the plains, and the rest is called the *sierra*. The plains are very dry and contain huge sandy deserts, for it never rains there, and there are no springs or wells or other sources to be found, only four or five swamps, whose water is very saline since they are close to the sea. The people draw their water from the rivers, which flow down from the mountains and are fed by the snow and rain that fall there; for even in the mountains there are very few springs. Sometimes the rivers lie twelve or fifteen or even twenty leagues apart, but usually there is no more than seven or eight leagues between them; so that travellers commonly make their daily stages from one to another, for there is no other water to drink. On the banks of these rivers for a breadth of a league, more or less according to the nature of the country, there are large belts of fresh shrubs and fruit trees and maize fields, sown by the natives. And since the Spaniards came to this land, wheat has been sown also.

All this land is watered by canals taken from the rivers, for the natives are very skilful and industrious irrigators. Sometimes they will take their canal six or eight leagues round to avoid an intermediate valley that may be no more than half a league across. The belts of cultivation lie along the rivers from the mountains to the sea. And the rivers, coming from such a height, are so fast that some – like the Santa and the Barranca – can only be crossed on horseback if natives stand downstream with long poles or sticks to prevent the Spaniards from being swept away by the current. Even so, when crossing these rivers, it is not safe to stop and take water or for any other reason since the stream is so fast that it will overthrow horse and rider, stunning the latter. The great danger is that if a horse and man fall the current may sweep them away before the man has a chance to get up. It is so violent that it often carries great stones along with it.

Travellers crossing the plains always go along the coast. They hardly leave it, or at least seldom lose sight of it. In the winter this journey is dangerous because the rivers are so swollen that they can also be crossed on balsa rafts, or on others which the natives make by stuffing nets full of gourds. On these they lie chest downwards, one Indian swimming in front and pulling with a rope while another pushes from behind.

On the banks of these rivers are different kinds of fruit trees, also cotton plantations, willows, canes, rushes, reeds, sedge, reed-mace and other kinds of grasses. The soil is very fertile, and wheat and maize are gathered throughout the year, without waiting for a fixed harvest.

The Indians do not live in houses, but under trees or in arbours. The women wear gown-like cotton robes to their feet, and the men aprons and shirts to the knee with a cloak on top. But although this way of dressing is common to all, they differ in their headgear according to the fashion of each country. Some wear woollen plaits, others a single woollen cord and others many cords of different colours. Everyone wears something on his head, but there are differences from province to province.

The Indians of the plains are divided into three tribes: the Incas, the Tallans and the Mochicas. There is a different language in each province. But the chieftains, captains and nobles speak the same tongue among themselves, though they also know and can speak the local one. This single language is that of Cuzco. Huayna Capac, the king of Peru and father of Atahuallpa, commanded all the chieftains, their brothers and relations to send their sons to serve him at court, so that they might learn the court language. For he considered it demeaning that he should have to speak through an interpreter to those nobles with whom he had most business. A more important reason for summoning these chieftains to court was, perhaps, to secure their lands by keeping their sons as hostages. In either case, he succeeded in making all the chief men of his kingdom speak the language of the court, just as the nobles and gentlemen of Flanders have been persuaded to speak French. As a result, a Spaniard who knows the language of Cuzco can travel throughout Peru, across plain and *sierra* alike, understanding and being understood by all the chiefs.

7. The wind that blows on the plains of Peru and the reason for their dryness

IT may be wondered why there is absolutely no rain on the plains of Peru, seeing that there are causes which should produce great rains. For on one side they are very close to the sea, which commonly engenders vapours and moisture, and on the other to high mountains where there is no lack of snow and water. Careful inquiry has shown the natural reason for this dryness. One wind, known to sailors as the South-Easter, prevails throughout the year over the whole plain and sea-coasts, and blows with such strength that it does not allow the clouds to pause, or rise from the land or sea and cool in the upper air. From the high mountains which look down on these vapours or clouds they seem like a second sky. Above them all is clear and cloudless.

This wind is also the cause of the predominant northward flow in those seas. Some however ascribe it to another cause: that since the waters discharge themselves into the Magellan straits, which are so narrow as to be barely two leagues across, they are far too great to go through. Moreover they meet there the waters of the Northern Sea, which force them back. Unable to enter the straits, they consequently surge backwards; which is why the current runs north. This makes an additional difficulty for ships on the voyage from Panama to Peru. Not only are the winds always against them, but for a large part of the year the currents too. Therefore, unless they sail close to the wind or in its teeth, they cannot make the voyage.

All along the coast of Peru there are great fisheries, which yield all kinds of fish and many seal. From the Tumbez river onwards there are none of those lizards.* Some say it is because the land is cooler, and they love the heat. But a better reason is the swiftness of the rivers, which does not allow them to breed. For they always breed in still waters.

On the plain there are five principal Christian settlements or cities. The first and nearest to the Equator is Puerto Viejo, which has few inhabitants because the soil is poor and sickly, although, as has been said, there are some emeralds. Fifty leagues further on and fifteen leagues inland is San Miguel, the Indian name for which is Piura. It is a cool and fertile place, though without gold or silver mines. There is a sickness, native to the district, which afflicts the eyes of all who pass through. Sixty leagues further on is a valley called Chimo and the city of Trujillo. This is only two leagues from the sea but its port is dangerous. Trujillo is in the plain on the banks of the river, and has plenty of water. It is rich in wheat, maize and cattle. It has been built on an ordered and regular plan and houses three hundred Spanish families. Eighty leagues further on is another city, two leagues from a good, safe port. It lies in a valley called Lima. But the city itself is called Los Reyes† (The Kings)

* Alligators.

† Referred to throughout this book as Los Reyes, it is now always called Lima.

because it was settled on the day of Epiphany. It lies on the plain beside a mighty river, and its soil is rich in corn, fruits of all sorts, and cattle. Los Reyes is so planned that all its streets are straight and lead into the central square. The country can be seen along them all, at both ends. The climate is temperate and it is a very pleasant place to live, for neither the heat nor the cold is oppressive at any time in the year. The four months corresponding to summer in Spain are a little cooler than the rest. At that time a frequent dew falls towards midday, which is like those mists that fall at Valladolid, except that it is not dangerous to the health; on the contrary people with headaches wash their heads in this dew.

All fruits grow well here that grow in Spain, especially oranges, citrons, lemons, grape-fruit both sweet and sour, figs and pomegranates. There would even be plenty of grapes but for the disturbances in the country which prevented the planting of vines. For some have actually been raised from raisin pips. There are also plenty of the pot-herbs of Spain, and beans, and every facility for cultivating them, since each house has a water conduit piped from the river, strong enough to drive a mill. In the river itself there are many mills built in the Spanish manner, at which the Spaniards grind their corn.

Lima is considered the healthiest and pleasantest place of residence in the country, both for its natural advantages, and because its port is a centre of great trade and commerce. Men come there from all the cities of the province to buy their provisions, bringing the silver and gold that is found in such abundance in their mines, and also for the reason that it is in the centre of the country and His Majesty has consequently chosen it as the seat of his Royal Chancery. It is therefore visited by all the inhabitants of the country who have business with the courts. Its population can be expected to grow continuously. It has now five hundred households but covers a much larger space than a Spanish city of fifteen hundred, because the streets and the square are very wide and each house occupies a plot eighty foot in frontage and twice as deep. The houses cannot be built of more than one storey since there is no timber in the land suitable for flooring, and none that does not rot within three years. Nevertheless the houses are very luxurious and imposing, and have many rooms. The walls are built of mud brick five feet thick; and the floors are formed of raised earth platforms, so that the windows looking on the street may be high above the ground. The staircases are in the open courtyard, and lead to terraces which serve as corridors or antechambers from which the rooms are approached. The roofing is of rough joists on which is hung a ceiling of painted canvas or else of coloured mats like those made at Almeria, which also covers the joists. On top of all this boughs are laid. The rooms are very high and cool, therefore, and well shaded from the sun. There is no need to protect them from the rain because, as has been said, it never rains at Los Reyes.

A hundred and thirty leagues further down the coast is another city, called the 'fair city' of Arequipa, which has about three hundred households, and is very healthy and rich in all kinds of foodstuffs. It is twelve leagues from the sea and for this reason its population can be expected to grow. Ships bring cloth, wine and other stores to its port for the city of Cuzco and the province of Charcas, where the majority of its inhabitants go to trade with the mines of Potesi and Porco. These mines send a great deal of silver to Arequipa, to be loaded on the returning ships which carry it to Los Reyes and Panama. This obviates a long and dangerous journey overland, which would be very laborious since by Royal ordinance Indians may no longer be employed as porters.

From Arequipa it is possible to travel overland, along the coast, for four hundred leagues, to the province which was discovered and settled by the governor Pedro de Valdivia and is called Chile, which in the Indian language means cold. The reason for this is the great cold suffered by travellers on their way there, as this history will relate, when I come to describe the expediion of the captain-general Don Diego de Almagro.

I have now set out the geography and population of the plains of Peru, and it will be assumed from my account that the seas are fair and clear of shoals all along the coast, for as far as I have described. There are no storms or weeds or shallows, or anything else to prevent ships from riding safely on only one anchor anywhere on the coast.

8. The sierra of Peru and its Indian and Christian population

THE Indian inhabitants of the *sierra* are very different from those of the plains in strength, courage and intelligence. They live in a more civilized manner in earth-roofed houses, and wear shirts and cloaks of the wool from the sheep they breed. They go bareheaded except for a band round their hair. The women wear slashed, sleeveless gowns with woollen belts round the waist, which they wear low, and woollen shawls over them secured at the neck by large gold or silver pins according to their means. These pins, which are called *topos* in their language, have large flat heads and are sharp enough to serve as knives. The women help their husbands greatly in the fields and at home; in fact they do most of the work. They are generally fair, and have much better faces and features than the women of the plains.

The soil here is very different from that of the plains. It is entirely covered with grass and has many cool streams and lakes, which join to form the rivers that flow across them. There are many flowers in the fields, and the same plants grow as in Spain. Everywhere there is watercress, nasturtium, wild chicory, verbena, blackberries and sorrel; and there are other plants with leaves like celery, which will clean even a suppurating wound. If put on sound flesh, they eat it to the bone. There are many kinds of local trees, whose fruit is as pleasant as we have in Spain, also alders and walnuts. The Indians have many sheep,* both domestic and free-ranging. There are also stags, deer, foxes and other small animals, which the Indians enjoy hunting. A hunt is called a *chaco* and is conducted in this way: four or five thousand Indians – more or less according to the population of the district – assemble and take up positions in a circle large enough to embrace two or three leagues of country. Then they gradually draw together, singing their hunting songs, till they are so close that they can clasp

* These are all of the llama family.

hands and link arms. In this way they drive a great quantity of game of various kinds into a sort of enclosure, and can capture and kill those they want. They make such a noise that not only do they scare the animals but they bring down partridges, falcons and other birds senseless at their feet. Stunned by the crowds and the shouting, they let themselves be picked up or caught in nets.

In the *sierra* there are lions,* black bears, wild cats, different sorts of monkeys and many other kinds of beasts; and in both *sierra* and plain there are eagles, pigeons and turtle-doves, woodpeckers, quails, parrots, butcher-birds, red owls, ducks and widgeon, white and grey herons, nightingales and many other fine birds. One kind are smaller than a grasshopper and have long feathers like a green sunflower. The vultures on the coast are so large that their wings measure fifteen or sixteen palms outspread.† These feed on seals, and when they find a seal on shore, one of them will seize him with his claws and tail while another pecks out his eyes. Then all the rest will peck him till he is dead, and feed on the corpse. There are some other birds called pelicans, which are like hens but much larger, for they can hold a peck and a half of corn in their bills. They are so common along the whole coast of the Southern Sea that for more than two thousand leagues there is always one in sight. They live on shellfish, but if they scent a human corpse they will go as much as thirty or forty leagues inland to find it. Their flesh is so foul and stinking that some who have been compelled to eat it have died as from poison.

Throughout the *sierra*, as has already been said, there is rain and hail, snow and great frosts. Yet it contains valleys so deep as to be out of the cold. Here there is great heat, and they grow a herb that the Indians value above gold and silver. It is called *coca*, and has a leaf like a *sumach*. We know by experience that anyone who chews this leaf feels neither hunger nor thirst.‡

In some parts of the *sierra* there are no trees. Travellers

* Pumas.

† A measure of 21 cm. (roughly 8¼ inches).

‡ For a fuller description of coca and its cultivation, see Cieza de León's chapter on the Andes, p. 170.

through these regions make their fires of the turf that grows there. There are beds of earth of various colours and veins of gold and silver which the Indians used to work and smelt better and more cheaply than Christians do today. High on the mountain they build little furnaces with doors facing south, the direction of the prevailing wind, and place the metal in them with sheep's dung. Then when the wind kindles the charcoal, the silver and gold are melted and refined. Even today when great quantities of silver are extracted from the mines of Potesi, the Indians never melt it with bellows but in these little furnaces which they call *guairas* – that is to say wind – because it is the wind that makes them burn.

This land is so fertile and yields such abundant crops that for a bushel of seed a hundred and fifty or even two hundred bushels of wheat may be reaped, whereas the ordinary yield is a hundred. Yet the Indians have no ploughs. They merely turn the earth over with pointed spades and drop the seed into the holes that they make with a stick, as we do in Spain when planting beans. Green vegetables and pulses grow so well that radishes have been seen in the city of Trujillo as fat as a man with leaves six feet round yet very sound and tender. Lettuces, cabbages and other garden produce have grown luxuriantly from seed brought from Spain. But when seed is gathered in the country, they do not grow so big.

The Indians eat boiled or roasted maize in place of bread, and venison cured like tunny-fish, also dried fish and roots of various kinds, which they call *yucca*, and peppers, *zapotes** and sweet potatoes, and many other fruits, vegetables and seeds, including lupin. In place of wine, they drink a beverage made by steeping maize in water and burying it in jars, which they leave in the earth to ferment. In addition to raw maize they put a quantity of chewed maize into each jar, to serve as yeast, and there are men and women who hire themselves out to chew it. They consider this drink better and more potent when made with stagnant water than with water from a stream. It is called *chicha* in the language of the islands, but *azua* in that of Peru; it is white or red according to the colour of the maize they use, and it is more quickly intoxicating than

* A fruit with a sweet, cloying taste.

Spanish wine. Nevertheless the Indians are so fond of wine that they would give up their native drink for it if they could get it. They make another drink also from the fruit of a tree which they call *molle*. But they think less of it than of *chicha*.

9. The Christian cities in the Peruvian sierra

IN the *sierra* of Peru there are some Christian settlements, beginning with the city of Quito, which is roughly four degrees south of the Equator. It was once a very peaceful place rich in corn and cattle, and became much richer in the years '44 and '45, when very valuable gold mines were discovered. Indeed it continued to increase in size and population until the fury of war struck it, and almost all its inhabitants were killed by Gonzalo Pizarro and his captain for taking sides with the viceroy Blasco Nuñez Vola and serving him during his residence in the city, as will be told at greater length.*

From Quito onwards there is no settlement in the *sierra* until you come to the province of Bracamors, which was discovered in part by Captain Juan Porcel and in part by Captain Vergara, who founded small settlements there on his way to make further discoveries, conquests and explorations. These settlements were broken up when Gonzalo Pizarro took these two captains with him to aid him in his wars. The original discovery had been made by order of Vaca de Castro when he was governor of that province. He had sent Captain Porcel from San Miguel and Captain Vergara from much further on in the province of Chachapeyas, hoping that they would take different routes. In fact they soon met and disputed the ownership of the province. Vaca de Castro summoned them to Los Reyes to decide the case, and they were there in his service when the civil war broke out. After his capture they remained with Gonzalo Pizarro, and the dispute about their expedition came to an end.

The land discovered by these two captains lies in the *sierra*, a hundred and sixty leagues from the city of Quito. Eighty

* This story is told in Book Five.

leagues further on is the province of Chachapeyas, where there is a Christian settlement called Levante. This province yields good crops and has fair mines. Its position is extremely strong since it is almost entirely surrounded by a deep gorge, through which flows a river. It is so nearly enclosed that if the bridges were cut it would be very hard to conquer. This province was later settled by Marshal Alonso de Alvarado, who received the grant of its population and revenue.

Sixty leagues further on is another Christian settlement called Huanuce, which was established at the command of Vaca de Castro, who named it Leon after his own native city in Spain. It yields good crops and is believed to have a great number of mines, especially in the part that is occupied by the Inca who has revolted and is fighting in the Andes, as will afterwards be told.

After this city there is no Christian settlement in the *sierra* before the town of Huamanga, called in Spanish San Juan de la Victoria, which is sixty leagues further on. This town has few Christian inhabitants, though it will probably grow much bigger if the Inca makes peace. For he is very close to the town and occupies its best land, which contains many mines and grows much *coca,* a herb whose utility has already been mentioned.

From this town of Huamanga to Cuzco is eighty leagues. The road is very rough and dangerous, and crosses many mountains and gorges. Before the coming of the Christians, Cuzco was the seat of the kings of Peru, who governed the whole land from there. Chieftains came to Cuzco from all parts, to bring tribute to their lord, to conduct their business and to get justice from him in their disputes. There was no other centre of population in the whole province, nor anything in the form of a town. It had a fine fortress built of squared stones so large that it was a wonder they could have been transported by the Indians alone, without help of oxen, mules or other beasts. Many of these stones ten yoke of oxen could not move. The houses and other buildings in which the Christians live today are the same that the Indians had, though some have been repaired and others enlarged. The city is divided into four residential quarters in which the king, called in Indian language the Inca, assigned lodgings to his visitors according to the quarter of his realm from which they came. The southern quarter was called Collasuyu, after its province of Collao which lies in the south; the northern quarter was called Chinchasuyu after the famous province of Chincha, which now belongs to His Majesty and was once wealthy, though today it is poor and thinly populated. The eastern and western quarters were called Antisuyu and Cuntisuyu. And no Indian might live in any other quarter than the one corresponding to his province, under pain of severe punishment. The land around this city is very fruitful in all crops and so salubrious that if a man arrives healthy he will seldom or never fall sick. All around are the many rich mines from which all the gold that has come to Spain was taken. But now, since the mines of Potosi have been opened, these gold workings have been deserted, because much more profit can be made from silver, at less risk to the Indians and Christians extracting it. From this city of Cuzco to the town of La Plata, which is in the province of Charcas, is more than a hundred and fifty leagues. In between lies a very large, flat province called Collao, which stretches for more than fifty leagues. The principal part, which is called Chiquito, belongs to His Majesty, and because there is such a large expanse without Christian population Pedro de la Gasca in the year '49 ordered that a place in this province should be settled, which is called Nuestra Señora de la Paz.

La Plata is extremely cold, colder than anywhere else in the *sierra*; it has few inhabitants, but they are very rich and even they have lived for the greater part of the year at the mines, first at the hill of Porco, and subsequently, when it was discovered, at Potesi. Going inland from La Plata, leftwards and towards the east is a province called Diego de Rojas, which was opened up at the command of Vaca de Castro, who sent Captains Diego de Rojas and Felipe Gutierrez to explore it. It is said to be a fine salubrious country, rich in foodstuffs. But despite expectations, no riches have been found there. In the year '49 Captain Domingo de Icala and his companions passed through it on their way to Peru. They had traversed the whole country between the Northern and Southern Seas, having first gone up the river Plate and explored the lands on that side.

This account covers all these parts of the province of Peru discovered and settled along the Southern Sea. Explorers have generally followed the coast without venturing far into the interior, where travelling is very difficult on account of the rough mountains, which lie in parallel ranges, the crossing of which involves great hardships from cold and lack of food. But Spanish courage and enterprise will overcome even these obstacles, provided there is no doubt that rich lands lie ahead.

10. Indian opinions on the subject of their creation, and certain other matters

NOT knowing the art of writing, the Indians are also ignorant of their origin. They have no knowledge of the story of the Creation or the Flood,* of which they have neither record nor memory. It is true that some kinds of traditions have been preserved among them, added to, changed or diminished from age to age according to the imaginations of the time. This is more or less what they amount to:

They say that there came from the north a man without bones or joints, who shortened or lengthened the road he walked according to his wishes, and raised or levelled mountains as he pleased; that this man created the Indians of that time, and that since the inhabitants of the plain had displeased him he made their country sandy, as it is to this day. He decreed that rain should never fall there, but sent them the rivers that flow there, so that they should at least have water to drink and to cool them. This man was called Con, and he was the child of the sun and moon. They considered him a god and worshipped him; and they say that to the people he created he gave the grasses and wild fruit for their nourishment.

Afterwards there came another man from the south, with more power than the first. He was called Pachacamac, which means creator, and was also the child of the sun and the moon. On his arrival Con disappeared, leaving the men he had made

* Zárate contradicts this statement later in this chapter.

without a leader or protector. Pachacamac then changed them into monkeys, cats, bears, lions, parrots and other birds of the country. Then Pachacamac created the Indians of today, and taught them how to till the earth and grow crops. They consider Pachacamac a god, and all the princes of the land wish to be buried when they die in the place which took its name from him because he dwelt there, and which lies four leagues from Los Reyes. The Indians say that Pachacamac lived there for many centuries, up to the time when the Christians came to Peru; but that he has not appeared since. This makes one think that it must have been some devil who thus unhappily deceived them, and put all these extravagant and foolish notions into their heads.

The Indians also believe that before all this there was a flood, and that when it came men took refuge in great caves which they had prepared in advance among the highest mountains, carrying all their necessities of life there. Having gone in, they so effectively sealed the entries and smallest openings of their retreats that the water could not get in. Then when they believed it had subsided, they sent out dogs who returned wet and with no mud on them, from which they concluded that the waters were still high. They dared not emerge from their caves until their dogs came back covered with mud. After the flood, it is said, the dampness engendered many snakes, which harassed them greatly until they succeeded in killing them.

It seems from this that the Peruvians have some confused knowledge of the Flood, though they do not know that Noah was saved in the ark. But it is possible that the flood they describe may have been some partial flood, like Deucalion's.

They think that the world will end, but that before this there will be a great drought and no rain at all for many years. For this reason the former lords kept barns stored with great quantities of maize to be eaten during the drought. And when there is an eclipse of the sun or moon the Indians cry and groan in great perturbation, thinking that the time has come in which the earth will perish, for then the orbs will lose their light, as they do in an eclipse.

11. The religious ceremonies and sacrifices of the Peruvians

THESE peoples worship the sun and moon as gods, and believe them to be actual divinities. They swear by the sun, and by the earth which they regard as their mother. They have certain stones in their temples that they honour and worship as representative of the orb of day. These they call *huacas*, a word which means to weep, since they actually do weep on entering these temples. No one approaches the *huacas* except the priests or sacrificers to these idols, who are always dressed in white. When they go up to the *huacas*, they carry white linen or cloths in their hands, and prostrate themselves, crawling on the ground. In addressing these idols, they use a language that the Indians do not understand. These officiants receive the offerings made to the *huacas* and bury them in the temples; for all the Indians bring figures or images of gold or silver, representing the objects for which they are praying to these gods. These same priests also sacrifice animals and men, and search the heart or entrails of their victims for the signs they desire; and having once begun these abominable sacrifices they make more and more till they find what they seek. They say that so long as these signs are not found, clearly their gods are not content with the sacrifice.

These priests hardly ever appear in public. During the times of their sacrifices they have no intercourse with women, and wander all night imploring and invoking these devils, in the country round the places where they dwell. There are very many *huacas* since there are many temples, each with its special idol. When the priests wish to speak with their devils they prepare themselves by fasting. Then they blindfold their eyes, and some even put them out. These wretched people are so superstitious that they have even been seen to tear or put out their own eyes.

The *caciques** and lords never undertake anything without

* A Caribbean term for a chieftain.

first consulting their priests, who then consult their idols or, more precisely, their devils. The Spaniards discovered in these temples to the sun a number of large earthenware pots full of dried children who had been sacrificed. Among the gold and silver objects with which these *huacas* were decorated were some in the exact shape of croziers and bishops' mitres; and some idols were found crowned with a mitre. Indeed when Tomas de Verlanga, Bishop of Tierra Firme, came to Peru, and the Indians saw him celebrating a pontifical mass with his mitre on his head, they said that he was like a *huaca* and asked if he was the *huaca* of the Christians.

The Peruvians have often been questioned on the subject of these mitres, their purpose and use. But their answers have been confused; all they have been able to say is that they have been so shaped since ancient times.

Besides the temples of the *huacas* there were also, all over Peru, houses or nunneries inhabited by women sacred to the sun, who never left them but spun and wove cotton and wool, and made very fine cloths. But once the cloths were finished they burnt them with the bones of white sheep and threw the ashes into the wind, in the direction of the sun. These women were obliged to live in perpetual chastity and continence, and if they erred they were put to death. Nevertheless if one was pregnant and swore on oath that the sun was the father of her child she was spared.

Every year at the time when the Indians of the *sierra* gathered their maize, there was a festival. They would erect in the middle of some public place two high trees, as straight as the masts of a ship, on the top of which they put the figure of a man surrounded by other figures decorated with flowers. After this they came in troops or bands, beating their drums and uttering loud cries. Then each band threw its darts or shot its arrows at these figures; and when all had done so the priests brought out an idol which they placed at the foot of these masts, and before which they sacrificed an Indian or a sheep, smearing the idol with the blood of the victim. Then, when they had examined the heart and entrails, and found good or bad signs, they announced their auguries to the people; and thus the festival was judged to be either lucky or unlucky. The whole day was spent in dancing and drinking, playing games and performing various feats, and some warriors would dance fully armed with their axes, clubs and other weapons.

12. The Indians of Peru believe in the resurrection of the flesh

THE *caciques* of Peru and all the chief men of the country were put in vaults after their death, seated in their chairs, which are called *duos*, and attired in all their richest clothing. It was customary also to bury with them one or two of their favourite wives. And there were often disputes among the women as to who should have this honour, for which reason it was generally settled by the husband before his death. Two or three boys who had been their attendants were generally buried with them also, and all their gold and silver vessels as well. This was done in the expectation that one day they would return to life, when they would wish to appear in the company of their women and officers. So when the Spaniards entered the tombs to take out the gold and silver that had been put there, the Peruvians begged them not to remove or disturb the bones, for fear that the dead person's restoration to life might be delayed or made more difficult.

In the funeral ceremony, the relatives pour the beverage they call *chicha* over the burial place, and it is conveyed by means of pipes to the mouth of the corpse. Over their graves they place wooden statues representing the deceased, though in the case of common people they are content to erect painted signs of their profession or trade, especially if they have been warriors.

13. The origin of the Kings of Peru, called Incas

IN every province of Peru there were chieftains called in their language *curacas*, who correspond to what in the islands are called *caciques*. For the Spanish conquerors of Peru were familiar with the names of ordinary things in the islands of Santo Domingo, Puerto Rico, Cuba and Tierra Firme, where they had lived, but did not know what they were called in Peru. So they used the words they had learnt, and these have been preserved. Indeed the Peruvians themselves when talking to Christians call these things by the names they have heard them use. Though their word for *cacique* is *curaca,* they use only *cacique;* they call their corn maize, though their own word is *zara,* and their beverage *chicha* instead of *azua,* and so on.

These chieftains kept the peace among the Indians and were their captains in the wars against their neighbours. There was no ruler-in-chief in the country until the coming of a very warlike people from the direction of Collao across a great lake called Titicaca which is eighty leagues across. These Incas wear their hair cropped and have pierced ears, in which they put round pieces of gold that gradually stretch them. They are called *ringrim,* that is to say *orejas* or 'ears'. The first of these was called Zapalla Inca – inca merely means lord – though some say they called him the Inca Viracocha, which signifies sea-foam or grease. Not knowing the origin of the world, they believed it had been created from that lake, which is drained by a great river running westward, which is in parts half a league across. It then flows into another smaller lake, forty leagues wide, in which it disappears, to the great amazement of those who cannot see how such a vast quantity of water can be contained in so small a reservoir. For the smaller lake has no outlet. Its bottom has never been found, however, and the water is believed to flow away under the sea like the river Alpheus in Greece.

These Incas began by establishing themselves in the city of Cuzco, and from there subjugated the whole country, from which they exacted tribute. Their rule was by succession, and this is the order they observed. When a king died he was immediately succeeded not by any of his children but by the eldest of his younger brothers, if he had more than one. Then after his death the succession returned to the eldest son of the previous ruler, from him to his brother, then straight from that brother to the eldest son of his elder brother, and so on. By this law of succession there could hardly fail to be an heir, nor could the line run out so long as it was observed.*

The insignia or diadem worn by these Incas as a sign of their office was a *borla* or fillet of red wool stretching from one temple to the other and almost covering the eyes. They governed the country and obtained their requirements merely by entrusting a strand from this *borla* to one of their *orejones*; and they were more scrupulously obeyed than many a king in other parts of the world. By sending one of their *orejones* they could have a whole province ravaged and every man and woman in it killed. No other force or commission was needed than one of these woollen threads, at the mere sight of which all would willingly offer themselves to be killed.

In the Inca succession, the lordship came to one Huayna Capac (which means 'rich youth') who extended the Peruvian empire to its greatest, and imposed his law and justice most widely, bringing order and civilization to distant frontiers. It is almost incredible that a barbarous and unlettered people could have been ruled in so orderly a way, or that the rulers could have been so loved and obeyed by their subjects, who built for them two very remarkable roads, of which an account must be given. For none of those accounted by ancient authors the seven wonders of the world was constructed with such labour and difficulty or at such cost as these.

When Huayna Capac left the city of Cuzco with his army to conquer the province of Quito, which is about five hundred leagues away, he took the mountain way. But such difficulties did he find in crossing the *sierra*, on account of the bad roads and great gorges and precipices, that the Indians decided to make him a new road by which to return when he had conquered the province. By the time he had won the victory, they had built a broad, smooth road over the whole range of the *sierra*, breaking and levelling the crags where necessary and

* Thus the Antwerp edition of 1555. The Seville edition of 1577, perhaps altered after Zárate's death, tells a different story, describing the succession in this way: 'After that, the succession to the country went to the most powerful, not by legitimate right of inheritance but by violence and tyranny. The only right was that of arms.'

filling the gorges with stones, sometimes to a depth of thirty or forty feet. This road is still to be seen for a distance of five hundred leagues, and it is said to have been so smooth when finished that a laden cart could be driven over it. But since that time, owing to the wars both of Indians and Christians, the paving is broken in many places and gaps at dangerous points prevent the passage of travellers.

The difficulties of this road building will be understood by anyone who thinks what it cost in money and labour to level the two leagues of Spanish road that lie between the thorn-woods of Segovia and the Guadarrama. The job has never been completed, although this is the route invariably followed by Kings of Castile travelling with their household and court each time they cross the passes on their way to or from Andalusia or the royal seat of Toledo.

The Indians were not content to have built this remarkable work. When Huayna Capac decided to return to the province of Quito, of which – since he had conquered it himself – he was extremely fond, and went by way of the plains, they built him another road which was almost as difficult an undertaking. The cool valleys through which the rivers run amidst trees and shrubs are generally a league wide. Yet across each one they built a road almost forty feet in breadth with stout mud-brick walls from end to end, as high as four or five such walls in Spain. And where these roads left the valleys, they continued them over the sandy desert, driving in lines of poles and stakes so that no one could lose his way or wander to either side. This road ran for five hundred leagues, also; and though the poles in the desert were broken in many places, because both in times of war and peace the Spaniards used them for firewood, the walls in the valleys for the most part stand complete to this day, as evidence of the greatness of these works.

So Huayna Capac went by one road and returned by the other; and wherever he was expected to pass, the way was always scattered with sweet-smelling flowers and branches.

14. *Huayna Capac's remarkable achievements in Peru*

IN addition to the building and upkeep of these roads, Huayna Capac ordered the construction of large palaces at each stage, with lodgings not only for himself and his household but for his whole army. He had them constructed on the plains as well as in the mountains, though on the plains they stood further apart since they could only be placed on the river banks which, as we have said, were eight or ten, and in places fifteen or twenty leagues apart. These lodgings are called *tambos*; and it was the duty of the Indians in whose district they stood to collect every sort of stores that his army might need, not only food but arms, clothing and provisions, so that if he needed replacements for twenty or thirty thousand fighting-men he could find them at any *tambo*.

The Inca was escorted on his journeys by a great number of warriors with pikes, halberds, clubs and axes of silver and copper, and sometimes even of gold, and with slings and arrows of palmwood with charred points. Where there was wood they built wooden bridges over the rivers, and where there was none they used thick cables of a plant called *maguey*,* which is stronger than hemp. They threw them from bank to bank and interwove them with a sort of brushwood. Their method of building these bridges was amazing, for some of them were more than a hundred feet in the air and two hundred yards long. Where they could not build bridges they crossed on these cables alone, in a basket provided with wooden flanges to prevent it from scraping and pulled by a rope from the other side. These bridges were maintained at their own cost by the Indians in whose territory they stood.

The Inca always travelled in a litter plated with gold. He took a thousand or more noblemen with him, merely as his bearers; these were the members of his council and his confidential officers. The *caciques* also travelled in litters, borne on

* Sisal.

the shoulders of their subjects. They treated the Inca with such respect that no one, however important, entered to speak to him except barefoot, and carrying some object wrapped in a cloak to be presented to him by way of duty. This rule was so strictly observed that though a nobleman might enter to speak to him a hundred times a day he would bring a fresh gift each time. They considered it most disrespectful to look their prince in the face, and if anyone stumbled and fell when carrying his litter he was immediately beheaded. Relays of Indian messengers were posted at intervals of half a league throughout the country, and they ran faster than our posthorses. On conquering a province, the first thing the lord did was to transfer his new subjects, or the most important of them, to some older settlement, and to populate his new territory with Indians who were already his subjects. In this way he kept the whole of his realm secure. The people who were transferred from old territories to new were called *mitimaes*. He received annual tribute from all the provinces of his realm in the produce of that province. From some places, three hundred leagues or more from Cuzco, which were so barren that they grew no crops, he received each year so many loads of lizards.

Huayna Capac rebuilt the temple of the sun at Cuzco, and had gold and silver plates made to line its roof and walls. After the rebellion of a lord of the plains called Chimocappa, who owned more than a hundred leagues of land, he not only attacked, conquered and killed the rebellious lord, but ordered that as punishment no Indian of the plains should carry arms. Nevertheless the rebel's successor was permitted to live in the province of Chime, where Trujillo stands today.

Huayna Capac and his father had large flocks of the native sheep maintained in the realm, so that each year a certain number could be let loose in the country as a tribute to the sun. And these multiplied until they became very numerous, for it was considered sacrilege for anyone to touch them except Huayna Capac himself, to feed his army. When he needed them and organized one of these hunts that were called *chacos*, twenty or thirty thousand of these animals might be taken in one day.

Gold was highly prized since the Inca and his nobles used it to make vessels for their service, jewels for decoration and offerings for the temples. He also had a chair of sixteen carat gold, which was worth thirty-five thousand ducats. Don Francisco chose this piece as his 'jewel' at the time of the conquest, since according to his articles of agreement he was entitled to a jewel of his choice before the general division of the spoil.

According to the report of many Indians still living, at the time of his eldest son's birth Huayna Capac had a golden cable made, so thick that six hundred Indian chieftains could scarcely lift it. And to commemorate this famous jewel, they called the boy Huascar (which in their language means rope), adding Inca, which was the surname of all those kings, as that of the Roman emperors was Augustus. I give this example to disprove a theory commonly held in Spain among people without knowledge of the Indies that the natives set no store by gold and did not know its value. They also had many barns and storehouses full of silver and gold, and large models of men, women and sheep and other animals, and of all the kinds of grasses that grew in that land, with their ears and shoots and nodes copied from nature. They had also great quantities of cloaks and slings threaded with gold wire, and logs also, like those they burnt on the fire, made of gold and silver.

15. The civil wars in Peru at the time of the coming of the Spaniards

ALTHOUGH the principal purpose of this history is to relate the adventures of the Spanish conquerors at the time of the conquest and afterwards, these cannot be understood without some knowledge of the affairs of the Indian rulers at the time. Without this, the reader will fail to see how providential it was that the Spaniards arrived at a moment when the country was divided between two factions. But for this division it would have been impossible – or at least very difficult – to conquer it. In order to clarify this history, therefore, I will give a brief account of the condition in which they found the country at this moment.

After subjugating to his empire many provinces extending for fifteen hundred leagues westwards from Cuzco, Huayna Capac decided to go in person to conquer the province of Quito, which bordered his empire on the north. He led out his army, conquered the country and, finding its climate very pleasant, lived there for some time, leaving in Cuzco some of his sons and daughters, among them his eldest son Huascar Inca, Manco Inca and Paolo Inca. In Quito he took a new wife, the daughter of the king of the country, and had by her a son called Atahuallpa, of whom he was very fond. Leaving Atahuallpa under tutors at Quito, he returned to visit Cuzco – and it was for this return journey that they built the difficult road over the *sierra* already described.

After he had been in Cuzco for some years, Huayna Capac decided to return to Quito, both because he found the country more agreeable and because he wanted to see his favourite son Atahuallpa. So he returned to Quito by the road across the plains, lived there and had his throne there for the rest of his life. At his death he decreed that this province of Quito, which he had himself conquered, should be left to Atahuallpa, since it had belonged to his maternal ancestors. When Huayna Capac was dead, Atahuallpa took over his army and the wealth that his father had brought with him. The principal and largest jewels, however, remained in the treasury at Cuzco in charge of his eldest son Huascar, to whom Atahuallpa sent ambassadors informing him of his father's death. Atahuallpa swore obedience to him, and begged that the province of Quito should be left to him, since his father had conquered it and it lay outside the realm to which Huascar succeeded by primogeniture. Moreover it had belonged to Atahuallpa's ancestors.

Huascar answered that Atahuallpa must come to Cuzco and hand over the army to him, in exchange for which he would give him land in which he could maintain himself very honourably. But Quito he could not give him since it was on the borders of his kingdom and he must maintain an army there to attack his enemies across the frontier. Huascar added that if Atahuallpa did not come he would regard him as an enemy and attack him.

Atahuallpa took counsel with two of his father's captains,

Quizquiz and Challcuchima, both valiant men and skilled in war. They advised him not to wait for his brother to attack but to strike first, for with his present army he could take possession of any province he invaded. Moreover he could add to his numbers daily. Therefore his brother would think it wise to come to an agreement with him. Accepting this advice, Atahuallpa left Quito and gradually took over the country. Huascar sent one of his captains or governors with some lightly armed troops on a rapid march to the province of Tumibamba, about a hundred leagues from Quito. But on hearing that Atahuallpa had already led his army forward, this personage sent a message to Huascar at Cuzco, asking for two thousand experienced captains and warriors, to whom he would add thirty thousand men of the very warlike people of Cañares, a province which was loyal to him.

Huascar sent two thousand men with great speed, and they were joined by the *caciques* of Tumibamba and by the Chaparras, Paltas and Cañares, the inhabitants of these parts. On receiving this news, Atahuallpa came out against them, and they fought for three days, many men being killed on both sides. Finally the Quito army was routed and Atahuallpa was captured at the bridge of Tumibamba. But while Huascar's men were celebrating their victory with a great drunken feast, Atahuallpa broke through the thick wall of the *tambo* of Tumibamba with a copper bar, which a woman had given him, and fled to Quito, about seventy-five leagues away. Collecting his people, he told them that his father had transformed him into a snake, which enabled him to creep out through a small hole, and that he had promised him victory if he would return to the fight. Thus inspired, his followers fell on the enemy, fought them, defeated and routed them, many men being killed on both sides in this battle also, so many indeed that great piles of bones still lie scattered on the battlefield.

Continuing and following up his victory, Atahuallpa decided to attack his brother. He advanced into the province of Cañares and killed sixty thousand of the army that had fought him, destroying with fire and sword the very large town of Tumibamba, which lies on a plain watered by three large rivers. From here he extended his conquests, executing all who resisted him and recruiting to his forces all those who made peace with him. In this way he continually increased his army and, arriving at Tumbez, decided to conquer the island of Puna which lies off it. But the *cacique* came out with many rafts and defended the island. So, knowing that his brother Huascar was advancing with his army against him, Atahuallpa decided that it would take him too long to capture Puna and continued on his way to Cuzco. Stopping at Cajamarca, he sent two of his captains ahead with four or five thousand men to make a rapid reconnaissance. When they came near to Huascar's army, they turned off the road along a by-way, to avoid notice. But it happened that Huascar himself had also taken this by-way with seven hundred of his best soldiers in order to avoid the bustle and congestion of the road. Coming upon Huascar by surprise, Atahuallpa's captains fought and routed his men, and took his brother prisoner. Then the whole of Huascar's army attacked them from all sides, and not one of them would have survived, for they were outnumbered thirty to one, if Atahuallpa's men had not put pressure on their prisoner. When they saw the attack coming, they told Huascar to order his men back, or they would cut off his head. In fear of death and trusting his brother's word that if he were left with the province of Quito he would acknowledge Huascar as his lord, for he had no other demands, Huascar ordered his men to fall back and return immediately to Cuzco, which they did.

When Atahuallpa was told of this great stroke of good fortune, he ordered his captains to bring Huascar as a prisoner to Cajamarca, where he awaited them. But at this juncture Don Francisco Pizarro arrived with the Spaniards whom he had brought to the land of Peru and seized the opportunity to make the conquest which will be described in the next book. For Huascar's army was defeated and in flight, and Atahuallpa's had for the most part dispersed after his victory.

BOOK TWO

THE CONQUEST OF PERU BY DON FRANCISCO PIZARRO AND HIS MEN

1. The expedition sets out

As was said in the last book, Francisco Pizarro had returned from Spain, and was now at Panama making preparations for the conquest of Peru. Don Diego was not acting with his accustomed vigour, however, although his cooperation was of prime importance since it was he who had both the wealth and the credit. The cause of his lukewarmness was that Don Francisco had brought him no favour from His Majesty. In the end, when Don Francisco had apologized, friendship was restored. But Don Francisco's brothers never had Almagro's goodwill. He harboured grievances against all of them, especially Hernando.

After some delay Hernando Ponce de Leon chartered one of his ships to Don Francisco Pizarro, who went aboard with his four brothers and as many foot and horsemen as he could collect. But recruitment was difficult because people had no confidence in this expedition on account of the great reverses it had suffered in previous years. It set sail however at the beginning of the year '31, and since the winds were adverse struck the coast of Peru more than a hundred leagues north of the place intended. Here Pizarro was forced to land his men and horses, and make his way along the coast, where they suffered great hardships and privations. For the rivers were so wide at the estuary that men and horses had to swim across. The skill and courage of Don Francisco's leadership counted for a great deal, however. He would himself make the crossing several times at great risk, carrying those who could not swim.

*

A FULLER ACCOUNT OF THE VOYAGE DOWN THE COAST BY DIEGO DE TRUJILLO

Those who had accompanied Francisco Pizarro in his first exploration of the coast refused to come, saying that it was a god-forsaken land and that any who went with him would go to their death. So many of those who came with him from Spain remained behind.

At the beginning of the year '31 we set sail, about two hundred and fifty Spaniards from the isle of Pearls. With us were three Dominicans, Fray Resinaldo, Fray Vicente de Valverde and Fray Juan. Once aboard we had very good weather and reached San Mateo bay in six days. It had never seen such a fleet. Bartolome Ruiz was our pilot, and was certainly of great help on the voyage.

We stayed ten days in the bay, resting our men, and many Indians came down the river in canoes to reconnoitre us; they were never willing to land. The country round the bay is mountainous and subject to frequent showers of rain. There was much local fruit, such as *guavas, guayabas, caimitos* and egg-fruit.*

On leaving the bay we came to a deserted village four leagues away, called Catamez. There were many *guayabas* and American plums and deep wells where we drank and drew water in shells. There were mosquitoes and showers, for this is still mountain country. From there we came to a large village on the coast called Cancevi, which was also deserted. It had many earthenware pots and fishing nets. There were maize fields, and although the grain was hardly formed we ate it, for we were very short of food. This country has no sweet water, and we suffered from thirst.

Since we had no guide who could tell us where we should go and rest, the Governor sent Captain Escobar into the mountains, to see if he could find an Indian. I went with him. We came to a dry, waterless gully, where we saw smoke, and we stayed in that gully until dawn in hopes of discovering their huts. It rained so heavily in the night that the gully was flooded, and one of our soldiers was drowned. The rest escaped by swimming. We did find their huts, and there were three or four Indians there. They had slung their beds at the top of high trees, like storks' nests, and were chattering like cats or monkeys. We captured one Indian, but had no way of understanding him, or he us. We took him to the camp and after a fortnight he told us by signs of a populous country ahead,

* The first two are the same, the third are called in America star apples and the last is unidentifiable.

where there was food, and now all that we wanted was to find food.

We went on down the coast and found a stream of sweet water falling down a gully into the sea. This delighted us hugely for we were very short of water. From here we marched on to the Quiximis rivers, where we made rafts to cross. When we reached here we were again very short of food and water, because the rivers have no sweet water except high up. But here Bartolome Ruiz joined us with the ship and the boat, and we received a meal of maize flour, half a pint for each man. After crossing these rivers, which were each a quarter of a league wide, we found plenty of sweet potatoes and yucca, from which we made cassava bread. And there was plenty of fruit, *guayabas* and other kinds. So our men were much restored.

There was another river in this country, further on than these and wider. Here they pulled a mare in, tied to a raft, and the horses immediately leapt in after her. Those who could not swim were taken over on rafts and on horseback, and since there were no beasts of burden each man carried his own possessions. Having crossed this river we went on down the coast, and struck some swamps where there were many crabs which had fed on the poison-tree. And that night everyone was at the point of death from eating poisoned crab.

We had now news of Coaque, a large village very rich in gold, silver, emeralds and other coloured stones, and gold, silver and bone beads. It had a large population. That night, when the men were still sick, the trumpet was sounded for an attack on the village. The attack took place and the *cacique* was captured, and kept imprisoned for a long time. There were large quantities of white cotton cloth, and the place had big temples with many idols and drums. There was plenty of maize and fruit to eat and sweet-basil, as in Spain, and chilis. The Indians were strong and warlike; the village had three hundred very large huts. It is rainy country with great thunderstorms and large snakes and toads; it is very wet. Once when there was nothing to eat, three soldiers ate a snake. Two of them died, and the third who had smeared his portion with garlic survived but lost all his hair and was left so ill that it was a long time before he recovered.

In this village they took eighteen thousand pesos of gold and some low-grade silver. The Governor then dispatched Bartolome Ruiz and Quintero, with the two ships, one to Nicaragua and the other to Panama, carrying the gold with which he hoped to attract more men. He and his followers stayed at Coaque for upwards of eight months, and during this time many died of sickness and of warts* which attacked the Spaniards.

After the ship had left for Panama the merchant Pedro Gregorio arrived at Coaque, bringing dried beef, hams and cheeses from the Canaries. And he brought some men also, of whom Pedro Diaz of Huamanga and Juan de la Terre of Arequipa and Yasasaga, who settled in Los Reyes, are still alive; all the rest are dead. On the ship that returned from Nicaragua came Sebastian de Benalcazar with a few more,† all of whom are dead.

The only person in the place who could identify emeralds was Fray Resinaldo, who collected upwards of a hundred and sewed them in his doublet.‡ He then returned in Pedro Gregorio's ship to Panama where he died. The emeralds were then taken from his effects and sent as a present to His Majesty.

In the meantime the Governor released the *cacique* of Coaque, who then revolted with all his people and burnt the village over our heads, leaving only a single hut in which we all took refuge. This we defended, and prevented them from setting it alight. The *cacique* then fled with all his people into the mountains. Taking with him an Indian who knew their hiding place, the Governor went out to look for them with a few men on foot, since the country was not fit for horses. But as they were crossing a river on rafts, their Indian guide

* This is again the local disease of deep seated warts, *verrugas*.

† Diego lists seven, of whom one, Miguel Estete, will describe his march with Hernando Pizarro to Pachacamac later in this book.

‡ He appears to have kept his knowledge to himself, since – as Zárate will tell us in his next chapter – the others destroyed their emeralds by testing them as if they were diamonds.

jumped in and was drowned. So the Governor and his men came back, having achieved nothing.

*

ZARATE CONCLUDES HIS CHAPTER WITH A BRIEF ACCOUNT OF EVENTS AT COAQUE, WHICH DIFFERS FROM DIEGO'S IN THE MATTER OF THE EMERALDS

Finally they came to a village called Coaque, which is near the sea and both populous and rich in merchandise. Here Pizarro was able to rest his men, who were very weak from the journey, and from here he sent two ships to Panama and Nicaragua with thirty thousand çastlins of gold which he had taken in Coaque. His purpose was to present an inspiring picture of the country which would induce others to join him in hopes of gain.

In Coaque we found some very fine emeralds, for the village is already south of the Line. But Pizarro's men shattered or chipped many of them, for they knew little about this kind of stone. They thought that, like diamonds, if genuine they would resist hammering. Believing that the Indians were passing off false jewels on them, they hammered them with stones, thus destroying emeralds of very great value. They were also attacked by an epidemic of warts, which spread right through the army so that none escaped it. The Governor persuaded them that this was due to the bad climate of the country and led them on to a province which they called Puerto Viejo, conquering and pacifying all that district. Here he was joined by Captain Benalcazar and Juan Flores who had come from Nicaragua in a ship with some foot and horsemen.

*

AN ACCOUNT OF THE INTERMEDIATE EVENTS BY DIEGO DE TRUJILLO

After the arrival of the ships from Panama and Nicaragua we left Coaque, though most of our men were sick. We then made for the Cape of Pascio but, being unable to pass the point, cleared a road across the mountain to the village of Pasao, and continued till we came to the bay of Caraquez, suffering great lack of drinking water. Here all the sick were put in a ship and sent to a village called Charapoto in the province of Puerto Viejo. Then the Governor and all his remaining men went along the bay shore to a place called Tecagua, and from here to another place in the same province which was ruled by a rich widow.

We spent more than two months in the Puerto Viejo country. There was maize and fish and a local fruit, the pawpaw. There was a syrup also, made from maize. The land is dry, and the heat opens great cracks in the soil. In some parts there are mountains. And there is chocolate like that of Mexico, though not much.

On leaving Puerto Viejo, we came to Picuaza and another port called Marchan, from which Captain Benalcazar made a foray inland, in which I took part. Here we found the first *lucumas** ever seen and many *caimitos*† and local duck. We took some prisoners and returned to the coast. From there we crossed a dry expanse that lies along the coast. The Governor sent Diego Maldenado to Nata to look for water since his men were almost dying of thirst, and he had decided that the best thing would be to turn back. But Hernando Pizarro was for going on, even at the risk of our lives. And the advance guard discovered a small pool of greenish water, where we all refreshed ourselves, although some pigs that Hernando had brought from Panama churned it up to such an extent that, except for the first of us, we drank pure mud.

From there we went to Santa Elena point, where the giants' bones were. We found that the inhabitants had taken to their rafts with their wives and children and all their animals, and would not come ashore. We were very hungry when we arrived, but we remedied that. Since the people had put to sea and the villages were deserted the dogs howled in the night, and we went after them. We kept ourselves alive by eating those dogs; we should have been very badly off without them.

From there we went to the province of Odon, in the Guam-

* A kind of fruit. † See above, p. 66

cavilcas, a land with plenty of food, and we spent a fortnight there recuperating both the sick and the sound. We then came to the straits of Huayna Capac, so-called because Huayna Capac crossed them to conquer the island of Puna. Tumbala, the ruler of the island, came out with many men and rafts and welcomed us with great feasts and rejoicing. We learnt afterwards that the men who steered the rafts intended to untie the cords when we were in the middle of the straits and drown us all. Only the raft carrying the Governor and the ruler of the island was to be left afloat. But the feasting was so excessive that the Governor said to Sebastian de Benalcazar: 'All this seems suspicious to me.' So he ordered the ruler and some other chiefs of the island to stay with him on the mainland, and said we must cross by another way. And so our men got over safely, and the rafts came back to take the Governor and those who had stayed with him.

We went ashore at a village called El Tucu. The straits were a league and a half across. And from there we went to a village called El Estero on the other side of the island. Here we found a tall cross and a small one painted on a door and a small bell hanging. It seemed a miracle. Then out of the house came thirty or more boys and girls crying 'Jesus Christ be praised, Molina, Molina!'

The fact was that at the time of the first voyage of discovery the Captain had left two Spaniards at the port of Payta, one of whom was called Molina. The other, whose name was Gines, was killed by the Indians at the village of Cinto for looking at a *cacique*'s wife. Molina came to the island of Puna which was held by the Indians for their captain against the Chonos and the people of Tumbez. But a month before we came he had been killed at sea by the Chonos while out fishing; and the people of Puna were greatly grieved by his death.

2. *The Governor conquers the island of Puna*

[Zárate describes the attempted treachery of the people of Puna, but gives a different and slightly fuller account of the crossing. He omits the story of Molina and his thirty children.]

...BUT the Governor got wind of the plot and ordered all his men to be very wary and to carry their swords unsheathed and not to let any Indian out of their sight. When they reached the island, the inhabitants came out peacefully and gave them a good reception though they kept an army in hiding all that night ready to kill them. But the Governor learnt of this and fell on them, routing them and taking the principal *cacique* prisoner. But when dawn broke next day the camp was surrounded by warriors. With great courage the Governor and his brothers swiftly mounted their horses and sent the Spaniards out in all directions. He also sent help to the ships which were lying close to land, for the Indians were attacking them in rafts across the sea. The Spaniards fought so hard that they routed the Indians, killing and wounding many. Only two or three Spaniards died here, though many were severely wounded, Gonzalo Pizarro in particular, who received a dangerous wound in the knee.

After this, Captain Hernando de Soto arrived with the reinforcements of horse and foot he had brought from Nicaragua. All the Indians of that island then boarded their rafts and took refuge in the mangrove-swamps, where they could not be attacked. Having made a division of the gold he had received here, the Governor decided to cross to Tumbez, because his men had fallen sick on this island, which is very unhealthy, being near the Equator.

3. The Governor crosses to Tumbez. His conquests up to the settling of San Miguel

MORE than six hundred men and women of Tumbez, including one chieftain, were held prisoner on the island of Puna. Don Francisco freed them all, and gave them rafts to carry them home. When he himself was embarking he sent three Christians ahead with some of these Tumbez Indians, and their raft was the first to reach port. On its arrival the men of Tumbez sacrificed three Spaniards to their idol as thanksgiving for the kindness Don Francisco had done them by freeing the prisoners; and they would have done the same to Captain Hernando de Soto, who had crossed on another raft with some local Indians and a single servant and was going up the Tumbez river, had it not been for Diego de Aguero and Rodrigo Lozano,* who had just disembarked and ran along the shore to warn them they must turn back immediately. Since all the country was up in arms, there were no rafts to help in the disembarkation of the men and horses. So no one landed with the Governor that evening except his brothers Hernando and Juan, Fray Vicente de Valverde, Captain Soto and two more Spaniards. They did not dismount from their horses all night, though they were very wet, for the sea had been rough and the raft had turned over as they landed. For the Spaniards could not manage these craft without Indian help and there were no Indians there.

Hernando Pizarro remained behind to receive the army, and the Governor rode ahead for more than two leagues without encountering an Indian. They were all in arms and had taken to the hills. He then turned back to the sea, where he found Captains Mena and Juan de Salcedo, who had come to look for him with some horsemen who had already disembarked. After this meeting, the Governor established his camp at Tumbez, where after some time Captain Benalcazar arrived. He and his men had remained on the island, since they could not cross in

* This is the man whom Zárate mentions as his chief informant.

the first raftloads but had to wait for the craft to return. The Indians had attacked them continuously.

The Governor remained at Tumbez for twenty days. During this time he sent an offer of peace to the ruler of the country, who refused his overtures. Instead he harried the camp servants when they went out to forage and inflicted heavy casualties on them. Being on the wrong side of the river, the Spaniards could not attack until the Governor sent for some rafts, which were brought along the coast without the Indians' knowledge. Then one evening Juan and Gonzalo Pizarro and Captains Soto and Benalcazar crossed the river with more than fifty horsemen and, after a difficult night ride, since the road was very narrow and led through thick woods and thorn patches, fell on the Indians' camp at dawn. Here they inflicted all the damage they could, and for a whole fortnight waged cruel war with fire and sword in revenge for the three Spaniards who had been sacrificed. Finally the chief of Tumbez came to make peace, bringing a present of gold and silver.

The Governor then set out with most of his men, leaving His Majesty's auditor Antonio Navarro and the treasurer Alonso Requelme behind with the rest. On reaching the river Poeches, thirty leagues from Tumbez, he made peaceable arrangements with the villages and their rulers on its banks, and went on in search of the port of Paita, the best on that coast. He sent Captain de Soto to the villages and chieftains on the banks of the Paita, and they too, after a few skirmishes, asked for peace.

During his stay at Paita messengers came to the Governor from Huascar, who was in Cuzco, to inform him of his brother Atahuallpa's rebellion and ask for his help. For Atahuallpa had not yet captured Huascar, as he soon did. The Governor sent Hernando Pizarro to Tumbez to fetch all those he had left behind, and on their arrival he founded the city of San Miguel at an Indian township called Tangarara, on the banks of the river Chira, near the sea, in order that ships coming from Panama should find a safe port. For some had arrived already. And when he had divided the gold and silver captured there, he set out with all the rest of his men for the province of Cajamarca, since he had heard that Atahuallpa was there.

4. The Governor's Journey to Cajamarca and events in that place

ON the way to Cajamarca the Governor and his army suffered greatly from thirst in a desert twenty leagues across in which there are no trees and no water. All is dry sand and it is very hot. This desert lies between the present city of San Miguel and the province of Motupe, where he found cool and populous valleys. Here he rested his men, and the abundant food of the district restored their strength.

*

AN ACCOUNT OF THE MARCH ACROSS THE SIERRA TO CAJAMARCA FROM FRANCISCO DE JEREZ, 'CONQUEST OF PERU AND THE PROVINCE OF CUZCO'

The Governor left the city of San Miguel in search of Atahuallpa on 24 September 1532. On the first day of his journey he and his men crossed the river on two rafts, the horses swimming. They spent the night at a village on the further side, and in three days' march reached the fortress of a *cacique* in the valley of Piura, where they found a captain and some Spaniards, whom the Governor had sent to impose peace on this *cacique* and to prevent him from harassing the *cacique* of San Miguel. The Governor remained here for ten days collecting supplies for his march. On reviewing the Christians in his company, he counted sixty-seven horsemen and a hundred and ten foot, including three gunners with guns and some crossbowmen. Hearing from his lieutenant at San Miguel that a few Christians remained behind, the Governor proclaimed that any who wished to return and settle in the town should have enough Indians assigned them to maintain them as well as the settlers then there. For himself, he intended to advance and conquer with such as stayed with him, whether many or few. Five horsemen and four foot turned back. Including them, the settlers at San Miguel amounted to forty-five, with ten or a dozen more who remained voluntarily unprovided for.

The Governor had now sixty-two horsemen and a hundred and two foot. He ordered that armour should be made for those who had none, both for themselves and their horses, and he reformed his crossbowmen, increasing their numbers to twenty and putting a captain over them.

Having made all necessary dispositions, he set out with his men and after marching till midday came to a great square surrounded by walls, belonging to a *cacique* called Pabor, where he and his men took up their lodgings. He learnt that this chief was a great lord, though at present in decline, since Atahuallpa's father, 'old Cuzco'* had destroyed twenty of his villages, killing their inhabitants.

Despite this disaster the *cacique* had many subjects, and bordering on his lands were those of his brother, as great a lord as himself. They both submitted peacefully and were assigned to the city of San Miguel. Like this settlement, Piura lies in a flat and fertile valley. The Governor made inquiries here about the local villages and chieftains and the road to Cajamarca. He was informed that two days' journey away was the large village of Cajas,† where Atahuallpa had placed a considerable garrison to await the Christians, should they come that way.

On receiving this information, the Governor ordered Captain Hernando de Soto‡ to go quietly to Cajas with some foot and horse and negotiate honestly with Atahuallpa's people if he found them there. He was careful not to provoke them, and if he could overcome their resistance, he was to bring them into His Majesty's service.

The captain departed immediately. Next day the Governor set out also for the village of Zaran, where he was to wait for Soto's return. The *cacique* of the place brought the Governor supplies of sheep and other things to a fortress where he

* Francisco de Jerez confuses the princes and their capital. He calls Huayna Capac 'old Cuzco' and Huascar 'young Cuzco'.

† Lying across the Andes in the Marañon watershed.

‡ Francisco de Jerez calls him 'a captain'. He seldom names anyone. I have however identified individual soldiers where possible without calling attention to the verbal changes I have made.

arrived at midday. Next day he left the fortress and came to Zaran, where he set up his camp and waited.

Five days later Soto sent a messenger to the Governor with news of events, and the Governor replied that he would stay at Zaran until negotiations were complete and he could return to join him. He instructed Soto to visit another place near Cajas called Huanca-pampa on his way back and reduce it to obedience also. The Governor informed him further that the *cacique* of Zaran was said to own several other villages and a fertile valley, all of which Pizarro had assigned to the settlers of San Miguel. During the eight days of the Governor's stay at Zaran, the Spaniards re-equipped themselves and refreshed their horses for the coming journey of conquest.

On returning with his men, Soto gave the Governor an account of all he had seen in the villages. The journey to Cajas had taken him two days and a night, with no pause except for meals, and they had climbed high mountains. They had hoped to take Cajas by surprise. But, although they had good guides, they would never have got there if they had not met some scouts from the place on the road. A few, whom they captured, had given them information. Soto had then marshalled his men and followed the road till they came to Cajas, which lies in a small valley surrounded by mountains. At the entrance to the place they found a military building which seemed to have been recently used. The people were in commotion, but Soto reassured them, explaining that he had come on the Governor's behalf to receive them as vassals of the Emperor. Then a captain appeared who stated that he was collecting tribute from these villages for Atahuallpa. Soto asked him about the road to Cajamarca, and whether Atahuallpa intended to receive the Christians peacefully, also about the city of Cuzco. The Captain answered that it was thirty days' journey away and a league in circumference, and that the *cacique's* lodgings were four bowshots long, and the great hall in which 'old Cuzco's' body lay had a floor paved with silver and walls covered with both gold and silver. He said that until a year ago these villages had belonged to 'Cuzco', the son of 'old Cuzco'. But then his brother Atahuallpa had rebelled and conquered the country, imposing heavy taxes and inflicting daily cruelties. He said that in addition to the tribute of valuables and stores, they had also to give their sons and daughters; that the military building the Spaniards had seen was Atahuallpa's, and that he had left with a division of his army only a few days before. There was a large, strong building in the village, surrounded by mud walls pierced with doorways, in which were many women who spun and wove for Atahuallpa's army, and no men with them except the porters who guarded them. At the entrance to Cajas some Indians were hanging by the feet. They had been executed at Atahuallpa's command because one of them had entered this house to sleep with a woman. Not only was he hanged, but the porters who had admitted him also.

Having established peaceable relations with the village, Soto went on to Nuanca-pampa, which is a day's journey away, and larger. It had better buildings and a fortress of fine masonry, the blocks of which were three foot six or four foot square, and so closely joined that there seemed to be no mortar between them. There was a high platform of hewn stone, with two stone staircases and a building on either side. Through both this place and Cajas runs a small river which supplies them with water and is crossed by bridges with well-paved footways. They are joined by the wide road which crosses the whole country from Cuzco to Quito for more than three hundred leagues. This road is smooth and well built where it passes through the mountains, being wide enough for six horsemen to ride abreast without touching. Alongside the road run channels of water drawn from a distance at which travellers can drink. At each stage there is a building where those who come and go may lodge. At the approach to this road from the village of Cajas, a toll-house stands at the head of the bridge, where a guard was posted to receive porterage in kind from those entering or leaving. No one could take a load out of the town without paying toll. This is an ancient custom, but Atahuallpa suspended it in regard to supplies brought for his troops. No passenger was allowed to take goods into or out of the town by any other road. Soto also found in both towns houses stocked with bread and footwear, salt and a food like *albondigas*,* and other stores for Atahuallpa's army. He re-

* Forced meat balls.

ported that these towns were well ruled and the people lived in an orderly manner.

With Captain Soto came an Indian chief and some others bringing a present for the Governor. The chief said that his master Atahuallpa had sent him from Cajamarca expressly to bring it. This present consisted of two drinking vessels carved in stone in the shape of fortresses, and two loads of skinned and dried goosemeat which is powdered and burnt as incense by the lords of that country. Atahuallpa also sent a message that he wished to be the Governor's friend and was waiting to receive him peacefully at Cajamarca.

The Governor accepted this present and caressed the messenger politely saying: 'I am delighted to receive you as a messenger of Atahuallpa. I have heard such good things of your lord that I long to meet him. I have been told that he is making war against his enemies. I have decided to visit him therefore as a friend and brother, and with the Christians of my company to aid him in his conquests.'

The Governor had food given to the messenger and his companions, and said that they should have all that they needed and be well lodged as ambassadors of so great a prince. Then, when they had rested, he sent for them again and told them they were free either to return at once, or rest for a day if they preferred. The ambassador said that he would carry the message back to his master immediately. The Governor then answered: 'Tell the prince in my name what I have said. Say that I will stop at no place on the way, but will come quickly to see him.' He gave the messenger a shirt and other articles from Spain to take with him.

The Governor stayed for two days after the messenger's departure, since the men who had been to Cajas were still tired from their journey. During this time he wrote to the settlers in San Miguel, setting down all he had learnt of the country and the news of Atahuallpa. He sent them the two fortress drinking vessels and some woollen cloth of the country, which had been brought from Cajas. This cloth aroused great admiration in Spain, where it was considered more like silk than wool and much admired for its applied figures and patterns in beaten gold.

Having dispatched his messengers to San Miguel, the Governor set out and marched for three days without finding a village or any water except at one small spring, from which it could only be got with difficulty.* At the end of three days he reached a great walled enclosure in which he found nobody. He learnt that it belonged to the lord of a village called Copiz in a near-by valley, and that the fortress was deserted because there was no water. Next morning, he got up early and set out in moonlight, since it was a long day's march to the next populated place. At midday he reached a walled house with very fine lodgings, from which some Indians came out to receive him. But because there were neither provisions nor water he went on two leagues further to the *cacique*'s village, and on arriving there had all his men lodged together in one part of it. Here he was informed by the chief Indians of the place, which is called Motupe, that the *cacique* was at Cajamarca and had taken three hundred warriors with him. But there was a captain in the place appointed by Atahuallpa. The Governor rested here for four days, during which he saw some of the *cacique*'s subjects, who seemed very numerous and lived in a fertile valley. All the villages from here to San Miguel lie in valleys, and so do all those known between here and the foot of the mountains, near Cajamarca.

All the people along this road have the same habits and customs. The women wear a long robe that drags on the ground like women's dresses in Spain; and the men wear short shirts. They are a dirty people. They eat flesh and fish always raw, and maize either boiled or toasted. They have other abominations, such as sacrifices and 'mosques',† which they hold in great veneration. Indeed they offer the best part of their wealth in them. Each month they sacrifice some of their own stock, smearing the faces of their idols and their 'mosque' doors with their blood, and pouring it over the graves of their dead. The victims they sacrifice go willingly to their deaths, laughing, dancing and singing. When they are full of drink they beg to be sacrificed and are then beheaded. These people also sacrifice sheep. Their 'mosques' differ from their other houses, being

* He was now crossing the great sandy desert of Sechura.

† Francisco de Jerez calls any pagan temple a mosque.

surrounded by well-built walls of stone and mud-brick and placed at the highest point in their towns. In Tumbez they wear similar clothes and practise similar sacrifices. They sow their crops on the plains beside the rivers and irrigate them by means of conduits. They grow maize and other grain crops, and edible roots in abundance. There is little rain in this country.

The Governor travelled for two days through thickly populated valleys,* spending the night in fortified houses, walled with mud-brick. The village chiefs told him that 'old Cuzco' used these houses as lodgings when he was travelling. The local population was friendly. Some days later he crossed a tract of dry, sandy country to reach another well-populated valley through which ran a large and swift river,† which was in spate. He spent the night here therefore and next morning ordered Hernando Pizarro and a few others who could swim to go across to the villages on the other bank and persuade their inhabitants not to oppose the Spaniards' passage. Hernando Pizarro crossed without opposition, and the people in the villages gave him a peaceful reception, lodging him in a walled fort. But despite this friendly welcome, he found that most of the villagers were in arms and had left their houses, taking their clothes with them. He inquired therefore about Atahuallpa's intentions. Was he preparing a peaceful or a warlike reception? No one was willing to answer, for they were afraid of Atahuallpa, till Hernando Pizarro took one of the chiefs aside and put him to the torture. The man confessed that Atahuallpa was preparing for war, and had divided his army into three detachments, one of which was at the foot of the mountains, another at the summit and the third at Cajamarca. He also said that Atahuallpa was waiting in great pride and that he had heard him boast that every Christian would be killed.

Next morning the Captain sent this news to the Governor, who ordered that trees should be cut down on both banks, so that the men and baggage could be brought across. Three boats were constructed and in the course of the day all the men were brought over, the horses swimming. The Governor took a

* The Motupe and Leche valleys.
† The Chincha river.

vigorous part in all this work and when the passage was complete went to lodge at the fortress where the Captain had stayed. He then sent for a *cacique,* from whom he learnt that Atahuallpa was now at Huamacucho on the other side of Cajamarca with a large army of about fifty thousand men. On hearing this figure, the Governor thought that the *cacique* must be mistaken and inquired as to their method of calculation. He was told that they count from one to ten, and from ten to a hundred, ten hundreds making a thousand and five ten thousands the number of men then with Atahuallpa. The Governor's informant, who was the chief *cacique* of that river, said that when Atahuallpa entered the country he had hidden out of fear. Then, furious at not finding him in any of his villages, Atahuallpa had killed four thousand of his five thousand subjects and taken six hundred women and six hundred boys to be divided among his warriors. He gave the name of the *cacique* of the village and fortress in which they were standing as Cinto, and said that he was with Atahuallpa.

The Governor and his men rested here for four days. On the day before his departure he took aside an Indian of the province of San Miguel, and asked him if he had the courage to go to Cajamarca as a spy and report what was going on there. The Indian answered: 'I should not dare to go as a spy. But I will go as your messenger to speak with Atahuallpa. I shall then find out what he intends and whether he has an army in the mountains.' The Governor agreed. 'And if there is an army in the mountains,' he said, 'as is reported here, send me warning by one of the Indians who will go with you. And when you speak with Atahuallpa and his people, tell them how well I and my fellow Christians treat those *caciques* who are friendly to us. Say that we only make war on those who attack us, and that you are telling the whole truth, according to what you have seen. Tell Atahuallpa that if he receives us kindly, I will be a friend and brother to him and aid and favour him in his war.'

The Indian departed with his message, and the Governor continued his journey across these valleys, arriving each evening at a village with its walled and fortified house. After three days he came to one at the foot of the mountains, where he left the road he had been following on the right, since it continued up the valley to Chincha, and turned along another road which goes straight to Cajamarca. The road to Chincha starts from the San Miguel river and passes through many villages. It is paved, and bordered on both sides with mud-brick walls, and can take two carts abreast. After leaving Chincha it goes on to Cuzco, and along a great part of its length it is bordered on both sides by trees, which have been planted to shade it. This road was made for 'old Cuzco' when he visited the country, and these walled houses were his lodgings.

Some Christians were of the opinion that the Governor should follow the Chincha road since there were difficult mountains to be crossed on the other, and before reaching Cajamarca they would meet an army of Atahuallpa, which might do them some harm. The Governor replied that ever since they left the San Miguel river Atahuallpa had known they were coming in search of him, and that if they did not follow that road the Indians would say they were afraid to come. At the conclusion of the Governor's speech, everyone agreed that he should take whichever road he preferred and they would follow with high courage. Then in due time each man would show him what he could do for God and His Majesty.

On reaching the foot of the mountains, they rested a day to make their dispositions for the ascent. After consulting experienced opinion, the Governor decided to leave the rearguard and baggage behind. Taking forty horse and sixty foot with him, he entrusted the rest to his brother Hernando, whom he instructed to follow at a regular pace until further orders. Having made these arrangements, the Governor began the ascent, the horsemen leading their horses. At midday they came to a walled fort on the top of a mountain, a dangerous place on the road, where a few Christians could have held off a great army. For the road was so steep that in parts it was cut in steps, and the only possible ascent was by following it. They had climbed this pass without meeting any resistance and arrived at the walled fort. The mountain on which it stands has precipitous crags on all sides. Here the Governor halted to rest and eat.

The cold in the mountains is so intense that, being used to

the heat of the valleys from which they had come, some of the horses caught cold. The Governor went on to sleep at another village, and sent a message to those in the rear telling them that they could safely climb the pass and should endeavour to arrive in time to sleep at the fort. He took up his quarters for the night in this village in a house surrounded by a masonry wall pierced with doorways. The enclosure was as large as a Spanish fortress, and the wall could not have been better built if the Indians had had Spanish tools and craftsmen. The villagers had taken up arms, and only some women and a few men remained. The Governor ordered a captain to take two of the chief Indians and ask each separately about the state of the country, and where Atahuallpa was, and if he intended peace or war. They both informed the captain that Atahuallpa had returned to Cajamarca three days before, and had many men with him, but they knew nothing of his intentions, though they had always heard that he wished to be at peace with the Christians. The people of the village were on his side.

Just as the sun was about to set one of the Indians who had accompanied the Governor's ambassador to Atahuallpa arrived, saying that his chief had sent him back from a place near Cajamarca where he had met two messengers from Atahuallpa travelling in the reverse direction, who would arrive next day. He reported that Atahuallpa was at Cajamarca and his master would not stop until he had spoken with him and could return with an answer. He added that he had met no soldiers on the road. The Governor sent all this news to his brother Hernando who was in charge of the baggage, and added that he would only make a short march next day in order to allow him to catch up, and that the whole force would then advance together. Next morning the Governor pressed on with his men still climbing, and stopped in a flat place at the top, beside some streams, to await the rearguard. The Spaniards camped in the cotton tents they carried, kindling fires to protect themselves from the great cold of the mountains. For it is not colder on the tableland of Castile than on these heights, which are bare and covered with a grass like short esparto. There are a few stunted trees, and the water is so cold that it gives men a chill to drink it.

When the Governor had rested here for a little the rearguard arrived, and from the opposite direction the messengers from Atahuallpa, bringing ten sheep. Being led before the Governor, they paid their respects, and said that Atahuallpa had sent these sheep for the Christians and wished to know on what day they would arrive at Cajamarca so that he could send them food on the road. The Governor welcomed them saying that he was glad to see them since his brother Atahuallpa had sent them, and that he would come as quickly as he could. After they had eaten and rested he inquired about the state of the country and the war in which Atahuallpa was engaged. One of them replied that Atahuallpa had been in Cajamarca for five days waiting for the Governor, and that he had only a few men with him, since he had sent his army to fight his brother 'Cuzco'. The Governor asked him more particularly about the state of this war and how Atahuallpa's campaign had begun. The Indian said: 'My master Atahuallpa is the son of "old Cuzco" who is dead and once ruled all these lands.' (The messenger then set out Atahuallpa's case against his brother, describing the war up to the moment of Atahuallpa's arrival at Cajamarca.) 'And when he came there the place seemed to him good and fertile, and he took up his residence there in order to complete the conquest of all his brother's land. He sent a captain with two thousand soldiers against the city where his brother was, and his brother, having a large army, killed those two thousand men. Then, six months ago, Atahuallpa sent more men under two captains who only a few days ago sent news that they had won all "Cuzco's" land as far as his city. They had defeated him and his army and taken him prisoner, and had captured much gold and silver.'

The Governor believed that all this had been said on Atahuallpa's instructions, for the purpose of striking fear and terror into the Christians and impressing them with his skill and power. He said to the messenger therefore: 'I can well believe that all you say is true. Atahuallpa is a great lord and I have heard that he is a fine soldier. But I must tell you that my lord the Emperor, who is king of Spain and all the Indies and the Mainland and ruler of the whole world, has many greater lords than Atahuallpa among his servants. He and his captains have defeated mightier rulers than Atahuallpa, his brother and his father. The Emperor has sent me to these lands to bring knowledge of God to their inhabitants and to make them obey Him. With these few Christians of my company I have overthrown greater lords than Atahuallpa. If he desires my friendship and will receive me in peace, I will be his friend and help him in his conquests, and he shall remain in his high estate, for I am crossing these lands to discover the other sea. But if he prefers war I will fight him as I fought the *cacique* of the island of Santiago and the *cacique* of Tumbez, and all others who have opposed me. But I neither fight nor molest anyone unless I am attacked.'

For a while the messengers remained speechless with amazement, unable to believe that so few Spaniards could have performed such great deeds. After a while they said they would like to carry this answer to their master, and tell him that the Christians would soon arrive, so that he might send them food on the road. The Governor then dismissed them. Next morning he resumed his march, still through the mountains, and slept the night in one of a group of villages which he found in a nearby valley. As soon as he reached it, there came the same messenger whom Atahuallpa had sent to Zaran on the Cajas road with the present of the fortress drinking vessels. The Governor expressed great pleasure at seeing him, and asked him how he had left Atahuallpa. He answered, 'Well,' and that Atahuallpa had sent him with twelve sheep for the Christians. He spoke very freely and, to judge by his expression, seemed an intelligent man.

On the conclusion of this messenger's speech, the Governor asked the interpreters what he had said. They answered: 'He says the same as yesterday's messenger, and much else in praise of his master's greatness and the vast power of his army. But in addition he brings an assurance that Atahuallpa will receive you in peace and wishes to have you as his friend and brother.' The Governor made the same speech to this messenger as to the last. This one was attended like a lord and had five or six fine gold vessels from which he drank and in which he proffered the *chicha* he brought with him to the Spaniards. He said that he wished to accompany the Governor to Cajamarca.

The Governor set out next morning and travelled through the mountains as before till he came to one of Atahuallpa's villages, where he rested. On the following day the chieftain from San Miguel whom he had sent as a messenger came to him there. On seeing Atahuallpa's messenger who was still in the camp, this man rushed upon him and seized him by the ears, tugging them violently till the Governor told him to let go. But for his interference indeed, there would have been an ugly scuffle. The Governor then asked his envoy why he had treated Atahuallpa's messenger so roughly. 'He is a great scoundrel, this runner* of Atahuallpa's,' he replied. 'He has come here to tell lies and pretends to be a great man. Atahuallpa is preparing war and has already led his army into the country. Finding Cajamarca deserted, I went out to the camp, where I saw a large army and many tents and sheep. All is ready for war. And they would have killed me if I had not threatened that you would kill Atahuallpa's ambassadors in revenge, and that you would in any case detain them till I returned. Then they released me, but they refused to give me food and said that I must pay a ransom. I asked to be allowed to see Atahuallpa and give him your message, but they refused. They said he was fasting and could not speak to anyone. An uncle of his came out to speak to me. I told him that I was your messenger and that I would tell him anything else he asked. He inquired what sort of men the Christians are and what weapons they carry. I told him: "They are brave men and very warlike. They have horses that run like the wind, and their riders carry long lances with which they kill everyone within reach. They catch them up in two leaps, and the horses kill many with their hooves and teeth. The Christians who fight on foot are very swift, and have wooden shields to protect them. They wear stout tunics lined with cotton, and carry very sharp swords that cut with both edges, and can slice a man in two at a single blow or cut the head off a sheep. They can pierce any Indian armour. Other Christians carry arquebuses that shoot from far away, and can kill a man with every shot, and yet others shoot with powder, sending out balls of fire that kill many men also."

* Presumably a runner of the post.

'They answered that all this is nothing, that the Christians are few, and that the horses have no armour and they will kill them with their spears. I replied they have thick skins which spears cannot pierce. They said that they are not afraid of the Christians' fire-shooters, since they have only two.

'As I was about to go I asked them once more to let me see Atahuallpa, since his messengers had come and spoken with you who are a greater man than he. But they refused, and so I came away. But should I not be right to kill this man? For he is one of Atahuallpa's runners (as I have been told) and yet he speaks with you and eats at your table, while I who am a chief was not allowed to speak to Atahuallpa and was given no food and only by argument prevented them from killing me.'

Terrified at hearing the other Indian speak with such assurance, Atahuallpa's messenger replied: 'If there are no people in the town of Cajamarca, it is in order that the houses shall be empty for the Christians to lodge in. Atahuallpa is in the field because that has been his custom since the beginning of the war, and if they would not allow this man to speak to him it was because he was fasting. On the days when he fasts he goes into retirement and no one may speak to him. No one dared to tell him that this messenger had come. Had he known he would have had him admitted and would have given him food.'

The man used many other arguments to convince the Governor that Atahuallpa's intentions were peaceful. If their whole conversation were to be reported it would fill a book. But, to be brief, the Governor said that he accepted the man's explanations, since he had not lost confidence in his brother Atahuallpa. He continued to treat the man as well as before and scolded his own messenger for attacking him in his presence. But secretly he was convinced that his own messenger's story was entirely true since he knew the deceitful ways of the Indians.

Next day the Governor departed, and slept the night on a treeless plain, expecting to reach Cajamarca at noon next day, since they told him it was near. Here messengers came from Atahuallpa with food for the Christians. And next day at dawn the Governor set out with his men in battle order and marched to within a league of Cajamarca. Here he waited for the rearguard to join him. All the troops and horses were then armed, and the Governor drew them up in three bands of foot and horse for their entrance into Cajamarca.

In this order the Governor marched on, sending messengers ahead to ask Atahuallpa to come and meet him in the town. When they reached the approaches, they saw that prince's camp a league away on the lower slopes of a mountain. The Governor reached the town of Cajamarca on the evening of Friday, 15 November 1532.

*

DESCRIPTION OF CAJAMARCA FROM PEDRO CIEZA DE LEON'S 'CHRONICLE OF PERU', I, CHAPTER LXXVII

The inhabitants of Cajamarca claim that they were greatly respected by their neighbours before the Incas became their masters, that they had temples and shrines on the hilltops, and that their dress was not as magnificent as it became later and is now. Some of the Indians say that the first Inca to conquer them was Yupanqui, and others that it was not he but his son Tupac Yupanqui. Whichever it was, it is well authenticated that before he conquered Cajamarca a large part of his army was destroyed in battle, and that it was by tricks and fine words and smooth protestations rather than force of arms that the people of Cajamarca were subdued. The native lords of this province were strictly obeyed by their subjects and had many wives. One of these was the chief wife, and her son, if she had one, succeeded to the lordship. When a chief died, they followed the custom of their former lords and buried his wives and treasure with him, observing a continuous mourning. Their temples and shrines were greatly venerated. Blood of lambs and sheep was offered in sacrifice and the priests are said to have conversed with the devil. On the occasion of their feasts a great number of people would assemble in their squares, which were swept clean. They performed songs and dances there during which they drank considerable quantities of their wine, which was made of maize and various roots. All wore cloaks and embroidered shirts and, as a distinguishing sign, slings or other cords in the form of a narrow band round their heads.

Once they had conquered the province of Cajamarca, the Incas are said to have set great store by it. They had palaces built for them and a very important temple for the worship of the sun, also a great number of storehouses. And the virgins who lived in this temple devoted themselves solely to spinning and weaving. The cloth they wove was the finest in the country, and indeed both for its colours and its perfect workmanship the equal of any in the world. This temple was very rich; magnificent vessels were used in its service. And here, on certain days, the devil was seen by its ministers, who conversed with him and confided in him.

Great numbers of the Indians of this province were *mitimaes*, and all obeyed their chief steward, whose duty it was to provide for them and command within the boundaries of the territory assigned to them. And the superintendent of the great stores and lodging-houses, which were all around in almost every village, came here to present their accounts. For this was the capital of the surrounding provinces and of many valleys of the plain. Though there were many other temples and shrines in the coastal lands, great numbers came to Cajamarca to worship the sun and sacrifice in its temple. There were many notable objects in the Incas' palaces also, especially the very fine bath in which the lords and chieftains bathed when they lodged here. But now (owing to the Civil War and the Spanish conquest) this province has fallen into great decay.

*

ZARATE, CHAPTER FOUR (CONT.)

[*Zárate tells the story of the march to Cajamarca very briefly, and his details do not entirely agree with those of Francisco de Jerez.*]

As he climbed the *sierra*, the Governor met a messenger from Atahuallpa who brought him a pair of painted shoes and some gold bracelets, with the request that he should wear them when he came before Atahuallpa in order that the prince might recognize him. The Governor received him joyfully and promised to wear the gifts. He said that he had not come to harm Atahuallpa, and would not do so unless the prince gave him overt cause. For the Emperor and king of Castile by whose command he came allowed no one to inflict harm without cause.

When the messenger departed, the Governor followed him, travelling very cautiously for fear the Indians might descend on the road and attack his men. And when he reached Cajamarca he met another messenger who came out to tell him that he must not take up his quarters without Atahuallpa's express command. The Governor's only answer was to do so immediately and to send Captain Soto with some twenty horsemen to Atahuallpa's camp, which was a league away, to announce his arrival . . .

*

THE 'TAMBO' AT CAJAMARCA AND HERNANDO PIZARRO'S VISIT TO ATAHUALLPA'S CAMP, FROM FRANCISCO DE JEREZ, 'CONQUEST OF PERU AND THE PROVINCE OF CUZCO'

In the middle of the town is a large square surrounded by mud-brick walls and lodging-houses. Finding it deserted, the Governor halted here, and sent a messenger to Atahuallpa announcing his arrival and asking the prince to come and see him and tell him where to lodge. He then sent his men to inspect the town and report if there was any stronger place in which he could camp. In the meantime he commanded his troops to stay in the square, and the horsemen to remain in the saddle, until he knew whether Atahuallpa would come. Those who had inspected the town reported that there was no better position in it.

Cajamarca, which is the principal place in that valley, lies at the foot of a mountain with a league of fields before it, which are crossed by two rivers. The valley is flat, with much populated land on one side and closed in by mountains on the other. It has two thousand inhabitants, and is approached by two bridges, one over each stream. The square is larger than any in Spain. It is entirely walled and has two doorways leading into the city streets. The houses have a frontage of more than two hundred yards and are very well built. The mud-brick walls round them are twenty feet high. The walls and roof are thatched with straw and the walls have wooden cappings. The houses inside are divided into eight rooms finer than those we had seen in other places. Their walls are of carefully worked blocks, and each lodging is surrounded by its own stone wall and doorways. In the courts are basins of water, which is piped from outside to serve the houses. On the field side of the square is a stone fort, which is connected with it by a stone staircase inside the walls. On the outside of the fort is another entrance, a small postern with its own narrow staircase entirely enclosed in the walls. On the mountainside above the town, where the houses begin, is another fortress perched on a rock and largely hewn out of it. This is larger than the other and surrounded by three walls, which ascend the hill spirally. Both forts are stronger than any we had seen in the Indies.

Between the mountain and the large square is another, smaller one, entirely surrounded by lodgings in which lived many women who were in Atahuallpa's service. Facing the entrance to the town is a house built in a mud-walled yard, in which there is a plantation of trees. They say that this is the house of the sun. For in each town they build 'mosques' to the sun. There are other 'mosques' in the town, for there is a great cult of 'mosques' throughout the land, and when they enter they take off their shoes at the door. The people of these mountain towns are superior to those of the plain, being both cleaner and more intelligent. The women are very modest and wear over their clothes most elaborate girdles which they tie at the waist. On top they have a cloak like a Spanish woman's shawl, which covers them from the head to half-way down their legs. The men wear sleeveless shirts and cloaks over them. All weave wool and cotton at home and make the cloth they need, also footwear of cotton and wool which the men wear instead of shoes.

The Governor and his Spaniards had now been waiting some time for Atahuallpa to come or send someone to show him to his lodgings. As it was now late, he sent Captain Hernando de

Soto with twenty horsemen to invite Atahuallpa to talk with him. He ordered Soto to proceed peacefully and not to pick a quarrel with Atahuallpa's men even if they should provoke one. 'It will be best,' said the Governor, 'if you speak to Atahuallpa and come straight back with his reply.'

The Captain was perhaps half-way on the road when the Governor, who had climbed up into the fort, saw a great number of Atahuallpa's men gathering in front of their tents. To save Soto's men from being overwhelmed should the Indians attack, and to protect their retreat, he sent his brother Hernando with another twenty horsemen, and strict instructions not to raise a disturbance.

A little later it began to rain and hail. The Governor ordered his men to take shelter in the lodging-house and Pedro de Candia, the captain of artillery, to carry his guns into the fort. As they were doing so, an Indian arrived from Atahuallpa to tell the Governor he could lodge where he wished, provided that he did not enter the fort on the square,* and that the prince himself could not come since he was fasting. The Governor accepted the lodgings, but remarked that he had sent his brother to invite Atahuallpa to visit him, since he had heard such good accounts of him that he greatly desired to meet him. The messenger departed with this message, and Hernando Pizarro returned at nightfall with his men.

On arriving before the Governor, they said that they had found a bad place in the road where it passed through a swamp. There is a broad stone and earth road leading from the town to Atahuallpa's camp, and it appeared to be entirely surfaced. But though it was paved at other bad spots, the pavement had been broken at this one, and they had been forced to make a detour. They had crossed two streams on their way to the camp, and found another in front of it, which the Indians crossed by a bridge, for the camp was surrounded by water. Captain Soto, who marched ahead, left his men on the near side of this river in order not to excite the Indians. He did not wish to cross the bridge for fear that his horse might slip and fall in. So he swam across, taking the interpreter with him, and, passing through a band of Atahuallpa's warriors, came to the

* Where Pedro de Candia was already concealed.

prince's lodging, which stood in the middle of the camp and, though small, was the finest of its kind he had seen in the Indies. It consisted of four rooms built around a courtyard, in which was a tank fed by water from a pipe. This water, which was so hot that it burnt the hand, flowed down from a spring on the mountain close by, and was joined on the way by cold water in another pipe, the two running into the tank together. But when they wanted the water from one pipe alone, they would divert the other. The pipe was large and made of stone. Outside the house, in a part of the yard, was another tank not so well made. Both had stone steps down which they went to bathe. The apartment in which Atahuallpa spent the day was a gallery looking down on a garden, and beside it was the room in which he slept, which had a window facing the courtyard and the tank. The gallery also had an entrance from the court. The walls were plastered with a red bitumen finer than ochre, which was very bright The wood used for the roofing of the house was stained with the same dye. The other room in front consisted of four bell-shaped vaults joined into one, and was washed with snow-white lime. The other two were service apartments. In front of these lodgings flowed the river . . .

On reaching this lodging a little ahead of Hernando Pizarro, Captain Soto had found four hundred men drawn up on a square, who seemed to be the guard. The tyrant was sitting on a low seat at the door of his lodging, with many Indians before him and women standing almost all round him. On his forehead he wore a woollen *berla* or fringe, crimson in colour, which looked like silk. It was tied to his head with cords and came down over his eyes, which made him look much graver than he was. His eyes were downcast and he did not raise them to look at anything.

On entering his presence Captain Soto said through his *faraute* or interpreter: 'I am one of the Governor's captains. He has sent me to visit you and say how much he desires to see you. He will be greatly delighted if you will be pleased to visit him.' And he said much more to the same effect. But Atahuallpa did not answer or raise his head to look at him. One of his captains, however, replied to Captain Soto's address.

Meanwhile Hernando Pizarro had reached the place where

Soto had left his men and, on inquiring for him, was told that he was speaking with the *cacique*. Leaving his men on the further side also, he crossed the river and came to where Atahuallpa was sitting. On his arrival, Soto said through the interpreter: 'This is one of the Governor's brothers. Speak to him, for he has come to see you.' Then the *cacique* raised his eyes and said: 'My captain Maizabilica, whom I have stationed on the Zuricara* river, has sent me a message to the effect that you have ill-treated the *caciques* of that province and put them in chains. He has sent me an iron collar and tells me he has killed three Christians and a horse. But I shall be pleased to go and see the Governor tomorrow, and to be a friend of the Christians since they are good men.'

Hernando Pizarro answered: 'Maizabilica is a rogue. A single Christian would be enough to kill him and all his men on that river. He could kill no Christians, nor a horse either. His men are a lot of chickens. Neither the Governor nor his soldiers harm *caciques* who do not make war on them. When they are good and friendly they receive good treatment. But if they attack him he fights them till they are all destroyed. When you see what help the Christians will give you against your enemies, you will know that Maizabilica has lied to you.'

Atahuallpa said: 'A *cacique* has disobeyed me. My people will come with you and you will make war on him.' Hernando Pizarro answered: 'There is no need for your Indians to go against any *cacique*. However great his army, the Christians on horses will destroy him.'

Atahuallpa laughed and invited them to drink.

*

DESCRIPTION OF THE REST OF THE INTERVIEW BY JUAN RUIZ DE ARCE, FROM HIS 'INFORMATION TO HIS HEIRS'

He then asked us to dismount and eat. We answered that we had not dismounted even at our lodgings and were pledged not to do so till we returned. He said that if we

* The Chira river, on which San Miguel stood.

would not eat we must at least drink. And we said that we would.*

Then the women who were with him went out to fetch the drink. There remained one of his uncles called Mateo Pangui and a lord of Quito. These two were his councillors and went over to him, as did many others. But he took no notice of them. The women entered each carrying two gold cups about eight inches high, full of wine.

It is the custom of the country that when drink is offered the attendant brings two cups and after taking a mouthful from one, hands it to the drinker; the attendant must also drink anything that is left in the cup.

After we had drunk, a woman took away the cups. Then they all returned to sit beside him. He was seated on a low chair. He wore a sleeveless shirt and a cloak which completely covered him. He had a cord tied round his head and a red fillet on his forehead. He did not spit on the floor; if he hawked or spat a woman held out her hand and he spat into it. And any hairs that fell from his head on to his clothes were picked up by the women and eaten. The reason for these customs is known: the spitting was out of majesty; the hairs because he was afraid of being bewitched. He required them to eat his hairs so that they should not be used in witchcraft.

When we had finished our drink† we begged leave to go, and he asked that one of us should remain with him. We replied that we dared not agree, for we had not the Governor's permission and if any of us were to stay behind he would be very angry. Atahuallpa gave us leave to go, saying that he would come next day to see the Governor. Before we left he asked us to gallop a horse, for he would very much like to see one run. So one of our companions started his mount two or three times. There were many Indians around looking at us from behind some reeds which grew very thick and high there. When the horse charged, some thirty or forty Indians who

* Francisco de Jerez says that the Spaniards swore they were fasting since they disliked the beverage offered them, which was *chicha*.

† Francisco de Jerez says that after the first round the Inca made a sign to the girls, who brought in another round in larger cups.

were near fled out of his way. Immediately we had gone, Atahuallpa ordered that they should be executed and their heads were cut off. He was very annoyed with his captains also for not having killed us all on our way to see him. They replied that they had not attacked us for fear we should flee back to the Governor, and had let us pass because they expected to capture us all next day. These were the excuses they gave him.

*

CONTINUATION BY FRANCISCO DE JEREZ

Atahuallpa's camp lay on the flank of a small mountain. His tents, which were of cotton, extended for a league, and his own was in the middle. All his men were standing outside the tents and their arms, which were spears as long as pikes, were stuck in the ground. There appeared to be more than thirty thousand men in the camp.

After hearing his brother's report, the Governor ordered a strong watch to be kept on the camp that night. He instructed his brother Hernando, the Captain-general, to post the sentries and to see that the whole circuit of the camp was patrolled from dusk to dawn. This was done, and on the morning of Saturday a messenger reached the Governor from Atahuallpa and said: 'My master wishes to visit you and to bring his men armed since you sent your men armed yesterday. He asks you to send a Christian to escort him.'

The Governor answered: 'Tell your master he is welcome to come when and as he will. However he comes, I will receive him as a friend and brother. I will not send a Christian to escort him, however, since it is not our custom to send one lord's man to another.'*

The messenger departed with his answer and the watchmen saw the army begin to move as soon as he reached the camp. Then, after a short while, another messenger came and said to the Governor: 'Atahuallpa sends me to tell you that he does not wish to bring his men armed. Although they are his escort, most of them will be without arms since he wishes them to

* Hernando Pizarro says in his *Letter to the Audiencia of Santo Domingo* that he *did* send a soldier.

come with him and lodge in the town. Let a place be prepared for him on the square where he may rest, and let it be the house that is called the House of the Serpent because there is a stone serpent inside.'

Shortly afterwards they saw the whole plain full of approaching soldiers who halted at intervals waiting for others to come out of the camp, and fresh troops continued to march along the road till the afternoon. They marched in bands and when they had passed all the bad places on the road drew up in the fields near the Christians' camp. And yet more men continued to come out of the Indians' camp.

Then the Governor ordered all the Spaniards to arm themselves in concealment, and every horse to be saddled and bridled, and the men to remain in the lodging under their three captains,* and none of them to appear on the square. Then he instructed the captain of artillery to train his guns on the enemy in the fields, ready to be fired when the moment came. After hiding more men in the streets leading into the square, the Governor entered his lodging, taking twenty men with him, whose task was to help him seize Atahuallpa if he intended treachery, as seemed likely from the great number of men accompanying him. The Governor's orders were that he should be taken alive and that no other soldier should come out of the buildings, even though they saw the enemy in the square, until they heard the guns fire. The sentries were to be on the alert and to give the signal if they saw any sign of treachery. Then on the cry of 'Saint James and at them!' all were to rush out of their lodgings, the horsemen already mounted.

Having made his dispositions and given his orders, the Governor awaited Atahuallpa's appearance, and no other Christian was in sight except the look-out who was observing the movements of Atahuallpa's army. The Governor and Captain-general inspected the Spaniards' quarters, to see that they were ready to come out when necessary. The Governor exhorted them to make fortresses of their hearts since they had no other, and no other help except from God who aids his

* Zárate says that the Governor entrusted his three squadrons each of twenty horse to his three brothers 'with Captains Hernando de Soto and Sebastian de Benalcazar'.

servants in their greatest need. 'Though there are five hundred Indians to every Christian,' he said, 'take courage as good men should in such times and trust that God will fight for you. Come out fiercely at the moment of attack, but fight steadily and when you charge take care that your horses do not collide.' Thus the Governor and Captain-general heartened the Christians, who would far rather have come out in the open than remain in their lodgings. For each man felt that he was equal to a hundred, and the sight of such great numbers frightened them hardly at all.

When the Governor saw that the sun would soon set, and that Atahuallpa had not moved from his position, although men continued to come out of the camp, he sent a Spaniard to ask him to come into the square and meet him before nightfall. When the messenger came before Atahuallpa he made a deep bow and asked him by signs to come where the Governor was waiting. Then he and his men began to move, and the Spaniard returned ahead of them to tell the Governor that Atahuallpa was coming, and to warn him that the men whom the *cacique* brought with him had arms concealed under the padded cotton jackets they wore as shirts, and carried slings and bags of stones; which made him think that they intended treachery.

Soon the advance-guard of Atahuallpa's army began to enter the square. First came a squadron of Indians dressed in a red and white check livery, who picked up the straws from the ground and swept the road; then more bands in different liveries, all singing and dancing, and after them a number of men with breastplates, medallions and gold and silver crowns, in the midst of whom came Atahuallpa in a litter lined with multicoloured parrots' feathers and decorated with gold and silver plates. The prince was borne on the shoulders of many Indians,* and behind him came two more litters and two hammocks containing persons of importance, who were followed by many more who wore gold and silver crowns and marched in bands. On entering the square, Atahuallpa made a sign for silence.

*

* An anonymous *Relacion* says that he was carried by 80 chiefs in blue livery.

A FULLER ACCOUNT OF THE MEETING BY DIEGO DE TRUJILLO

Seeing no Christians, Atahuallpa asked the Inca who had accompanied us from Maricavilea and Carran:

'What has become of the bearded ones?'

And he answered: 'They are hidden.'

And so, though the Governor persuaded him, Atahuallpa refused to descend from his litter.*

5. *The struggle with Atahuallpa and his capture*

...ATAHUALLPA had spent a great part of the day making his dispositions and choosing the place from which each captain should attack. He commanded one of them, called Ruminagui, to take up a concealed position behind the Spaniards, in the direction from which they had come and to kill them all as they turned and fled. Then he moved his army, but so slowly that they took more than four hours to cover one short league.

[*Zárate then describes the advance and the litters.*]

They thought so little of the Christian army that they expected to capture it with their bare hands. For an Indian governor had

* Accounts of Atahuallpa's intentions in visiting the Spaniards differ. Zárate, who was not of course present, believes that his intention was to destroy them. Francisco de Jerez makes him insist that he desired peace, but was overruled by bad advisers. Unlike Zárate he does not mention the Inca's demand for the gold and silver the Spaniards had taken. But Atahuallpa's true intentions remain in doubt. Those of the Spaniards do not. Atahuallpa's seizure of the breviary provided an opportune excuse and a godly cloak for a massacre that was clearly planned. The model was provided by Pizarro's distant relative Hernando Cortes, who had massacred the people of Cholula in this way, and at a later date had seized Moctezuma under similar circumstances. We now return to Zárate's narrative, which has been very sparing from the departure from San Miguel to this point but now expands.

sent to inform Atahuallpa that the Spaniards were very few and so despicably lazy that they could not walk without getting tired, for which reason they rode on a sort of large sheep that they called horses.

When Atahuallpa entered the square in front of the *tambo* of Cajamarca and saw so few Spaniards, all of them on foot since the horsemen were concealed, he thought that they were afraid to appear before him and would not resist an attack. Rising in his litter, therefore, he said to his people: 'They are our prisoner,' and they all answered, 'Yes.'

Then the bishop, Fray Vicente de Valverde, came forward with a breviary in his hand and expounded how One God in three persons had created heaven and earth and all that was in it, and had made Adam, who was the first man on earth, taking his wife Eve from his rib, whereby we were all engendered, and how by the disobedience of our first parents we had fallen into sin and could not achieve the grace of seeing God or going to heaven until our Redeemer Christ was born of a virgin to save us, as a result of which He received His death and passion; and that after His death He was reborn in glory, and remained in the world for a short time before rising to heaven, leaving in His place Saint Peter and his successors who lived at Rome and whom we Christians called popes; and how the popes had divided the whole world between the Christian princes and kings, entrusting each with a task of conquest; and that this province of Atahuallpa's had been assigned to His Majesty the Emperor and King Don Carlos, our master; and that he had sent Don Francisco Pizarro to represent him as governor and inform Atahuallpa on behalf of God and the Emperor of all that he had just said; that if Atahuallpa chose to believe and receive the waters of baptism and obey him, as did the greater part of Christendom, the Emperor would defend and protect him, maintaining peace and justice in the land and preserving his liberties as he did those of other kings and lords who accepted his rule without the risk of war; but if Atahuallpa were to refuse, the Governor would make cruel war on him with fire and sword, and lance in hand. As for the matter of Jesus Christ and His evangelical law, if on being well informed of it he chose of his own will to believe, he would be acting rightly and securing the salvation of his soul, but if he did not they would not compel him.

*

THE DIFFICULTIES ARISING FROM THE MISTRANSLATION OF FRAY VICENTE DE VALVERDE'S SPEECH, FROM 'GARCILASO DE LA VEGA, ROYAL COMMENTARIES', PART II, BOOK I, XXIII

...All authorities agree that Fray Vicente de Valverde's speech was extremely harsh and abrupt without any redeeming charm or kindness, and that the translation made it even worse. Many consider that subsequent expositions to Atahuallpa made by Hernando de Soto and Hernando Pizarro were more temperate than Valverde's.

As for the translation, it must be observed that the *faraute* or Indian interpreter Young Felipe was from the island of Puna and of very plebeian stock. He was a lad of under twenty-two with as little knowledge of the common language of the Incas as of Spanish. The Inca language he had learnt not in Cuzco but in Tumbez, from the Indians there who spoke it as foreigners. For, as has already been remarked, it is a foreign tongue to all Indians except the natives of Cuzco. He had learnt Spanish also without proper instruction, merely from hearing Spaniards talk, and the words he heard most often were those used by rough soldiers: 'I swear to God! By my blessed soul' and suchlike and worse, and also of course the names of things that he had to find and bring, for he was a servant in the Spanish camp. And even what he knew he spoke as badly as a Negro straight from Africa. Although he had been baptized, he had received no instruction in the Christian faith, and knew nothing of our lord Christ or the Apostles' creed.

Such was the education of the first interpreter in Peru. So of course when he came to translate Fray Valverde's sermon he did so badly, often reversing the sense, not willingly and out of malice, but because he did not understand what he was translating, but repeated like a parrot. Thus for 'One God in three persons' he said, 'God three and one are four', adding the numbers to explain the proposition. This follows the convention of the *quipus* of Cajamarca, in which the knots for each year are added in this way. He could not have translated in any other way because there are no words or expressions in the language of Peru for such elements of the Christian faith as Trinity, Three in One, Person, Holy Ghost, Faith, Grace, Church, Sacraments and such things, since these pagans are utterly ignorant of them . . .

In speaking of Adam's generation Young Felipe, out of ignorance and through no fault of his own, said that once upon a time all human beings born or yet to be born piled all their sins upon Adam instead of 'partook of Adam's sin'; and of Christ's divinity he said no more than that he was a great hero who died for men; and of the virginity and purity of Our Lady he said even less. In fact he interpreted most of the religious truths in a contrary sense. When he came to the second part of the speech, on the other hand, he did rather better, because here he was dealing with the material matter of war and arms. He insisted so vehemently on the power and might of the Emperor Charles and his resolution in sending captains and soldiers to conquer the world that the Indians believed him to be superior to all the powers in heaven . . .

*

ZARATE CONTINUES

After listening to all this, Atahuallpa replied that these lands and all that was in them had been won by his father, and his ancestors, who had left them to his brother Huascar Inca, and that, since he had conquered him and now held him prisoner, they were his possessions, and he did not know how Saint Peter could give them to anyone; and that even if he had given them, he Atahuallpa did not acknowledge the gift and would give the Emperor nothing. As for the bishop's statement that Jesus Christ had created the heavens and men and everything else, he knew nothing about it. He had never heard of anything being created except by the sun, whom they worshipped as they did the earth their mother and their *huacas*; and that Pachacamac had created everything in that country, though he knew nothing about Castile, never having seen it. He asked the bishop how he could know that all he said was the truth and how he could prove such statements.

The bishop said that it was written in this book, which was God's scripture. And Atahuallpa asked him for the Bible or breviary he held in his hand. The bishop gave it to him, and Atahuallpa turned over the leaves from end to end, saying that it said nothing to him. In fact it did not speak at all. And he threw it on the ground.

Then the bishop turned towards the Spaniards and cried 'At them! At them!'*

Then, realizing that if he were to wait for the Indians to attack first, they would very easily rout him, the Governor forestalled them by sending a message to Hernando Pizarro that he must now carry out his instructions. He immediately ordered a gun to be fired, and the horsemen attacked the Indians from three sides. The Governor himself advanced with his infantry in the direction from which Atahuallpa was coming, and on reaching his litter they began to kill the bearers. But as fast as one fell several more came with great resolution to take his place.

The Governor realized that if the defence were to be at all prolonged his men would be defeated. For though they might kill many Indians a single Christian death would count for more. So he attacked the litter with great fury, seizing Atahuallpa by the hair (which he wore very long) and dragging him roughly towards him till he fell out. Meanwhile the Christians were slashing the litter – which was of gold – so fiercely with their swords that they wounded the Governor in the hand. But in the end Francisco Pizarro threw Atahuallpa to the ground and, though many Indians rushed forward to rescue him, took him prisoner.

* Various versions of Valverde's words are given. The anonymous *Relación* makes him say: 'Fall upon him. I absolve you', and Don Alonso Enriquez says, 'Then the rascally friar, who was certainly the peace-breaker, began to cry in a loud voice: "Christians, I call on you to avenge this insult to the faith of Jesus Christ." '

When the Indians saw their lord lying on the ground a prisoner, and themselves attacked from so many sides and so furiously by the horses they so feared, they turned round and began to flee in panic, making no use of their arms but running away so fast that they bowled one another over. So many of them were driven into one corner of the enclosure in which the battle had taken place that they knocked down a piece of the wall through which to escape.

The horsemen continued to chase the Indians till night turned them back. Ruminagui also took to flight with all his men. For when he heard the shot from the gun and saw a Christian throw down the watchman who was to give him the signal for attack he realized that the Spaniards had conquered. He did not stop till he came to the province of Quito, which is more than two hundred and fifty leagues away.

The morning after Atahuallpa's capture, the Spaniards went to pillage his camp, and were amazed at so many fine gold and silver vessels, also at the tents and robes and other valuables that they found in the royal quarters. The gold vessels alone that Atahuallpa carried with him weighed more than sixty thousand pesos, and fifty thousand women who accompanied the royal train came over to the Spaniards of their own free-will.

When everything had been taken, Atahuallpa said that being the Governor's prisoner he hoped to be well treated, and promised as ransom to fill a certain room in the *tambo* with gold vessels and pieces and more silver than could be carried away. When this offer was interpreted to him the Governor was amazed and quite incredulous. Atahuallpa repeated it, however, and said that he would give even more. The Governor promised to treat him very well, and Atahuallpa expressed great gratitude. He then sent messengers to all parts of the country, and to Cuzco in particular, to collect the gold and silver he had promised as his ransom. The promise was so great that its fulfilment seemed impossible. For he had undertaken to fill a very large room in the royal apartments of Cajamarca with gold vessels to the height his hand could reach when he stood upright; and although every day great quantities of gold and silver were brought into the camp the Spaniards never considered it enough even for a beginning. So they began to grumble and complain that the time proposed by Atahuallpa for delivering his ransom had expired and they could see no possibility of the required amount being brought. They inferred that the delay was for the purpose of collecting an army to attack and destroy them.

Being a man of intelligence, Atahuallpa realized that the Christians were dissatisfied and asked the Marquis* the reason. When he heard it, he answered that they were wrong to complain of the delay, which was not enough to justify suspicion. They must realize that the chief place from which the gold must be brought was the city of Cuzco, which was about two hundred very hard leagues' journey away along a bad road; and that since everything had to be carried on the backs of Indians, the time should not be reckoned long. Atahuallpa insisted that in the first place the Spaniards should satisfy themselves as to whether the promise could be fulfilled or not. Then if they considered it possible a month more or less was of very little importance. And they could satisfy themselves on this point if they would trust him with one or two men who could go to Cuzco and see and bring back news.

There were differences of opinion in the camp about this inspection that Atahuallpa requested, for it was considered very dangerous to trust an Indian to the extent of putting anyone in his power. Atahuallpa laughed a great deal at this, and said he did not know why any Spaniard should refuse to accept his word and go to Cuzco under his protection, so long as he remained imprisoned there with his wives and children and brothers, as hostages for him. Upon this answer Captain Hernando de Soto and Pedro del Barco decided to make the journey; and Atahuallpa sent them, each in a hammock with a great number of Indian bearers, who travel with these hammocks almost as fast as the post. For they are incapable of going slowly, and though only two men carry the hammock, the whole body of bearers (who will be at least fifty or sixty for each hammock) goes at a run. Then, after a certain distance

* From this point Zárate sometimes calls Pizarro by his subsequent title.

another two take over, which they do so skilfully that they change without stopping.

Hernando de Soto and Pedro del Barco set out for Cuzco in this way, and when they had covered a few stages of the road met Atahuallpa's captains and soldiers bringing his brother Huascar as a prisoner. On hearing of the Christians' presence, Huascar asked to speak with them, which he did, and they gave him all the information he asked for. When he learnt that His Majesty's intention, and the Marquis' on his behalf, was to do equal justice to the Christians and the Indians they had conquered, so that all should have their rights, Huascar gave them an account of his dispute with his brother, saying that not only did Atahuallpa wish to deprive him of the kingdom which was his by right of succession as the eldest son of Huayna Capac, but for this reason had taken him prisoner and intended to kill him. He begged them to return to the Marquis and inform him, on his behalf, of the wrong he had suffered, and beg him, since both princes were in his power and he was master of the country, to decide the case between them and adjudge the kingdom to its rightful possessor. For did the Spaniards not claim that the Marquis' chief purpose was to do justice? In exchange he pledged himself to fulfil his brother's promise, and more. Not only would he fill the *tambo* or apartment of Cajamarca with gold vessels to the height of a man, but to the very roof, which was three times as high. And he claimed that he could do this more easily than his brother could fulfil his promise, as they could confirm for themselves if they would make the investigation. To collect as much treasure as he had offered, Atahuallpa would have to strip the temple of the sun at Cuzco of its gold and silver panels. He had no other resource. But Huascar possessed all his father's jewels and treasures, and could easily provide far more than Atahuallpa. He was speaking the truth. But no one in the world knew where he had buried all this, and it has never been discovered to this day. He had loaded it on the backs of many Indians who had carried it to its place of burial, and he had killed them all afterwards so that no one should reveal its hiding place and no one should ever find out. And although since the country was pacified, and indeed till the present day, Spaniards have been most carefully inquiring every day and digging in every place where they think it might be concealed, nothing has ever been found.

Hernando de Soto and Pedro del Barco answered Huascar that they could not break off their present journey, but would make the investigation on their return, which would be very soon. So they travelled on. But their refusal led to Huascar's death and the loss of all the gold he had promised them. The captains who held him immediately sent a runner of the post to report this meeting to Atahuallpa, and Atahuallpa was wise enough to know that if Huascar's request were presented to the Governor, he might lose the kingdom. For not only was his brother in the right, but he had promised a greater quantity of gold (and the Christians' avidity for gold was already well known). He feared indeed that he might be killed as an embarrassment, on the pretext that he had wrongfully imprisoned his brother and usurped the kingdom. He decided therefore to have Huascar killed, though fear prompted him to refrain, since he had often heard that one of the chief laws of the Christians was that he who killed another was executed for it. He decided therefore to test the Governor's opinion on this matter, which he did very cunningly. One day he pretended to be sad, crying and moaning and refusing to speak to anyone. The Governor several times asked him what was wrong, but despite his persuasions Atahuallpa would not reply. Finally he allowed himself to say that he had received distressing news. On learning that he was a prisoner, one of his captains had killed his brother Huascar; which distressed him greatly since he regarded Huascar not only as his elder brother but in some respects as his father also, and if he had taken him prisoner it had been with no intention of harming him in his person or kingdom, but only so that his brother should leave him in peace in his province of Quito, which his father had left to him, having himself conquered and won it and it being no part of his hereditary domain. The Governor comforted him, telling him not to grieve, for death was a natural thing, and came to all alike, some soon and others a little later, and that when the land was pacified he would inquire who the murderers were and punish them.

When Atahuallpa saw that the Marquis took the matter so lightly, he decided to carry out his plan, and sent orders to the captains who held Huascar that they should kill him immediately. This was done with such speed that it could hardly be discovered afterwards whether Atahuallpa had made his pretence of grief before or after Huascar's death.

This whole evil business was commonly blamed by the soldiers on Hernando de Soto and Pedro del Barco. But ordinary soldiers do not understand the obligations of persons entrusted with commands – especially in time of war. They are bound to carry out these commands to the letter, and are not free to vary their conduct according to time and occasion unless they have express instructions to do so.

The Indians say that when Huascar saw he was to die he said: 'I have been lord of this land for a short time only. But that traitor my brother who has ordered my death, though I am his natural lord, will rule for a shorter time still.' For this reason, when they afterwards saw Atahuallpa killed, the Indians believed that Huascar was truly a son of the sun since he had prophesied his brother's death. And Huascar also said that his father, on his deathbed, had commanded him to make friends with a white and bearded people who would one day come to the land, since these men would become lords of the kingdom. This may well have been a trick of the devil, since before Huayna Capac's death the Governor was already traveling down the coast of Peru, conquering the country.

Now while the Governor was at Cajamarca, he sent his brother Hernando with some horsemen to explore the land.

*

MIGUEL ESTETE'S ACCOUNT FROM FRANCISCO DE JEREZ, 'CONQUEST OF PERU AND THE PROVINCE OF CUZCO' OF HERNANDO PIZARRO'S JOURNEY FROM CAJAMARCA TO PACHACAMAC, AND FROM THERE TO JAUJA

On Wednesday, 5 January 1533, the feast of Epiphany (or as it is commonly called of the Magi) Captain Hernando Pizarro left Cajamarca with twenty horsemen and some arquebusiers, and slept that night in some huts five leagues from the town. Next day he dined at another village called Icocha, where he was welcomed and given all that he needed for himself and his men. That night he slept at another small place called Huancasanga, which is subject to the village of Huamachuco. Next morning he reached this town, which is a large place lying in a valley surrounded by mountains, and has fine views and lodgings. The captain and his men were well received here also by the ruler, whose name was Huamanchoro. Here they met a brother of Atahuallpa* who was hastening with a load of gold and told the Captain that Captain Challcuchima was twenty days' journey away and was bringing the full quantity that Atahuallpa had sent for. Learning that the gold was so far away, the Captain sent to the Governor for further instructions, saying that he would advance no further till he received them. He made further inquiries in the village as to whether the gold was really so far away, and on pressing certain chiefs, was told that Challcuchima was actually at the town of Andamarca seven leagues away, and was coming with twenty thousand warriors to kill the Christians and free his master. The chief who made this admission said that he had dined with him on the day before. The Captain took one of this chief's colleagues aside and he made the same statement.

On receiving this news the Captain decided to go and meet Challcuchima. Having prepared his men for battle, he started on the road, sleeping that night in the small village of Tambo, which is subject to Huamachuco, where he inquired again. All the Indians told the same story. Having kept strict watch that night, he continued on his way next morning, exercising great precautions, and before noon reached the town of Andamarca, where he found neither Challcuchima nor any more news of him than Atahuallpa's brother had brought in the first place: that he was on his way with much gold and had reached the town of Jauja. While at Andamarca, the Captain received the Governor's answer that since Challcuchima and his gold were far away he now had the bishop of the 'mosque' of Pachacamac in his power and the large quantities of gold that this dignitary was sending. He was therefore to inquire about the

* Called by Zárate, Illescas. His actual name was Quilliscacha.

road to Pachacamac and if it seemed good to him to go there, for the gold from Cuzco would arrive in due course.

The Captain inquired about the road and the number of stages to the 'mosque', and though both men and horses were ill shod and ill equipped for so long a journey he decided that he would be serving His Majesty if he were to go for the gold and prevent the Indians from hiding it, and also inspect the land and see if it was fit for Christian settlement. He was told that the road was long and had many difficult places and there were many rivers to be crossed on woven bridges. But he decided to go and took some chiefs with him who had been in that country.

He began the journey on 14 January, and on that first day crossed some bad passes and two rivers, and slept at the village of Totopamba, which is on a steep slope.* There the Indians welcomed him, giving him plenty of food and all that he needed for the night, also porters to carry his baggage. He left next day and spent the night at another village called Coronga. Half-way on the road was a high snow-covered pass, and all along it were many flocks with their shepherds, who have their houses in the mountains, as in Spain. The village is subject to Huamachuco. He left next day and spent the night in another small village called Pinga, which they found deserted, because all the inhabitants had fled out of fear. This day's journey was very bad, since it led down a series of steps cut in the rock, which were very tiresome and dangerous for the horses. Next day at dinner-time he reached a large village in a valley. Half-way on the road was a wide and very rapid river crossed by two woven bridges, constructed in this fashion: they raise a stout foundation at water level, building it very high; and from one side of the river to the other they stretch cables of reeds plaited like osiers, as thick as a man's thigh, which they secure with very large stones. These bridges are wide enough to take a small cart and are formed of tough cords closely woven between the cables and weighted down by very large stones, which keep them firm. The edges are raised. One bridge is for the use of the common people and is kept by a porter who

* Here the road crossed from the Marañon to the coastal watershed.

collects a toll; the other is for lords and captains. This is ordinarily kept closed. But it was opened for the Captain and his men, and the horses crossed it easily.

The Captain stayed two days in this village, since both his men and horses were exhausted by the bad road. The villagers received them well and gave them food and all necessities. The ruler of this place was called Pumapaecha. On the third day the Captain left that place and dined in a small village, where they gave him all necessities. Near this place he crossed another network bridge like the last, and he slept at another village two leagues further on, where they came out to receive him and gave him food both for the Christians and the Indian porters. That day's journey was down a valley with maize fields and small villages on both sides of the road.

On the next day, which was Sunday, he left this village and reached another during the morning, where they were very well received, and at nightfall came to another where their treatment was just as good. The Indians gave them sheep and *chicha* and everything else they needed. This whole land is very rich in flocks and maize, and as they went on the road the Spaniards met flocks of sheep wandering across it. Next day the Captain left that village and went down the valley to arrive at dinner-time at another large one called Huaras, whose ruler was called Pumacapillay, where they were well supplied with food and porters. This valley lies on a plain with a river close by; and from it can be seen others with their flocks and maize fields. They had two hundred head of sheep in a pen, merely as food for the Captain and his men.

The Captain left this place late and spent the night in another valley called Sucaracoray, where he was well received; the ruler of this place was called Marcocana. Here the Captain rested for a day, because both men and horses were exhausted by the bad road. He had to keep a strong guard, for the place was large and Challcuchima was near with fifty-five thousand men. Next day he marched on along a valley which had both flocks and tillage, and slept two leagues further on at a small village called Pachicoto. Here he left the royal road that leads to Cuzco and took the road across the plain, which he followed next day to spend the night at a place called Marcara where the chief's name was Corcora. It belongs to the great sheep farmers who lodge their shepherds here when at certain seasons of the year the flocks are brought to graze, as they are in Castile and Estremadura. From here the rivers run to the sea, and the road becomes much more difficult. For all the country inland is very cold and wet and snowy, and the coast is very hot, with so little rain that they have to irrigate their fields with the water that comes down from the mountains. So though there would not be enough rain for the crops, the land yields an abundance of fruit and foodstuffs.

The Captain left Marcara next day, and followed a river past orchards and tillage to sleep in the village of Huaracanga, from which he set out in the morning to spend the next night in the large town of Parpunga, which is on the sea coast. It has a fortress with five blind walls, with many painted devices inside and out and finely carved gates in the Spanish manner, with two tigers at the main entry. The Indians of this town were alarmed by the sight of men like none they had seen before and the horses surprised them even more. The Captain spoke to them through the interpreter of the party, which calmed their fears, and they served us well. At this place he turned on to another, wider road, which was built by the people of the coast, and bounded by mud walls on both sides.

The Captain stayed in this town of Parpunga for two days, to rest his men and get them reshod. On leaving, they crossed a large river on rafts, the horses swimming, and went on to spend the night at the town of Huamanmayo* which lies in a cleft near the sea. Near it they swam another river with great difficulty for it was very fast and swollen. There are no bridges over these coastal rivers, since they are very wide and flood their banks. The ruler of this place and his people did good service in helping to get their baggage across; they gave them plenty of food and porters.

The Captain left this place with his men on 9 January and slept that night in a village subject to Huamanmayo, three leagues away along a clear rolled road, the greater part of which was bordered by tillage, trees and orchards. They spent that night in a very large town on the sea coast called Huara,

* Now called La Barranca.

which has a fine position, and possessed large lodging-houses. The Spaniards were well served by the rulers of this place and their Indians, who gave them all that they needed that day. On the morrow they marched to a place called Llachu, which they named the Partridge town, since there were partridges in cages in all the houses, and here they spent the night. The Indians came out to welcome them and made much of the Captain, serving him well. But the *cacique* of the place never appeared.

Next day the Captain started rather early, for he had been told that the stage was long, and reached a large village called Suculacumbi, five leagues on the way. The lord of the village and the inhabitants came out to welcome the Spaniards and gave them enough food and necessities for that day; and at the hour of vespers they set out once more in order to reach the town where the 'mosque' was next day. They forded a large river and after following a walled road slept the night at a village a league and a half short of that town, which was a dependency of it. Next day, Sunday, 30 January, the Captain marched out and passing through a succession of villages and plantations reached Pachacamac, where the 'mosque' stands, after dining at another village on the way.

*

DESCRIPTION OF PACHACAMAC FROM CIEZA DE LEON'S BOOK, CHAPTER LXXII

Four leagues down the coast from the city of Los Reyes is the valley of Pachacamac, which is very famous among these Indians. The valley is fruitful and pleasant, and is the site of one of the grandest temples to be seen in these parts. It was said that though the Inca kings built many temples beside that of Cuzco and laid them out and decorated them richly, none was so fine as this temple of Pachacamac. It was built on the top of a small mound, entirely made of earth and mud-brick, and though it stood on the top the edifice began at the base. It had several doors which, like the walls, were painted with the figures of wild beasts. Inside the temple, where they kept the idol, were the priests, who made a great display of sanctity.

When they performed sacrifices before the people, they faced the doors of the temple and turned their backs on the idol. They looked down on the ground and were seized with a mighty trembling. Indeed from the accounts of Indians still living, they might be compared to those priests of Apollo when the Gentiles awaited their vain replies. The priests are also said to have sacrificed animals and even the blood of human victims, whom they killed before the effigy of this devil; and at their most solemn feasts to have pronounced oracles which were listened to and implicitly believed by the people. Beneath the terraces of this temple and under the base itself a large quantity of gold and silver was buried. The priests were greatly reverenced, and the lords and *caciques* obeyed their commands. Tradition says that beside the temple they had many great lodging-houses for those who came on pilgrimage; and that no burials were allowed in the neighbourhood except of lords or priests, or pilgrims who brought offerings to the temple. No others were considered worthy. On the occasion of their great annual feasts many people came there, and danced to the sound of the Indian instruments of music.

When the mighty Incas became lords of the kingdom and reached this valley of Pachacamac, they respected this temple. Though it was their custom to build temples and shrines to the sun in all the lands they conquered, in view of its size and antiquity, and the reverence in which it was held, they felt that it would be very difficult to wean the people from their great devotion to it. So they are said to have agreed with the native lords and the priests of this god or devil that the temple of Pachacamac should retain its cult and authority, on condition that another large temple should be built to the sun. This temple to the sun was built according to the Incas' orders and endowed with great riches and tended by many virgins. The demon Pachacamac is said to have been delighted with this arrangement and to have said so in his oracles, because now he was worshipped by both parties, and the souls of the simple and unfortunate people remained in his power. Some Indians say that this accursed demon Pachacamac still speaks to the old people in secret places. Knowing that he has lost credit and authority and that many of those who used to worship him now recognize their error and hold contrary beliefs, he tells these old people that he and the God of the Christians are one, and much else to the same effect. Thus by deceits and shams the adversary tries to prevent the Indians from receiving baptism, but with little success. For God, taking pity on the souls of these sinners, vouchsafes that many shall come to know Him and call themselves sons of the Church; and so there are baptisms every day.

These temples have been so dismantled and ruined that the principal building has now disappeared and, despite the demon, in the place where he was once so worshipped and adored stands the cross, to his great terror and the comfort of the faithful.

The name of this demon meant creator of the world, for *Camac* means creator and *pacha* the world.*

*

MIGUEL ESTETE'S ACCOUNT CONTINUED

The lord and chief men of Pachacamac came out to welcome the Christians and showed great goodwill. The Captain went to lodge with his men in some very large apartments which lie in one quarter of the town. On his return he said that he had come at the governor's command for the gold of that 'mosque', and that they must either collect it and give it to him or carry it themselves to where the Governor was. The chiefs of the town and the servants of the idol assembled and promised to hand the gold over. But they continued to dissemble and delay. Finally they brought a very little and said they had no more. The Captain then contrived a ruse. He said that he wanted to see their idol and asked them to lead him to it, which they did. The idol was in a finely painted house, but in a very dark chamber with a close fetid smell. It was a very dirty wooden object, which they said was their god who created and sus-

* For an archaeological account of the site see G. Kubler: *Art and Architecture of Ancient America* (Pelican History of Art) and J. Alden Mason: *The Ancient Civilizations of Peru* (Penguin Books).

tained them and assured their subsistence. At its feet lay an offering of golden jewels.

They held this god in such veneration that only his attendants and servants, whom they said he himself chose, were allowed to wait on him. No one else was considered worthy to enter his house or touch its walls. The truth is that the devil assumed the shape of this idol to speak with those who were in league with him and proclaim his wicked oracles throughout the land. They considered him a god and made him many sacrifices. Pilgrims came to this devil from a distance of three hundred leagues with gold and silver and cloth. On arrival, they went to the gate-keeper and offered their gift. He then went in and spoke with the idol, and said that the offering might be presented. Before one of his ministers entered to serve him, it was said that he must fast for some days and refrain from women. In all the streets of this town, at the principal gates and all around the temple, there are many wooden idols which they worship as they do this devil.

Many important men of this country have stated that from the town of Catamez,* at which this province begins, all the people of this coast brought gold and silver to this 'mosque', paying a fixed tribute each year. They had houses in charge of officials, to which they brought their tribute; and in them Hernando Pizarro found a little gold and signs that much more had been taken away. On inquiring from many Indians he learnt that it had been removed on the devil's orders.

Much could be said about the idolatries practised before this idol. But for brevity's sake I will only say that it compelled them to accept it as their god, and persuaded them that if they offended it or failed to worship it properly, it could destroy them, and that everything in the world was in its hands.

The people were shocked and alarmed merely that the Captain should have gone in to see it, for they thought that when the Christians departed it would certainly destroy them all. The Christians explained that they were much mistaken, and that what spoke from inside this idol was the devil, who greatly deceived them. They admonished the Indians that henceforth they should neither believe in him nor follow his counsel, and

* Atacames, on the coast of Ecuador.

they said more on the subject of idolatry. The Captain ordered that the vault in which the god stood should be pulled down and the god broken up in front of them all. He then explained our holy catholic faith and taught them the sign of the cross which they must use to defend themselves against the devil.

This town of Pachacamac is of considerable size. Beside the 'mosque' is a temple of the sun, standing on a hill; it is of fine masonry and is surrounded by five walls. There are also houses with terrace roofs as in Spain. The town appears to be old, for it has many ruined buildings and the greater part of the outer wall has fallen. The chief lord of the place is called Taurichumbi.

The lords of the neighbouring districts came here to see the Captain, bringing presents of the produce of their lands and gold and silver. They were greatly astonished that he had dared to enter the sacred chamber and demolish the idol. The lord of Malaque, whose name was Lincoto, came to swear obedience to His Majesty and brought a present of gold and silver; the lord of Poax, called Alincay, did the same, and Huarilli, lord of Hualco, brought gold and silver. The lord of Chincha, attended by ten of his chieftains, came with a present of gold and silver also. He said that his name was Tambianvea. And Huaxchapaicho, lord of Huara, and Aci, lord of Celixa, and Ispilo, lord of Sallicaimarca, and other lords and chiefs of the surrounding country brought presents of gold and silver, which added to the amount taken from the 'mosques' made up ninety thousand pesos.* The Captain spoke most courteously to all these chiefs

* In his *Historia general* Antonio de Herrera says that the priests concealed four hundred loads of gold and silver, and that Hernando collected only nine hundred castlins.

Cieza de Leon says, later in his chapter on the town: 'Although Hernando Pizarro succeeded in reaching the town very quickly, it is common knowledge among the Indians that the chiefs and priests of the temple took away more than four hundred loads of gold, which have never been discovered. No Indian living today knows where they are. Hernando Pizarro found a certain quantity of gold and silver, however. And in the course of time, Captain Rodrigo Ordonez and Francisco de Godoy and others have taken a great sum of gold and silver from their burials. But it can be taken as certain that there is much more. As no one knows where it is buried however, it is lost and is not likely to be recovered, unless by chance.'

and thanked them for coming. He commanded them in His Majesty's name always to behave in this way and dismissed them, well satisfied.

While at Pachacamac, Captain Hernando Pizarro received news of Atahuallpa's captain Challcuchima. He was four days journey way with the gold and silver and a large army, and was refusing to go any further. He proclaimed his intention of coming to fight the Christians. The Captain sent him a friendly message, urging him to bring the gold since he knew that his master was a prisoner and had been waiting for him many days, and that the Governor also was annoyed with him.

He said much else with a view to persuading him to come, being himself unable to make the journey to meet Challcuchima since the road was too bad for the horses. And with this in mind he designated a village on the way as a meeting place, where whichever party arrived first should await the other.

Challcuchima sent back the message that he would do as the Captain said, and had no other intention. And so the Captain left the town of Pachacamac to meet Challcuchima, returning by the same stages as he had come as far as the town of Huara, which lies on the plain beside the sea, and there turning inland. He left Huara on 3 March, and marched up a river through much woodland for the whole of that day, sleeping that night at a village called Huaranga, which is subject to Huara and lies on the river bank. Next day he marched on, to sleep at another small village called Aillon, which lies near the mountains and is subject to a larger place called Aratambo, which is rich in flocks and maize.

Next day, 5 March, he slept at Chincha, which is subject to Caxatambo. On the road they had to cross a very difficult snow-covered pass, where the snow came up to the horses' girths. This village has large flocks, and the Captain stayed there two days. He left on Saturday, 7 March, and slept at Caxatambo, a large place, which lies in a deep valley where there are many flocks, and all along the road they passed sheep-folds.

The lord of this village was called Sachao and he was very serviceable to the Spaniards. Here Hernando Pizarro turned on to the broad road by which Challcuchima would be coming. The distance across is three stages. Here the Captain asked whether

Challcuchima had passed on his way to the agreed meeting place. The Indians all replied that he had done so and was carrying the whole of the gold with him. But, as afterwards transpired, they had been instructed to give this answer in order that the Captain might march on. But in fact Challcuchima was still at Jauja and had no intention of coming. Knowing that these Indians seldom speak the truth, the Captain decided, despite all hardships and dangers,* to march as far as the royal road by which Atahuallpa's captain should pass, in order to find out if he had indeed done so and, if not, to go and meet him wherever he was, in order not only to get the gold but to disperse his army, either by winning him over to peace, or by attacking and capturing him, if he proved recalcitrant.

So the Captain and his men set out for a large village called Pombo, which lies on the royal road. On Monday, 9 March, he slept at Cyus, a village lying in the mountains, whose chief welcomed the Christians and gave them all that they needed for the night. Early next day he marched on to sleep the next night at a small village of shepherds which lies near a sweet-water lake three leagues in circumference,† on a plain where there are many medium-sized sheep like those of Spain, with very fine wool. Next morning, Wednesday, the Captain and his men reached the village of Pombo‡ where they were welcomed by the local chieftains and some of Atahuallpa's captains, who were there with troops. Here the Captain found about thirty hundredweight of gold which Challcuchima had sent while he himself remained with his army at Jauja. When the Captain had taken up his quarters he asked Atahuallpa's captains why Challcuchima had sent the gold but not come himself as he had promised. They answered that it was because he was much afraid of the Christians, but also because he was waiting for

* One of the Spaniards' main troubles was that the horses' shoes had worn out, and there was no iron. The historian Oviedo reports: 'They had shoes and nails for their horses made of silver by very good Indian smiths, who made as many as they wanted. These shoes lasted them for the next two months.' Oviedo: *Historia de los Indias*, III, 8. 16, quoted by Prescott. Another account says that the shoes were made of an alloy of silver and copper.

† The lake of Lauricoche, source of the Marañon.

‡ The modern Bombon.

more gold that was on its way from Cuzco and dared not come with so little. Captain Hernando Pizarro sent a messenger from the village to Challcuchima, telling him in a friendly way that since he had not come to meet Hernando Pizarro, Hernando Pizarro would go to meet him, and that he need have no fear. The Captain stayed for a day at Pombo, to rest the horses in case they might have to fight.

On Friday, the fourteenth of this same month of March, the Captain left Pombo with all his foot and horse to march to Jauja. He spent the night at a place called Xacamalca, six leagues away across the plain. Here is another sweet-water lake which begins near the village and is eight or ten leagues in circumference. It has villages all round its shores and large flocks, and houses waterbirds of various kinds and small fish. Atahuallpa's father used to keep a fleet of rafts on this lake which were brought from Tumbez for his amusement. A river flows out of it to the village of Pombo, and one branch is very calm and deep. This is used by boats which unload at a bridge close to Pombo, where passengers pay a toll, as in Spain. There are many flocks along the river, which we called the Guadiana, on account of a resemblance to that river of Spain.

On Saturday the fifteenth the Captain left Xacamalca and, after marching three leagues, came to a house, where he was welcomed with a good meal. He marched on to spend the night three leagues beyond at a place called Tarma, which lies on the slope of a mountain. Here he was lodged in a painted house which had very fine apartments. The chief of this place received him well, giving him both food and men to carry his baggage. On Sunday the Captain left this place early because the next stage was rather long. He set out with his men in battle order, since he suspected that, having sent no messenger, Challcuchima intended some treachery. At the hour of vespers he reached the village of Yanaimalca, where they came out to receive him. Here he learnt that Challcuchima was not at Jauja, which increased his suspicions. Being only a league from the town, he resumed his march as soon as the meal was finished and, arriving within sight of Jauja, saw from a hill several groups of men who might have been soldiers or townsfolk. On arriving in the main square he discovered that they were townsfolk assembled for a festival.

Immediately on his arrival and before dismounting, the Captain asked for Challcuchima, and was told that he had gone to another village and would be back next day. He had absented himself on the excuse of some business and was waiting to learn from the Indians who had come with the Captain what the Spaniards' purpose in coming might be. For realizing that he had done wrong in breaking his promise and that the Captain had come eighty leagues in pursuit of him, he supposed that he must have come to capture or kill him. So he had gone away out of fear of the Christians, and especially of their horses.

There travelled in the Captain's company a son of 'old Cuzco' who, when told that Challcuchima had gone away, offered to go after him. He departed in a litter. All that night the horses were kept saddled and bridled, and the chiefs of the town were instructed that no Indians must appear on the square, since the horses were angry and would kill them. Next day 'old Cuzco's' son returned bringing Challcuchima with him, both in litters and with a large escort. On entering the square Challcuchima got down, left his soldiers and went with a few companions to Hernando Pizarro's lodgings, to see him and present his excuses for breaking the promised appointment and not having come out to welcome him. He pleaded this was unavoidable since he had heavy duties. The Captain asked him precisely why he had not come to meet him as he had promised, and Challcuchima answered that his master Atahuallpa had sent him orders to stay where he was. The Captain then said that he was not annoyed with him, but that he must now prepare to come back with him to the Governor, who held his master Atahuallpa prisoner and would not release him until he handed over the gold Atahuallpa had sent for, for he knew that he had much gold. If Challcuchima would hand it all over, then he and the Captain would travel together and he would be well treated. Challcuchima answered that his master had sent him orders to stay where he was, and that unless these orders were countermanded he dared not go, because this was newly conquered country and might rise again in rebellion if he left. Hernando

Pizarro urged him strongly, and in the end they agreed that he should consider the matter in the night and they would talk again next morning. The Captain was anxious to persuade him by argument in order not to excite the country, since this might endanger the three Spaniards who had gone to Cuzco.

Next morning Challcuchima went to the Captain's lodging and said that in view of the Captain's wishes he could not do otherwise than obey. He was willing to accompany him therefore, and would leave another captain in charge of the soldiers at Jauja. That day he collected about thirty loads of low-carat gold and they arranged to leave two days later, during which time some thirty or forty loads of silver arrived. Throughout these days the Spaniards kept a strong guard and the horses remained saddled day and night. For this captain of Atahuallpa's had clearly a large force, and would do the Christians great damage should he attack them in the night.

This town of Jauja is very large and lies in a beautiful valley. A great river passes near it, and its climate is most temperate. The land is fertile. Jauja is built in the Spanish manner with regular streets, and has several subject villages within sight of it. The population of the town and the surrounding countryside was so great that, by the Spaniards' reckoning, a hundred thousand people collected in the main square every day. The markets and streets were so full that every single person seemed to be there. Certain officials were required to count all these people, and find out how many came to serve the soldiers. Others had the task of examining everything that entered the city. Challcuchima had stewards whose duty it was to supply provisions for his army, and many craftsmen who worked in wood, and great numbers of other servants and personal attendants. He had three or four personal porters, and indeed in his household and all other respects he imitated his master. He was much feared throughout the country, since he was a very brave warrior and, in fulfilment of his master's orders, had subdued more than six hundred leagues of land in the course of a victorious campaign in which he had fought many engagements in the plains and passes, and won them all. He had now nothing left to conquer in the whole country.

On Friday, 20 March, Hernando Pizarro left the town of

Jauja accompanied by Challcuchima, on his return journey to Cajamarca. He marched by the same stages as he had come as far as the village of Pombo, where he joined the royal road from Cuzco. Here he stayed on the day of his arrival and one day more. On the Wednesday they left Pombo and marched across the plains on which there were great flocks of sheep and where they spent the night in a large inn. That day there was heavy snow. They spent the next night at the village of Tambo, where there is a deep river with a bridge, which is approached by a flight of very steep stone steps. If these were defended from above casualties would be heavy. The Captain was liberally provided by the chief of this village with all that he needed for himself and his men. A great feast was provided in honour of Captain Hernando Pizarro, and because he was accompanied by Challcuchima, who was generally welcomed in this way. Next night they slept at another village called Tomsucancha, where the chief was called Tillima. They were welcomed here also, and there were many servants available, since though the village is small the people had crowded in to see and greet the Christians. Here there are flocks of small sheep with very good wool like that of Spain. They slept the next night at another village called Huanuco after a march of five leagues along a road that was mostly paved with flagstones and had water conduits on both sides. These were said to have been made on account of the snows that fall in these parts at certain seasons of the year. Huanuco is a large village and lies in a valley surrounded by steep mountains which is three leagues round. On one side, on the road to Cajamarca, there is a very sharp ascent. The Captain and his men were very well received and during the two days of their stay there several feasts were given. Huanuco has some subject villages lying round it and is rich in sheep.

On the last day of March the Captain left this place and reached a bridge over a large river, built of heavy timbers. Guards were stationed there whose task it was to collect the customary tolls. They slept at a place four leagues from the villages where Challcuchima had provided them with all that they would need for the night. Next day, 1 April, they left this place and slept at another called Picosmarca, which lies on the slope of a very steep mountain. Its *cacique* was called Parpay. The Captain left this place on the morning of the second and spent the night three leagues further on at a considerable village called Huari, where there is a deep and wide river with another bridge. Its position is very strong, for it has ravines on two sides. Challcuchima said that he had fought a battle here with the Cuzco army, which had waited for him at the pass and defended it against him for two or three days. When he had defeated them and some of his men had got across, they had burnt the bridge. But he and the rest of his men had swum the river and killed many of them.

Next day the Captain left this village and slept at another called Huacango, five leagues along the road, and on the following day he reached the large village of Piscobamba, which lies on the slopes of a mountain. The *cacique,* whose name was Tanguamo, welcomed the Captain and treated his men well. Half-way between this place and Huacacamba is another deep river with two woven bridges side by side which, like those they had met before, rested on stone foundations rising from beside the water. The horses crossed the bridge easily though at a walking pace. For though it is alarming to one who is crossing for the first time, there is no danger since the fabric is very strong. At all these bridges there are guards as in Spain, whose duty it is to collect tolls. Next day the Captain left Piscobamba, and after a march of five leagues came to a group of huts. Next day he came to a village called Agoa, which is subject to Piscobamba. It is a good village, lying in the mountains with maizefields all round it. The chief and his people supplied him with all that was needed for the night and porters to carry the baggage next day, when they marched a further four leagues along a very rough road, to pass the night at Conchuco. This place lies in a hollow, and half a league before it the road descends in a series of broad steps cut in the rock. There are many difficult places on this stairway, which would make strong defence points. Leaving Conchuco, they marched next day to a place called Andamarca, which is the point where they had turned off to go to Pachacamac. Here the two royal roads to Cuzco join. From Andamarca to the village of Pombo there are three more leagues of very rugged road, with steps cut in the rock at all the climbs and descents and a stone wall on the outer side to save the traveller from slipping. For there are places where anyone who fell would be dashed to pieces. These walls are a great advantage to the horses also, which would fall if they were not there. In the middle of the road there is a very well-made bridge of stone and wood, joining two rocks, and at one end of the bridge some very good buildings and a paved courtyard where, according to the Indians, the lords of the land were entertained with feasts and banquets when they travelled that way.

From this place Captain Hernando Pizarro went, by the same stages as he had come, to the town of Cajamarca, which he entered with Challcuchima on 25 April, 1533. Here a scene took place unparalleled since the discovery of the Indies and impressive even to Spaniards. As Challcuchima entered the doors of the house where his master was imprisoned he took a fair-sized load from the back of one of the Indian porters and put it on his own. And other chieftains of his company did the same. Thus laden, they all entered their master's presence, and when Challcuchima saw Atahuallpa he raised his hands to the sun, and gave thanks for having been permitted to enjoy the sight. Then very reverently, and with tears in his eyes, he approached his master and kissed his cheeks, his hands and his feet; and all the chieftains of his company did the same, and Atahuallpa preserved so majestic a mien that though he loved no one so much in the whole of his kingdom he did not look Challcuchima in the face or take any more notice of him than of the humblest Indian who might come before him. This taking up of a load before entering Atahuallpa's presence is a ceremony that has been performed for every lord who has reigned in that land.

This is an account of events set down exactly as they occurred by me, Miguel Estete, overseer to the treasury, who accompanied Captain Hernando Pizarro on his journey.

*

ZARATE CONTINUES

When Challcuchima went in to see Atahuallpa he took off his shoes, laid the customary present before him, and told him with tears in his eyes that if he had been at his side the Christians would never have taken him. Atahuallpa replied that it had been the judgement of the gods that he should be taken since he had not paid them sufficient respect; and that the chief reason for his capture and defeat had been the flight of his captain Ruminagui with the five thousand men whom he should have brought up at time of need.

7. Don Diego de Almagro returns to Peru and Atahuallpa is killed under the pretext that he intended to kill the Christians

WHILST the Governor Don Francisco Pizarro was in the province of Poechos, before his march to Cajamarca, he received a letter without signature, which as he afterwards learnt had been written by a secretary of Don Diego de Almagro in Panama, informing him that Don Diego had built a large ship and was about to embark, with himself (the secretary) and as many others as he could recruit, in order to take command and possession of that larger part of the country which lay outside the boundaries assigned to Don Francisco. For, according to the concession which Don Francisco had brought from His Majesty, his government extended only two hundred and fifty leagues north and south of the Equator. But the Governor had shown his patents to nobody.

It was said and believed therefore that Don Diego had sailed from Panama equipped with ships and men for this purpose. On landing at Puerto Viejo, however, and learning that the Governor's luck had been so good, and of the great quantity of gold and silver he had won – half of which belonged by right to him – Almagro changed his plan (if this had been his plan) and, learning that his secretary had warned the Governor of his coming, hanged the secretary. He then took all his men to join the Governor at Cajamarca. Here he found that, to the general amazement, a considerable part of Atahuallpa's ransom had been collected. Never before had so much gold and silver been seen anywhere in the world. On the day when they assayed and melted the amounts assigned to the company, the quantity of the gold alone was assessed at more than six hundred million maravedis. And even so the metal had been assayed very hastily and by a rough and ready process, for they had no acid with which to refine the assay. For this reason they reckoned the gold to be two or three carats less than it afterwards proved on a true assay, and the value was consequently increased afterwards by more than a hundred million maravedis. As for the silver, the quantity was so great that the share which fell to His Majesty as the royal fifth was thirty thousand marks of refined silver, a large part of which subsequently proved to be three- or four-carat gold. In gold the royal fifth amounted to a hundred and twenty million maravedis.

In the division every horseman got upwards of twelve thousand pesos in gold, and silver in addition; and their share was more by a quarter than that of the foot soldiers. Yet all this did not amount to a hundredth part of what Atahuallpa had promised to provide for his ransom. And because no part of this treasure was due to the many very important soldiers who had come with Diego de Almagro, since this was Atahuallpa's ransom and they had played no part in his capture, the Governor ordered that they should be given a thousand pesos each towards their expenses; and he decided to send his brother Hernando Pizarro to inform His Majesty that this enterprise had met with this great success. And since the melting and assay had not yet been made, and the amount of His Majesty's fifth was still uncertain, he sent a hundred thousand pesos of gold and twenty thousand marks of silver, choosing the most massive and handsome pieces which would be valued most highly in Spain. So Hernando Pizarro took many wine-jars, braziers and drums, and figures of sheep and men and women, up to the weight and value decided; and with these he went down to the coast to embark, to the great grief of Atahuallpa, who was very fond of him and discussed all his affairs with him. On bidding him farewell, Atahuallpa said: 'I am sorry that you are going, Captain. For I know that when you have gone this fat man and this one-eyed man will kill me.' By this he meant Don Diego de Almagro, who had, as we have said, only one eye, and Alonso de Requelme, His Majesty's treasurer, whom he had seen muttering against him for reasons which will soon be explained. And so it was. Indeed once Hernando Pizarro had departed they immediately plotted Atahuallpa's death.

*

ALONSO DE GUZMAN'S ACCOUNT OF ATAHUALLPA IN CAPTIVITY

Atahuallpa was so intelligent that in twenty days he understood Spanish and learnt to play chess and cards... During the two months between his capture and his death he learnt many things. He was greatly astonished at the Christian way of communicating by writing. But he responded very differently from that other king who was captured by Hernando Cortes in New Spain,* who believed that the letters spoke and asked them to tell him what they had said to the Christians. Atahuallpa, on the contrary, asked a man to write down certain words at his dictation, and then asked another man privately to read them, and thus he learnt to understand this marvel.

*

AN ACCOUNT OF ATAHUALLPA'S TRIAL AND EXECUTION FROM FRANCISCO DE JEREZ, 'CONQUEST OF PERU AND THE PROVINCE OF CUZCO'

One of the *caciques* of Cajamarca came to the Governor and said to him through the interpreters: 'I wish to inform you that after he was taken prisoner Atahuallpa sent orders to his native land of Quito and to all the other provinces that a large

* Moctezuma.

army should be collected to attack you and your men and kill you all. This army is approaching under the command of a great captain called Ruminagui and is now very near. It will come by night and attack the camp, and set fire to it in many places. The first man they will try to kill will be yourself, and they will take their lord Atahuallpa out of prison. Two hundred thousand warriors are coming from Quito and thirty thousand Caribs, who eat human flesh, and a great number of soldiers from the province of Pazalta and other parts.'

On receiving this warning, the Governor thanked the chief and did him much honour, and sent for a clerk to write it all down. Then he made further inquiries and took the statement to an uncle of Atahuallpa and some principal chiefs and some women, and learnt that all the chief of Cajamarca had said was true.

The Governor then spoke to Atahuallpa: 'What treason is this you have been plotting against me? I have treated you honourably as a brother and have trusted your word.' Then he told him of the information he had received. 'Are you mocking me?' Atahuallpa replied. 'You are always making jokes at my expense. How can I and all my people possibly cause any anxiety to valiant men like you? Do not talk such nonsense.' He said all this without betraying the least sign of disturbance. Indeed he laughed and, to conceal his wicked purpose, practised such other tricks of dissimulation as would occur to a ready-witted man. Indeed the readiness of his wit had surprised those Spaniards who had heard his conversation in captivity. They were amazed to find so much intelligence in a savage.

The Governor ordered a chain to be brought and fastened round Atahuallpa's throat, and he sent two Indians as spies to find out where this army was, for it was said to be only seven leagues from Cajamarca. He wanted to know whether it was in such a position that he could send a hundred horsemen against it. As soon as Atahuallpa was put in chains, he had sent a messenger to his great captain to say that the Governor had killed him, and when this news had reached the Captain and his army they had begun to retreat. Then he had sent other messengers with orders that they should advance immediately, and instructions how and from what direction and at what hour they should attack the camp, since in fact he was still alive, but they would find him dead if they delayed.

The Governor was informed of all this and ordered that careful watch should be kept in the camp, and that the horsemen should go the rounds three times each night, fifty horsemen on each round and the whole hundred and fifty at dawn. During these nights the Governor and his captains did not sleep but supervised the round and saw that all were on the alert. Those soldiers who were not on patrol slept with their arms by their sides and their horses saddled. These precautions were observed in the camp until at sunset on Saturday evening two of the Spaniards' Indian servants came in and reported that they had been pursued by the hostile army, which was only three leagues away and would attack the Christian camp that night or the next. For they were approaching at great speed in obedience to orders from Atahuallpa.

Then the Governor, with the agreement of His Majesty's officers and the captains and persons of experience, sentenced Atahuallpa to death.

*

PEDRO PIZARRO 'RELACIONES' QUOTED BY PRESCOTT

Atahuallpa wept, and begged that they should not kill him, for not an Indian in the land would move without his orders, and since he was a prisoner, they had nothing to fear. I saw the Marquis weep with sorrow that he could not spare his life because of the danger that he might escape.

The sentence was that for the treason he had committed he should die by burning unless he chose to become a Christian; and this was for the safety of the Christians and the good of the whole land, and to secure its conquest and pacification. For once Atahuallpa was dead, the whole of that army would immediately disperse, since they would lack the courage to attack and carry out the order he had given them.

They brought Atahuallpa out to execution, and when they carried him into the square he said that he wished to become a

Christian. The Governor was immediately informed and said that he must be baptized. He was baptized by the reverend father Fray Vicente de Valverde, who comforted him. The Governor then ordered that he should not be burnt but tied to a post in the square and strangled. This was done, and the body was left there till the next morning, when the friars, the Governor and other Spaniards carried him to be most solemnly buried in church, with all possible honours. Such was the end of this man who had been so cruel. He died with great courage, showing no emotion and saying that he entrusted his children to the Governor. When they took his body to be buried there was much wailing among his women and household servants. He died on a Saturday, at the same hour that he had been defeated and taken prisoner. Some said that it was for his sins that he died on this day and at this hour. He was punished for the great wrongs and cruelties he had committed on his subjects. For all said with one voice that he was the cruellest butcher that had ever been known, and that he would raze a village to the ground for a petty crime committed by one of its inhabitants, and kill ten thousand people. He subjected the whole country to his tyranny and was universally loathed.

[*Such is the official account as given out by Francisco Pizarro and repeated by his secretary, Francisco de Jerez. Without closely examining the details of the frame-up, Zárate looks for reasons of self-interest. In fact Atahuallpa was executed after a mock-trial against which many of the Spaniards themselves protested. There was no Indian army on the point of attack, and Hernando de Soto had reported as much. The accusations against Atahuallpa were fraudulent and as Hernando de Soto pointed out when he returned to Cajamarco, Pizarro had no jurisdiction over a foreign king. Soto was the chief of the twelve Spaniards who protested; the rest were for the most part Almagro's men. When they accused Pizarro, he attempted to shift the blame on to Valverde and the royal treasurer Riquelme. One of the chief criminals Sancho de Cuellar was afterwards executed by Atahuallpa's brother Titu Atauchi at the same spot and in the same way.*]

*

ZARATE'S ACCOUNT OF THE MOTIVES FOR ATAHUALLPA'S EXECUTION

The instigator of the plot was the Indian interpreter Young Felipe, who had accompanied the Governor to Castile. He said that Atahuallpa intended to murder all the Spaniards by stealth, and had placed a great number of Indians in hiding for this purpose. And since all information concerning the matter was interpreted by this same Young Felipe, he was able to frame it as he would in the interests of his own plan. The reason that prompted him was never really discovered. Two stories were told: the first that Young Felipe was in love with one of Atahuallpa's wives and wished by Atahuallpa's death to enjoy her in safety. For the prince had been informed of the intrigue and had complained to the Governor, saying that he resented it more bitterly than his imprisonment itself, or any misfortunes that might befall him, even if they were to lead to his death. He was outraged that this despicable man should treat him with such disrespect. Not only was this a gross insult, he protested, but the fellow knew that by the law of the land anyone found guilty of this offence, or of merely attempting it, was burnt alive, with the woman too if she were guilty. Indeed his parents, children, brothers and sisters and all his near relatives were put to death with him, and even the adulterer's sheep were slaughtered. The country from which he came was ravaged and sown with salt, its trees felled, and all the houses of his village demolished; nor was this an end of the punishment meted out for such a crime.

The second story was that the chief cause of Atahuallpa's death was the cunning and persistence of Don Diego's men, who contrived it out of private interest. Those who had marched with the Governor not only claimed that no share was due to Almagro's men of all the gold and silver gained so far, but that they would get no share in any future booty until the whole sum of Atahuallpa's ransom money was complete; and it seemed impossible that this could ever be even if all the gold in the world were collected for it. Atahuallpa's captors claimed the whole of the prince's ransom for themselves since it was by their toil and cunning that he had been taken, with no help from Don Diego's men. So Don Diego's men thought that it would suit their interest to contrive Atahuallpa's death. For so long as he was alive any gold that was brought in would be taken as his ransom money and they would get no share in it.

Whichever story was true, Atahuallpa was condemned to death. The sentence utterly amazed him since, as he said, he had never even thought of the crime of which he was accused. He asked them to double his fetters and guards, or put him on one of their ships at sea. To the Governor and his chief lords he said: 'I do not know why you think me a man of such little judgement that I should wish to commit treason against you. You have no reason to believe that these men who, you say, have been collected are under my orders or have my authority. This would be absurd, for I am in your power, bound with iron chains, and the moment these men appear or you hear that they are coming you can cut off my head. And if you think they will come without my permission, you have little knowledge of my power in this land, and the fear and obedience in which I am held by my subjects. If I do not wish it, no bird will fly and not a leaf will stay on the trees throughout my land.'

But all this was of no avail, nor was the offer of princely hostages for the life of every Spaniard in the country. For on top of these suspicions, the death of his brother Huascar was counted against him. The Spaniards sentenced him to death and executed him, and as he was taken away he cried repeatedly to Hernando Pizarro, saying that if he had been there they would not have killed him. And at the time of his death he was baptized, by permission of the Governor and the bishop.

8. Atahuallpa's captain Ruminagui raises a rebellion in the province of Quito, and the Governor goes to Cuzco

ATAHUALLPA'S captain Ruminagui fled from Cajamarca, as we have said, with five thousand Indians. On reaching the province of Quito, he assumed the governorship of Atahuallpa's children and took possession of the country, exacting obedience as its ruler. A little before his death, Atahuallpa sent his brother Illescas to Quito to fetch his children. But Ruminagui killed him and refused to give them up. After Atahuallpa's death, some of his captains, in obedience to his will, took his body to the province of Quito to be buried beside his father Huayna Capac. Ruminagui received them all with honour and affection, and had the body most solemnly buried according to the custom of the country. Then he ordered a great carousal to be held, and when the captains who had brought the corpse were drunk he killed them all. Among them was Atahuallpa's brother Illescas,* who was flayed alive. His skin was afterwards made into a drum from which his head was left hanging.

When the Governor had divided all the gold and silver that was in Cajamarca, he set out to attack one of Atahuallpa's captains called Quizquiz. Reports had reached him that this man was travelling about with some soldiers, rousing the land. But he was not brave enough to wait for the Governor in the province of Jauja. So the Governor sent Captain Soto ahead with some horsemen, himself following in the rear. In the province of Viscacinga Soto was suddenly attacked by a large army and almost defeated. Five or six Spaniards were killed. When night fell the Indians retired into the mountains, and the Governor sent Don Diego de Almagro with some horsemen to Soto's aid. Then when the fighting was resumed at dawn next day, the Christians cunningly gave ground in order to lure the

* Zárate has just reported his murder as taking place on an earlier occasion. There is clearly some confusion of names.

Indians on to the plain and get out of range of the stones they hurled from the clifftops. But the Indians saw the ruse. They refused to come out and fought where they were. They did not see Almagro's reinforcements, however, because of the mist, which was thick that morning; and the Christians fought so bravely that day that they defeated the Indians, killing many. And shortly afterwards the Governor arrived with the whole rearguard. Then a brother of Huascar and Atahuallpa called Paulo Inca who at Atahuallpa's death had been made Inca or king of the land and given the *borla* – the royal insignia or crown – came out to sue for peace. He told the Governor that a large army was waiting for him at Cuzco.

*

A DESCRIPTION OF CUZCO AND NOTE ON THE 'MOLLE'* FROM PEDRO CIEZA DE LEON, 'CHRONICLE OF PERU', CHAPTERS XCII AND XCIII

The city of Cuzco stands in a very rugged spot entirely surrounded by mountains. There are two rivers near-by, one of which flows through it. The city has buildings on both sides. A valley on the east opens out from Cuzco, so that the two rivers flow west. This valley is so intensely cold that it grows no fruit trees except a few molles.

In most inhabited parts of the country there are large and small trees called molles.* They have small leaves which smell rather like fennel. Their bark has the virtue of relieving pain and reducing swellings . . . The twigs are used for cleaning the teeth. The natives also make a very good drink from the small berries, and vinegar too by steeping and boiling these berries in water. The Indians value these trees most highly.

* The molle (*schinus melle*), which looks something like a walnut, has red berries and evergreen leaves. It grows freely in Mexico, where it is called the *piru*, also around the Mediterranean. Translator's note.

To the north of the city, on the highest hill in the neighbourhood stands a fortress, once a building of size and strength and still impressive. Though it is largely in ruins, its massive foundations and principal stone blocks are still standing.

On the east and north are the province of Antisuyu, which contains the forests and mountains of the Andes, and the still larger province of Chinchasuyu, which comprises the lands lying towards Quito. To the south are the provinces of Collao and Cuntisuyu. Collao lies between east and south and Cuntisuyu between south and west. There was a part of the city called Hanancuzco and another called Hurin, where lived the noblest families, some of which were of ancient descent. In another part is the hill of Carmenca on which stood a number of small towers, spaced at intervals and used to observe the movement of the sun, to which the Peruvians attached great importance. In the space between the hills, where the majority of the population lived, there was a large square. This was said once to have been a marsh or lake, which the founders filled in with stone and earth to make it as it is now. From this square issued four royal roads. These were called: Chinchasuyu, which led to the plains and the whole mountain range as far as the provinces of Quito and Pasto; Cuntisuyu, which led to the provinces subject to Cuzco and Arequipa; Antisuyu, which led to the provinces on the skirts of the Andes and some villages on the further side; and Collasuyu, which led to the provinces in the direction of Chile. As the Spaniards of old divided their whole country into provinces, so the Indians apportioned their very large territories according to the roads that led to them. The river that passes through the city had bridges connecting one district with another. Nowhere in the kingdom of Peru was there another city of noble architecture like Cuzco, which was the capital of the Inca empire and the royal seat. Most of the other Indian provinces are collections of villages. If there are any towns they have neither plan nor order, nor political organization worthy of remark. Cuzco had the manner and quality of greatness, and must have been founded by people of great character. Its streets were grand, though rather narrow, and the principal houses were of finely jointed stone blocks which showed the antiquity of the building. The rest of the houses were entirely of wood and thatched with straw or terrace-roofed, for there are no remains of tiles or brick or plaster. In various parts of the city stood the principal apartments of the Inca kings, in which they held their feasts on succeeding to the kingdom. There was also a magnificent and stately temple of the sun, which was called Curicancha and was richer in silver and gold than almost any other temple in the world. The greater part of the city was inhabited by *mitimaes*. It was governed by mighty laws and statutes set out in a form that all could understand. These regulated both its temples and ceremonies and its political organization. It was the richest town of any we know in the Indies. For treasures had been brought there for the greater glory of its lords over a long space of time. No gold or silver that had once entered the city could be taken out again, under pain of death. The rulers' sons came from every province at certain times, to reside at the court with their attendants and servants. There were a great number of silversmiths and goldsmiths capable of undertaking any work the Incas might require of them. In the chief temple lived one whom they called Huillac-umu. He was their high priest.

At the present day there are very fine houses in Cuzco with upper storeys roofed with tiles. Although the city is cold it is very healthy and the largest in the whole kingdom. It is also the best supplied with provisions and has the largest number of Spaniards possessing *encomiendas* of Indians. It was founded and populated by Manco Capac, the first Inca king to enter these parts, and, after passing under the rule of ten other lords in succession, was refounded and rebuilt by the Adelantado Francisco Pizarro, governor and captain-general of these kingdoms, in the name of the Emperor Charles in October 1534.

Since Cuzco was the chief and most important city in the kingdom, Indians flocked in from the provinces at certain seasons of the year, some to repair the houses, others to clean the streets and suburbs and perform other duties. Near the city, on either side, stand many buildings which were once lodgings and store-houses. All are constructed and planned like those in the rest of the kingdom, though they are of different sizes and some stronger than others. Since the Incas were so rich and powerful, some of these buildings were once gilded and others panelled with gold. Their predecessors held sacred a large hill called Huanacaro, which lies near the city. They are said to have sacrificed the blood of human beings and many sheep and lambs there. And as the city was full of strange and foreign people, for Indians came there from Chile and Pasto, also Cañaris, Chachapoyas, Huancas, Collas and other peoples of the Inca empire, each nation lived apart in the place and quarter assigned to it by the governors of the city. All kept their ancestral customs and the way of life of their lands, and although there were a hundred thousand male inhabitants in all, the nations could easily be recognized by the distinguishing marks which they wore on their heads. Some of these foreigners buried their dead on high hills, others in their houses, and others in ancestral tombs together with their wives, still alive, some of their most precious possessions, and quantities of provisions. The Incas, as I learnt, forbade none of these customs so long as all adored and worshipped the sun, a cult which they called Mocha. In many parts of the city there are large underground buildings, in which we still discover stone flags and conduits, and even jewels and pieces of gold that they once buried there. Indeed there must be great treasures still buried within the confines of this city, of which no living person has any knowledge. And since there were so many inhabitants, and the devil, by God's leave, had such power over them, there were many magicians and diviners and idolaters, and the city is still not fully cleansed of them, especially of practisers of witchcraft.

Near the city there are many temperate valleys with fruit and other trees, which grow well, the timber and fruit being, for the most part, brought to sell in the city. And at the present day much wheat is grown there also for bread. And many orange and other fruit trees, from Spain and other parts of the land, have been planted also. Their mills are driven by the river that passes through the city, and four leagues away can be seen the quarries from which they took the blocks, slabs and facings for their building. In addition they rear hens and capons as good and fat as those of Granada; and in the valleys are herds of cows and goats and other cattle both Spanish and native. And although there are no trees in the city, Spanish pot herbs grow very well.

*

ZARATE, CHAPTER EIGHT CONTINUED

When, after many days' journey, the Governor was approaching the city of Cuzco, much smoke was seen rising from it. Supposing that the Indians were burning it, he sent certain captains and horsemen in haste to prevent them; and when they reached the place, great numbers of Indians fell on them and began to attack them so hard with stones and slings and other weapons that they were forced to retire in haste for more than a league to a flat place, where the Governor joined them. He sent his two brothers Juan and Gonzalo with most of the cavalry to attack the Indians from the direction of the mountains, which they did with such bravery that they forced the enemy to retire, followed them and killed many in the pursuit. When night fell, the Governor collected all the Spaniards and kept them under arms; and next day, when they expected to encounter resistance at the entrance of the city, they found no one defending it and entered peacefully.

Twenty days after this, news arrived that Quizquiz was marching with many warriors through the province of Cuntisuyu, looting and destroying as he went; and the Governor sent Captain Soto with fifty horsemen to stop him. Quizquiz did not wait for Soto, but took the road to Jauja to attack some Spaniards whom he knew to have remained there guarding their baggage and treasure, and the royal fifth which was in charge of the treasurer Alonso de Requelme. Warned of his advance, the Christians, though few, defended themselves courageously in a strong place that they had chosen for the purpose. And so Quizquiz passed on along the Quito road.

The Governor once more sent Captain Soto with some horsemen to pursue him, and later sent his brothers to reinforce him. All together, they followed Quizquiz for more than a hundred leagues, but were unable to overtake him and returned to Cuzco. Here they found as great a booty of gold and silver as at Cajamarca. The Governor divided it among his men and settled the city, which was the Indian capital of the country and remained the Christian capital also for some time. The Governor divided the Indians among the Spaniards who had decided to stay there. Many did not wish to settle in the country, however, but preferred to bring back what they had won at Cajamarca and Cuzco and enjoy it in Spain.

9. Captain Benalcazar's conquest of Quito

WE have already said that on entering Peru the Governor settled the city of San Miguel, in the province of Tangarara near the port of Tumbez, in order that those coming from Spain should have a safe port at which to disembark. And since he thought he had not left enough horsemen there, after the capture of Atahuallpa he sent Captain Benalcazar from Cajamarca with a company of ten as his lieutenant at San Miguel.

On his arrival the Cañaris Indians came to complain to him that Ruminagui and other captains from Quito were making continuous attacks on them. Just at this time a great number of men arrived from Panama and Nicaragua; and Benalcazar took two hundred of them, including eighty horsemen, and advanced towards Quito, both to protect the Cañaris Indians, who had made a treaty with him, and because he had received a report that Atahuallpa had left great quantities of gold at Quito.

Now when Ruminagui heard that Benalcazar was approaching he came out to block his advance and fought him with more than twelve thousand Indians at many dangerous passes. He laid ambushes on the road, all of which Benalcazar avoided with great prudence and cunning. He would himself remain facing the Indians, but would send a captain with fifty or sixty horsemen riding through the night either above or below the road to seize the narrow place before daybreak. In this way he drove the Indians back on to the plains, where the horsemen could inflict great losses on them. When they awaited his attack it was because they had dug deep and wide pits set with sharp poles and stakes and covered with turf or grasses on very thin canes, which were much like those dug by the people of Alexia for the defence of their city, as described by Caesar in his seventh Commentary.

Whatever they did, however, the Indians could never deceive Benalcazar; his men did not fall into any of these traps, and received no harm from them. He never atacked the Indians frontally when they faced him, but made a detour of a league or two to attack them from the rear or the flank. He took great care never to ride over turf or grass that had not grown naturally on the spot. So when they saw that this stratagem did not work, the Indians contrived another. Everywhere where they supposed the horses would have to pass they dug holes the width of a horse's hoof so close together that there was almost no space between them. But they could not deceive Benalcazar with any of these tricks, and he gradually conquered all their territory as far as the principal town of Quito.

Here one day, as we afterwards learnt, Ruminagui said to all his wives (of whom he had a great number): 'Now you'll be glad because the Christians are coming, and you'll have some sport with them.' They all laughed, thinking that this was a joke, but their laughter cost them dear, for he had almost all of them beheaded. He had decided to leave the city, but first he set fire to a room full of very rich cloth that had been there since the time of Huayna Capac; and before he fled he made a surprise attack on the Spaniards at night, but inflicted no damage. Benalcazar then took possession of the city.

About that time the Governor sent Don Diego de Almagro with some men to the city of San Miguel and the coast to discover whether it was true, as he had heard, that Don Pedro de Alvarado, governor of Guatemala, had sailed for Peru with a great number of men and horses to explore the country. On reaching San Miguel, Don Diego learnt no certain news of Alvarado, but heard that Benalcazar was approaching Quito and Ruminagui was resisting, and decided to go and help. So he rode the whole hundred and twenty leagues to Quito, where he joined Benalcazar and took command of the army. He captured some towns and stockades that had resisted till then. But, finding that the country contained none of the gold and riches of which he had heard, he then returned to Cuzco, leaving Benalcazar governor of the province of Quito, as he had been before.

10. Pedro de Alvarado's landing and the events that followed

WHEN Don Hernando Cortes, Marques de Valle, had conquered and pacified New Spain, he received news of a neighbouring land called Guatemala, and sent one of his captains, Don Pedro de Alvarado, to discover it. With the army he took from Mexico, Alvarado conquered and won the country, and as a reward for the labours and perils of the conquest, His Majesty gave him the governorship of Guatemala. But, once established there, he received news of the land of Peru and begged the king for a share in its conquest. His plea was granted and an agreement drawn up by virtue of which he sent a gentleman of Caceres called Garcia Holguin with two ships to explore and seek information on the coasts of Peru. This gentleman returned bringing such good news of the great quantity of gold that the Governor Don Francisco Pizarro had won, that Alvarado decided to come himself. It seemed to him that while Don Francisco Pizarro and his army were terminating their affairs at Cajamarca he might be able to sail down the coast and seize the city of Cuzco which, as has already been said, was understood to fall outside the government of Don Francisco Pizarro, this being confined to two hundred and fifty leagues.

In pursuance of his plan, being afraid that help might subsequently be sent to Don Francisco Pizarro from Nicaragua, Alvarado descended one night on the Nicaraguan coast and seized three large ships that were being fitted up to carry men and horses to Peru as reinforcements for the Governor. On these and those he had brought from Guatemala, Alvarado then embarked fifteen hundred foot and horsemen, and went by sea as far as the province of Puerto Viejo, from which he took the road to Quito, near the Equator, along the edge of the plain and skirting some wooded hills called the Arcabuces.* On the way his men suffered great hardships from hunger and worse from thirst. There was such a shortage of water that if they had not found some reed-beds they would have perished. The peculiarity of the reeds that grow there is that when each knot is cut it is found to contain a hollow full of very good sweet water. They are generally as thick as a man's leg, and so each section yields more than two pints. These reeds have the property of collecting the night dews where the earth is dry and there are no springs or streams.

The men and horses of Alvarado's army refreshed themselves with this water along a considerable stretch of the road. But they were driven to such straits by hunger that many of the horses were eaten, though they were worth four or five thousand castlins each.

Along most of the road a very fine warm dust fell on them. This, they discovered, came from a high volcano near Quito, the fires of which are so great that they throw ash for a distance of eighty leagues. Their thunderings are sometimes so great that they can be heard upwards of a hundred leagues away.

In all the towns through which Pedro de Alvarado passed below the Equator, he discovered great stores of emeralds. When he came to the end of his road, most of which he had been forced to clear with axe and machete, he found himself faced by a chain of snow-covered mountains, on which the snow was still falling. It was very cold. But, choosing a favourable hour, he set out to cross them by a pass. Every man put on all the clothes he had, and they marched fast without a pause. Indeed no one stopped even to help a comrade. Nevertheless sixty men died of cold. One Spaniard, who was accompanied by his wife and two small daughters, seeing them sit down too tired to go on and being himself too weary to carry or help them, stayed with them until all four were frozen to death. Though he could have saved himself he preferred to perish with them.

At the cost of great toil and peril Alvarado and his men crossed the pass; and they counted themselves extremely lucky

* The Thickets.

to reach the other side. The province of Quito is surrounded by high snow-clad mountains, but between them are cool and temperate valleys in which men live and sow their crops. During their passage, the snow of one of these mountains melted, and a vast quantity of water came down with such violence that a village called Contiego was covered and submerged. The streams were seen to be carrying down in their current stones twice as big as those in a wine-press, as easily as if they were corks.

11. The meeting between Don Diego de Almagro and Don Pedro de Alvarado

As we have already said, Don Diego de Almagro left Captain Benalcazar as governor of the province of Quito and, having had no news of Don Pedro de Alvarado's landing, returned to Cuzco. On his way back he captured some crags and strong points in which the Indians had fortified themselves and took so long in doing so that Don Pedro had time to land and march to the province of Quito before Don Diego heard about it. For the distance was great and no Christians or Indians were travelling the road. One day, however, when engaged in the conquest of a province called Liribamba, he had to cross a full river by a very dangerous ford since the Indians had burnt the bridges and there was a host of them waiting to engage him on the other side. He had great difficulty in overcoming them, for the women fought too, shooting most accurately with slings. But when he finally captured the chief, this man told him that Pedro de Alvarado was marching speedily through the country, and at that moment was fifteen leagues away besieging a crag that had been fortified by an Indian captain called Zopazopagui.

On receiving this information Don Diego sent seven horsemen to discover the situation, and these were taken prisoner by Don Pedro's men and subsequently released. Don Pedro then took up his quarters five leagues from Don Diego's camp. When the news reached Don Diego, in view of his opponent's great advantage he decided to return to Cuzco, taking only twenty-five men with him and leaving the rest under Captain Benalcazar to defend the country. At this juncture the Indian interpreter Young Felipe (who was, as has been said, the cause of Atahuallpa's death and was afraid of the punishment that he knew he deserved) fled from Don Diego's camp to Don Pedro's taking a principal *cacique* with him, having arranged with the rest who were following Don Diego that they would come over when he sent them a summons. On reaching Don Pedro's camp therefore, he offered to bring the whole land over to Don Pedro peacefully. He told him that Don Diego was making for Cuzco, and that if he wanted to capture him he could easily attack him and do so, because he had no more than two hundred and fifty men, only ninety of them horsemen.

On receiving this information, Don Pedro de Alvarado immediately fell on Don Diego de Almagro, whom he found at Liribamba resolved to die defending the land. Don Pedro de Alvarado drew up his men and attacked with banners flying, and Don Diego, having few horsemen, waited for him on foot behind some walls. He had divided his men into two squadrons, the first under Captain Benalcazar and the second under his own command. When the two armies came within sight of one another they started to discuss peace, and for that day and night observed a truce. A lawyer called Cordera reconciled the two captains on these terms: that Don Diego de Almagro should give Don Pedro de Alvarado a hundred thousand gold pesos for the ships and horses and other furniture of the fleet; and that together they should go to the governor Pizarro to receive the payment. This agreement was made and observed with great secrecy, since if Don Pedro de Alvarado's men (among whom there were many gentlemen and persons of importance) had heard of it they might have rebelled, there being no reward provided for them. So the two captains announced that they were travelling together to a port where Don Pedro de Alvarado could continue his voyage of discovery by sea.

Leave was given to all those who wished to stay with Captain Benalcazar in Quito, for now all were united in peace and amity. Many of Don Pedro's followers remained at Quito, therefore, while Don Diego and he, with all the rest, went to Pachacamac, having learnt that the Governor had gone there from Jauja, where he had been staying, in order to meet them. Before leaving Quito, however, Don Diego burnt alive the *cacique* who had fled from him in the night, and would have done the same to Young Felipe if Pedro de Alvarado had not interceded for him.

12. Don Diego de Almagro and Don Pedro de Alvarado meet Quizquiz

As Don Diego de Almagro and Don Pedro de Alvarado were on their way from Quito to Pachacamac, the *cacique* of the Cañaris informed them that Atahuallpa's captain Quizquiz was approaching with an army of more than twelve thousand warriors, having collected all the Indians and flocks that he had found from Jauja onwards. He promised that, if they would wait, he would deliver Quizquiz into their hands. But, putting no trust in this promise, Don Diego continued on his way, and when they reached the province of Chaparra they unexpectedly encountered two thousand Indians who were marching two or three stages ahead of Quizquiz under a captain called Sotaurco.

Quizquiz's dispositions were as follows: Sotaurco and his troops marched ahead; on the left flank went another three thousand men gathering food in the neighbouring districts, and in the rear, two stages behind, were another three or four thousand men. Quizquiz himself marched in the middle with the main body, the sheep and the prisoners. His army therefore covered more than fifteen leagues of country from front to rear.

Sotaurco was about to occupy a pass through which he thought the Spaniards would come, but Don Pedro de Alvarado arrived first and captured him. Learning Quizquiz's dispositions from Sotaurco, he made a night march with such of his horsemen as could follow him. They were forced to halt in the night, however, because as they rode down to the river the horses cast their shoes on the great boulders and had to be reshod by torchlight. They then continued on their way with great speed for fear that some of the many Indians whom they had met might go back to Quizquiz and tell him that the Spaniards were coming. They did not stop once until late next day they came in sight of Quizquiz's camp.

When Quizquiz caught sight of the Spaniards he went by one road with all his women and servants, and sent a brother of Atahuallpa called Guaypalcon with the soldiers by another, which was rougher. Don Diego went to meet those soldiers on the slopes of a hill, where he outflanked Guaypalcon and attacked him from the rear. Finding themselves surrounded, Guaypalcon and his men fortified themselves in a wild and rocky place and defended themselves till night. Don Diego and Don Pedro then collected all their Spaniards and Indians and went out into the darkness in search of Quizquiz, whom they found. But not before the three thousand Indians who formed his left flank had beheaded fourteen Spaniards whom they had taken in an attack. In the course of their march the two Spanish captains ran into Quizquiz's rearguard. The Indians took up a defensive position on a river bank, and prevented the Spaniards from crossing all that day. They themselves crossed the river upstream of the Spaniards and seized a hill. The Spaniards advanced to fight them, though they would have preferred to retire. But they could not do so since the ground was covered with thorny shrubs. So they suffered heavy casualties. Many were wounded, notably Captain Alonso de Alvarado, who was pierced in the thigh, and a certain Master of the Order of St John.

All that night the Indians kept careful watch. But when dawn came they had retired from the river crossing and fortified themselves on a high peak, where Don Diego de Almagro left them in peace, not wishing to stay any longer. That night the Indians burnt all the clothing that they could not carry away. There remained in the camp more than four thousand men and women who had been Quizquiz's prisoners and who came over to the Spaniards.

When the Christians reached San Miguel, Don Diego de Almagro sent Captain Diego de Mora to Puerto Viejo to take possession for him of Don Pedro de Alvarado's fleet, and Don Pedro sent Garcia de Holguin to hand it over. And when Don Diego had distributed additional supplies of arms, money and clothes at San Miguel, both to his own men and Pedro de Alvarado's, they continued on their way to Pachacamac. On the road Don Diego left Captain Martin Estete to settle the city of Trujillo by order of Don Francisco Pizarro.

*

THE FOUNDATION OF THE CITY OF TRUJILLO, FROM PEDRO CIEZE DE LEON, 'CHRONICLE OF PERU', I, CHAPTER LXIX

The city of Trujillo was founded in the valley of Chimu, beside a large and beautiful river, from which water is drawn by means of conduits with which the Spaniards water their gardens and orchards. This water is piped to all the houses in the city, whose gardens are always green and full of flowers. Trujillo stands on a site that is considered healthy, and is surrounded on every side with what in Spain would be called granges and farms. Here the citizens graze their cattle and sow their crops. And as all the land is irrigated, vines, pomegranates, figs and other fruit trees from Spain have been planted everywhere. There are many wheat fields, and orange groves whose blossom is most beautiful. There are also citrons, grape-fruit, limes and lemons, and many very good native fruit. The citizens also keep hens, capons and other poultry. In fact the Spanish settlers at Trujillo have such an abundance of all these things that they can be said to lack for nothing. They have no lack of fish either, since the sea is only half a league away.

Trujillo lies among luxuriant trees in a level part of the valley, though there are barren and rocky mountains near-by. It is well planned and built, with broad streets and a large main square. Indians come down from the *sierra* to serve the Spaniards who hold them in *encomienda* and provide the city with the things they make and grow in their villages. Ships sail from Trujillo laden with cloth made by the Indians to be sold abroad. The Adelantado Don Francisco Pizarro, Governor and

Captain-general in the kingdom of Peru, founded and settled the city of Trujillo, in the name of the Emperor Charles, our lord, in the year 1530.

*

ZARATE, CHAPTER TWELVE CONTINUED

At about this time, as Quizquiz was approaching Quito, one of Benalcazar's captains defeated the soldiers of his advance guard, which so distressed him that he was uncertain what to do. His captains advised him to make peace with Benalcazar, whereupon he threatened them with death and ordered them to prepare to turn back. But as the army had not enough food to advance, certain captains came to him under the leadership of Guaypalcon, saying that it was better to die fighting the Christians than to retire and die of hunger in the desert. Quizquiz answered rudely, and Guaypalcon thrust a spear through his chest. Then other captains attacked him, and hacked him to pieces with clubs and axes. And they dispersed the army, letting each man go where he would.

13. The Governor pays Pedro de Alvarado the hundred thousand pesos agreed, and Don Diego de Almagro decides to have himself made Governor of Cuzco

WHEN Don Diego and Don Pedro reached Pachacamac, the Governor who had come there from Jauja received them joyfully and paid Don Pedro the hundred thousand pesos he had agreed to give him for his fleet, though many advised him not to pay since the fleet was worth less than fifty thousand. These advisers said that Don Diego had made this agreement out of fear, in order not to break with Don Pedro who had a great advantage over him, and that it would be better to send Don Pedro as a prisoner to His Majesty. And although the Governor could have done this very easily and without danger he decided that he would rather honour his partner Don Diego's promise, and liberally paid Don Pedro the hundred thousand pesos in good coin, which he let him take to his province of Guatemala. He himself remained behind to settle the city of Los Reyes to which he transferred the settlers he had planted at Jauja, for it seemed a more peaceful place and more suitable for trade of all kinds, since it had a seaport.

*

THE SITE AND FOUNDATION OF THE CITY OF LOS REYES (LIMA), FROM CIEZA DE LEON, OP. CIT., I, CHAPTER LXXI

The valley of Lima is longer and broader than any southward from Tumbez, and therefore had a larger population. At present it has few Indian inhabitants, since when the city was settled on their soil and their fields and irrigation ditches were taken over, they went off, some to one valley, some to another. The few who remain still keep their fields and conduits to water their crops. At the time when the Adelantado Pedro de Alvarado entered the kingdom, he found Don Francisco Pizarro, His Majesty's governor, in the city of Cuzco. And when Marshal Don Diego de Almagro had gone off to Riobamba, fearing that he would come down to these plains and try to occupy some part of the coast, Don Francisco decided to found a city in this valley. At that time neither Trujillo nor Arequipa nor Huamanga were settled,* nor any of the other cities, which were founded later. When considering the placing of a settlement, Don Francisco surveyed the valley of Sangalla and other places on the coast. But one day, when he and some companions came down to where the city now stands they were struck by the suitability of the site, which had all the necessary advantages. A plan was then drawn, and Los Reyes was built on a level part of this valley, two short leagues from the sea.

A river rises in the mountains to the east, which carries little water when it is summer up there, but is very full when it is winter. It flows out to sea in the west. Los Reyes is so situated

* They were in fact settled in the same year.

that the sun never strikes across the river, but follows the length of the city. Los Reyes is so close to its banks that a good marksman could drop a small stone into the water from the main square. The city can never be extended on this side in such a way as to leave the main square out of centre. The river must always remain the boundary. After Cuzco, Los Reyes is the biggest and most important city in Peru. It has many fine houses, some of them most splendid, with towers and roof terraces. The square is large and the streets wide. Most of the houses have water-conduits, which are extremely pleasant, and cool and delightful gardens and orchards, which are watered by them. At present the city is the site of the court and royal chancery; for which reason, and because it is the centre of trade for the whole Tierra Firme, it is always crowded with people and has shops full of merchandise. In the year I left the kingdom [1548] those many citizens who had *encomiendas* of Indians were so rich and prosperous that their estates were worth anything between 50 and 150 thousand ducats. Nearly everyone was very wealthy when I left. Ships often sail from the port of Los Reyes carrying 800,000 ducats, and some have carried more than a million. May the Lord always grant the city increase, for the service and growth of our holy faith and the salvation of our souls.

Above Los Reyes to the east stands a very large and very high hill on which a cross has been planted. Outside the city, on both sides, are many farms and estates, on which the Spaniards keep their flocks and dovecots. Here they have vines and fresh delightful orchards, teeming with the fruit of the land, also figs, bananas, pomegranates, sugar-canes, melons, oranges, limes, citrons, grape-fruit and pot-herbs from Spain, so good and succulent that they have no fault, but by their beauty give thanks to the Lord who produced them. Indeed, if only brawls, uprisings and wars would end, Los Reyes would be one of the finest places in the world in which to spend one's days. There is neither hunger, nor plague, nor rain, nor lightning, nor thunderbolt. The sky is always clear and very beautiful. More could be said but I will pass on, noting in conclusion that the city was founded and settled by the Adelantado Francisco de Pizarro, Governor etc. ... in the year of our salvation 1530.

From Los Reyes Don Diego marched to Cuzco with many soldiers, and the Governor went down to Trujillo to resettle the place and divide the land. And here news reached him that Don Diego de Almagro was trying to take possession of the city of Cuzco, having learnt that his Majesty, on receiving Hernando Pizarro's report, had conferred on him the governorship for a hundred leagues beyond the boundaries of Don Francisco's territory, which was said to end before Cuzco. The Governor's brothers Juan and Gonzalo with many soldiers who joined them had resisted this attempt, and every day they were skirmishing with Don Diego and Captain Soto, who was of his party. In the end Don Diego had received a setback, for the majority of the city council sided with the Governor and his brothers.

On hearing this news, the Governor travelled post-haste to Cuzco and imposed a general peace by his presence. He pardoned Don Diego who was much upset at having acted without grant or title, merely on the verbal statement that the territory had been granted to him. So they signed a new agreement and deed of partnership to this effect: that Don Diego de Almagro should go and discover the country towards the south, and if he should find good land he should beg His Majesty for the governorship of it, and if he did not receive it they would divide Don Francisco's governorship between them. The two captains then swore on the consecrated host that they would no longer oppose one another. Some people say that Almagro swore also not to set foot in Cuzco or within a hundred and thirty leagues of it even though His Majesty should make him governor of the city. They said that he swore on the Holy Sacraments: 'May it please you, Lord, to confound me, body and soul, if I break this oath', and having done so, he marched away with his followers, of whom he had upwards of fifteen hundred. The Governor then returned to the city of Los Reyes, sending Alonso de Alvarado to conquer the land of Chachapoyas, which lies sixty leagues into the mountains from Trujillo. Don Alonso and his company underwent great hardships in their conquest of this country, but finally settled and pacified it, whereupon the governorship and chief magistracy of the province were assigned to him.

BOOK THREE

DON DIEGO DE ALMAGRO'S JOURNEY TO CHILE, EVENTS IN PERU DURING HIS ABSENCE AND THE REVOLT OF THE INDIANS

1. *Don Diego de Almagro sets out for Chile*

DON DIEGO DE ALMAGRO set out to explore his conquest with five hundred and seventy well-equipped horse and foot; and some colonists, attracted by the great quantities of gold to be found in those parts, left their houses and *encomiendas* of Indians to accompany him. He sent Juan de Saavedra of Seville in advance with a hundred men, and in what was afterwards called the province of Charcas Saavedra met some Indians coming from Chile to pay tribute. The Adelantado* himself took about two hundred foot and horse with him and conquered the land for the distance of three hundred and fifty leagues, as far as the province of Chicoana, where he received news that another fifty Spaniards under Noguerol de Ulloa were following him. He sent them orders to join him, and together they advanced as far as the province of Chile, another three hundred and fifty leagues on. Here Almagro stayed with half his men, and sent Gomez de Alvarado forward with the other half, who advanced a further sixty leagues and returned to Don Diego at the onset of the winter rains.

At the time of Almagro's departure from Cuzco, Mango Inca and his brother Huillac Umu had planned to massacre all the Christians in Peru on a certain day. Huillac Umu himself was to account for Don Diego and his people, which he was unable to do. But his brother raised a rebellion in Cuzco of which more will be told. Having heard of the plot, the Indian interpreter Young Felipe fled from Don Diego's camp. But Don Diego sent to pursue him, and he was captured, executed and quartered. At the moment of death he confessed that he had been the cause of Atahuallpa's unjust execution, out of desire for his wife.

When the Adelantado had been in Chile two months, one of

* Almagro had been appointed Adelantado (the chief of a frontier province) in contrast to Francisco Pizarro who, though sometimes referred to as Adelantado, was a Governor. Alvarado was also adelantado.

his captains, Ruy Diaz by name, arrived with a reinforcement of a hundred men and categorically stated that all the Indians of Peru had rebelled and killed most of the Christians in the country. This news greatly distressed Almagro, who decided to return and attack the Indians and restore the country to obedience to His Majesty. Then, when he had done so, he would send one of his captains back to Chile with men to settle the province. So he set out and on the way received letters from Rodrigo Orgoñez, who was following after him with twenty-five men. And a little later he encountered Juan de Herrada, who was bringing him a further reinforcement of a hundred men, and carried a royal patent making him governor for two hundred leagues beyond the boundaries of the Marquis' territory. Almagro's governorship was called New Toledo, since the Marquis' was called New Castile.

Now although at the beginning of this chapter, it was said that Don Diego took five hundred and seventy men on his expedition, this is merely an estimated number; for in actual reality only two hundred men set out in the first place, to be followed by the reinforcements of which mention has been made.

2. The difficulties which Don Diego and his men encountered in the conquest of Chile

DON DIEGO and his men underwent great hardships on their expedition to Chile, both from hunger and thirst, and in their encounters with the Indians. Parts of the country were inhabited by men of very large stature who were excellent bowmen and dressed in sealskins. But the Spaniards suffered worst from the extreme cold they met on their way, both from cold winds and afterwards when they crossed snow-clad mountains. Here Ruy Diaz, who was following after Don Diego, lost several men and horses from frostbite. No clothes or armour were sufficient to keep out the icy wind which pierced and froze them. And the ground was so cold too that when Don Diego returned to Cuzco five months later he found in various places men who had died on the way out frozen hard to the rocks with the horses they were leading; and their bodies were as fresh and free from corruption as if they had only just died.

The carcases of these horses provided the main part of the food of Almagro's army on the way back. In all these wild places where there was no snow there was a great shortage of water, which the Spaniards carried in sheepskins, each living sheep carrying the skin of a dead one on its back filled with water. One of the characteristics of these Peruvian sheep is that they can carry a load of fifty or sixty pounds, like camels, which they much resemble in build though they have no hump. The Spaniards have since used them as horses, for they can carry a man four or five leagues in a day. When they are tired and lie on the ground, they will not get up even if beaten or pulled; the only thing to do is to take off their load. If they grow tired when ridden and the rider urges them on, they will turn their heads and spatter him with a very evil smelling liquid which they seem to carry in their crops.

These animals are of great use and profit, for they have very fine wool, especially the kind that they call alpaca, which have long fleeces. They require little food, especially those that work; they eat maize and can go for three or four days without drink. Their flesh is as clean and succulent as the very fat mutton of Castile. There are now public slaughterhouses throughout the land, but in the early days none were necessary. As every Spaniard had his own herd, when he killed a beast he would send his neighbours what they needed, and thus they supplied one another in turn.

In one part of Chile there were many ostriches on the plains, and these were hunted in this way: several horsemen would take up positions at various spots and would chase the birds from one to another. No horse could keep up with them otherwise, for they run very fast, taking great strides though they never leave the ground.

There are many rivers on this coast that flow by day but are quite dry at night. This greatly surprises those who do not understand the reason: that by day the snow on the mountains is melted by the heat of the sun, and so the water runs, whereas at night it is frozen by the cold and so the flow stops. Five hundred leagues down the coast, that is to say thirty degrees south of the Equator, there is rain and all the same winds blow as in Spain and other lands to the east. The whole of Chile is well populated and roughly divided into two parts, the plain and the mountain, and although the bays and inlets run in different directions into the land, the general line of the coast is from north to south from Los Reyes southward through forty degrees. It is a very temperate country, and has both summer and winter, though at the opposite times to those of Spain. There is no star corresponding to our North Star; there is only a small white cloud which revolves in a day and a night around the place where the pole should lie, which astronomers call the Antarctic Pole. There is also a cross with three other stars following it, making seven in all, like the seven stars that turn round our North Star. These are called by the astronomers Triton, and are placed much like ours except that the four which form the Southern Cross are closer together than our northern constellation. Our North Star entirely disappears from sight a little less than two hundred leagues from Panama. It then sinks below the horizon, and the two tritons or companions of the Pole remain visible, though only when they stand highest above the Pole in the northern hemisphere. But for a long distance still all that is visible of the Antarctic constellation is the four stars that form the cross, and pilots take their bearings from these. Then, when the traveller has passed thirty degrees south, all seven stars are visible.

In this land of Chile the length of day and night vary according to the season as in Spain, but in contrary fashion, as has been said. In Peru, in the province of Tierra Firme and in all the lands close to the Equator night and day are equal throughout the year; and if there is any divergence at any season it is not very noticeable in the city of Los Reyes.

The Indians of Chile dress like those of Peru; they are a handsome people, both men and women, and eat the same food as the Peruvians. Beyond Chile, thirty-eight degrees below the line, there are two great lords who are at war with one another, each of whom can field an army of two hundred thousand warriors. One of them is called Leuchengorma, and has an island two leagues from the mainland sacred to his idols, where there is a great temple served by two thousand priests. And Leuchengorma's subjects told the Spaniards that fifty leagues further on there is a great province between two rivers entirely populated by women, who will only allow men to come near them at the times most suitable for conception; and if they bear sons they send them to their fathers, if daughters they bring them up themselves. They are subject to Leuchengorma; and their queen is called Gaboimilla, which means in their language 'golden sky', because great quantities of gold are said to be mined in that land; and they make very fine cloth and pay tribute of all their commodities to Leuchengorma.

Though reliable news of all this has often been received, there has never been an opportunity for a journey of discovery, since Don Diego de Almagro did not wish to settle, and Don Pedro de Valdivia, who was afterwards sent to make a settlement, never had enough men to go exploring and still leave populated the settlements he had made. The town founded by this captain is thirty-three degrees south of the Line. The whole coast is thickly inhabited till beyond forty degrees south of the Line, as was reported by a ship of the expedition sent by Don Gutierre de Carvajal, Bishop of Plasencia, which went through the Magellan Straits and coasted northwards as far as the port of the city of Los Reyes. This ship brought the first mice to Peru, where there had been none before. But since then they have spread in great numbers in all the cities of Peru. It is believed that the litters travelled in boxes or bales of merchandise which were carried from one town to another. The Indians call them *ococha* which means something that has come out of the sea.

3. Hernando Pizarro's return to Peru and the dispatches he brought. The Indian uprising

AFTER Don Diego de Almagro's departure from Cuzco, Hernando Pizarro arrived from Castile where His Majesty had made him a Knight of Santiago and granted him other favours. He brought an extension by a hundred leagues of his brother

Francisco's governorship and the patent that we have mentioned for the new governorship of Don Diego de Almagro.

Now at this time Manco Inca, lord of Peru, was a prisoner in the fortress of Cuzco, on account of the plots, already mentioned, that he had made with Paulo Inca and Huillac Umu to kill the Christians. He wrote to Juan Pizarro, asking to be set at liberty so that Hernando Pizarro should not find him in prison, and Juan, who was in the *sierra* capturing an Indian rock-fortress, ordered his release. So when Hernando Pizarro arrived in Cuzco, he made great friends with the Inca and treated him very well, though he still had him watched. Probably the reason for his kindness to the Inca was to obtain gold from him, either for His Majesty or for himself. When Hernando had been in Cuzco for two months, the Inca asked his permission to go to the land of Yucaya to celebrate a feast. He promised to bring back a life-sized statue of his father Huayna Capac, a figure of solid gold. On the way to Yucaya, Manco Inca put the finishing touches to the plot he had been nursing ever since Don Diego left for Chile; and when he arrived he ordered the killing of some miners and servants who were out in the country, on the estates and in the mines. He sent a captain with a large army, who made a surprise attack on the fortress of Cuzco, which they captured, and which the Spaniards took almost a week to win back. During the recapture Juan Pizarro was killed in the night by a stone, which struck his head. He was wearing no helmet owing to a recent wound. His death was a great loss to the country, for he was a very brave man with great experience of fighting the Indians and well liked and respected by everyone.

*

ALONSO DE GUZMAN'S DESCRIPTION OF THE INDIAN REVOLT

The object of my journey was the conquest of a province called Chiriguana,* which I was unable to effect owing to the Indian rising.

* An Indian people inhabiting the Gran Chaco, allegedly cannibals before their conquest by the Inca Yupanqui.

I arrived at the city of Cuzco, worn out by the long and rugged road, and the difficulty of getting provisions, for we had to seize what we wanted from the Indians, and they killed one of my slaves who had cost me more than six hundred castlins.

The Spaniards had ill-treated the *caciques* and Indians, overworking, burning and torturing them for gold and silver; and one day Manco Inca, son of the great lord Huayna Capac, on pretence of seeking gold for the Governor's brother Hernando, who was acting as his lieutenant at Cuzco, left the city and did not return. He raised the country against us, collecting 50,000 armed men, against no more than 200 Christians, half of whom were lame or disabled. One morning the Indians broke into Cuzco at more than seven points, burning as they advanced and fighting so fiercely that they gained half the city; and there was little that did not burn since the houses were thatched with straw.

God and some strength of our own assisted us. For not only were the Indians fierce and numerous, but the smoke was so dense that we could not see each other. The battle lasted from that morning to the next. And then, with God's aid, we drove the Indians back towards the fortress, which we then attacked and captured, killing 3,000 of them. But they killed the Governor's brother Juan Pizarro, a youth of twenty-five who possessed 200,000 ducats in money. During the fighting in the city the Indians killed four Christians, in addition to the thirty or more whom they killed on the *caciques*' lands where they were collecting tribute.

I accepted the office of master of the camp, and was given Rodrigo de Pineda as my lieutenant. This is why I abandoned my intention of undertaking the service to which the Governor had appointed me.

The Indians of Cuzco are better dressed than those of any other province, both because it is colder here, and because, the land being more fertile, the people are richer. They are very much afraid of our horses, but their mountains offer an excellent protection against them. They have no defensive but many offensive weapons such as lances, arrows, clubs, axes, halberds, darts and slings, and another weapon which they call *ayllas*.

This consists of three round stones sewn up in leather and each attached to a cord about eighteen inches long. They throw them at the horses and so bind their legs together; and sometimes they will tie a man's arms to his sides in the same way. They are so expert with this weapon that they will bring down a deer with it when they are hunting. Their principal weapon, however, is the sling, with which they will hurl a huge stone with such force that it will kill a horse. In fact it is not much less effective than an arquebus. I have seen a stone from a sling break a sword in a man's hand in two pieces at thirty paces. The Indians also adopted the trick of digging great numbers of deep holes, in which they set stakes, and which they covered with earth and straw. Horses often fell into them, and the rider was generally killed.

This, as I know from experience, was the most fearful and cruel war in the world; for between Christians and Moors* there is some fellow-feeling, and both sides, acting in their own interests, spare their prisoners for the sake of the ransom. But in this Indian war there is no such feeling on either side; both kill as savagely as they can.

*

ZARATE, CHAPTER THREE, CONTINUED

After the recapture of the fortress the Inca descended with his whole army and besieged the city for more than eight months. At every full moon he attacked it from several sides. Hernando Pizarro and his brothers defended it most valiantly, however, with the many other gentlemen and captains in Cuzco, among whom Gabriel de Rojas, Hernan Ponce de Leon, Don Alfonso Enriquez and Riquelme the treasurer were outstanding. They and many others stayed fully armed by day and night, and throughout this time they were quite certain that the Governor and all the other Spaniards had been killed by the Indians, for they had news that there had been uprisings everywhere. Thus they fought and defended themselves like men who had no hope of help except from God and their own

* Alonso de Guzman had taken part in the conquest of Granada.

strength, though their numbers were reduced daily by death and wounds.

During the siege Gonzalo Pizarro broke out several times with twenty horsemen to raid the country as far as the lake of Chinchero, which is five leagues from Cuzco. Here he was attacked by so large a force that, hard though he fought, the Indians would have overwhelmed him if Hernando Pizarro and Alonso de Toro had not rescued him with their horsemen. For he had ridden further into the enemies' ranks than was wise, considering how few men he had with him. His conduct was indeed more courageous than prudent.

4. Don Diego brings his army to Cuzco and captures Hernando Pizarro

WHEN Hernando Pizarro brought His Majesty's patent making Don Diego governor of the territory outside Don Francisco Pizarro's province, Almagro decided to return from Chile and seize the city of Cuzco; and he was greatly encouraged in this project by the principal soldiers of his army, especially by Gomez de Alvarado, brother of the Captain-general Don Pedro de Alvarado, and Rodrigo Orgoñez. Some were greedy to obtain a share in the land of Cuzco, and others ambitious to remain in sole possession of the government of Chile. So, each for his own purposes, they persuaded the interpreters to say that Governor Pizarro and every other Spaniard in Peru had been killed by rebellious Indians, for news of the Indian uprising had already reached Chile.

So, urged by his entire army, Don Diego returned; and having arrived within six leagues of Cuzco without informing Hernando Pizarro of his approach, he sent a letter to the Inca promising to pardon him for all he had done if he would be his friend and take his side, since this land of Cuzco was in his governorship and he was returning to assume possession of it. The Inca cautiously sent him a message proposing an interview, which Don Diego accepted, suspecting no treachery.

Leaving some of his men with Juan de Saavedra, he took the rest with him. But, when he saw the opportunity, the Inca attacked Don Diego so violently that he inflicted heavy casualties.

Meanwhile, hearing of Don Diego's approach and that Juan de Saavedra was waiting with his contingent at the village of Hurcos, Hernando Pizarro came out of Cuzco with a hundred and seventy fully armed men. When this news came to Juan de Saavedra, he drew up his army of three hundred Spaniards and put them in a strong position. On reaching Hurcos, Hernando Pizarro sent to invite Saavedra to a private interview, at which they could discuss terms of agreement. Saavedra accepted the invitation, and at the meeting, Hernando Pizarro – so the story goes – offered him a very large sum in gold, if he would hand over his army. Saavedra refused, as would hardly have been surprising for he was a man of fine feeling and incapable of performing a mean action even in secret. It is however impossible to ascertain what actually took place, except from what the parties said and what the soldiers suspected, and from the few indications on which their suspicions were based.

Diego de Almagro returned from his encounter with the Inca and, joining his men with Juan de Saavedra's, marched towards Cuzco. On the way, having heard that four horsemen had been sent to spy on them, they ambushed and captured these men, from whom Don Diego learnt the full story of recent events in the country: that the Incas had rebelled and killed more than six hundred Spaniards and burnt a large part of the city of Cuzco; at which he showed great emotion. He then sent to inform the council of Cuzco of the royal patents, requesting them to accept him as governor of the city since the boundaries of the Marquis' government fell far short of it. His request was heard by the council of Cuzco who asked him to calculate the boundaries of the Marquis' government, offering to accept him as their governor if it was confirmed that the city fell outside them. Neither then nor subsequently has this confirmation been made; though very skilful men have met to make the calculation, they have never been able to agree on the form of measurement. Some have said that the leagues specified as the extent of Don Francisco's government should be measured along the coast taking in all the bays and inlets, or along the royal road with all its curves. In either case the boundaries would fall short not only of Cuzco, but, according to some, of Los Reyes also. The Marquis claimed that his leagues should be measured aerially, as along a cord stretched straight, without twists or turns, through the upper sky, the degrees being measured by the height of the sun and so many leagues agreed for each degree.

To resume our history, Hernando Pizarro sent to inform Don Diego that he would have part of the city cleared for him, where he and his men could lodge in security while an account of all these events was sent to Don Francisco Pizarro who was in Los Reyes. For some accommodation could certainly be arranged since they were friends and comrades. Some say that for these negotiations a truce was arranged, under which Hernando Pizarro thought it safe to send his settlers and soldiers home to rest, since they were exhausted by their long spell under arms during which they had taken no rest or sleep by day or night. When Don Diego learnt that the army had been stood down, in the darkness of the night and favoured by some heavy clouds he made an assault on the city. Hernando and Gonzalo Pizarro heard the noise, however, armed at great speed and, since their house was the first to be attacked, defended themselves fiercely with their servants until the fabric was set alight in many places and they were finally captured.

Early next day Don Diego compelled the council to accept him as governor and throw Hernando and his brother into prison. Many advised him to kill them, but Don Pedro de Alvarado urgently counselled him not to, and he refused. The immediate cause of Don Diego's violation of the truce was, undoubtedly, the information given him by some Indians and certain Spaniards also, that Hernando Pizarro had ordered the bridges to be broken and was fortifying himself in Cuzco. This seems clearly proved, for on entering the city he exclaimed: 'I have been deceived! All the bridges are intact!' The Governor heard nothing about this at the time, nor for many days afterwards.

Don Diego made Paolo Inca and invested him with the *borla*.

For on seeing what had happened, Manco Inca had fled with many soldiers to some very rugged mountains called the Andes.

*

AN ACCOUNT OF THE ANDES AND THE GROWTH OF COCA BY CIEZA DE LEON, 'CHRONICLE OF PERU', CHAPTERS XCV AND XCVI

The range of mountains called the Andes is accounted one of the greatest in the world, for it is known to begin at the straits of Magellan and stretches right through this kingdom of Peru, traversing innumerable lands and provinces. It contains great numbers of high mountains, some of them covered with snow and others belching fire. These highlands and mountains are very difficult for travellers since they are densely wooded and it rains there for most of the year. The ground is consequently so dark that one has to proceed with great care. For the roots of the trees come up through it, covering the whole mountain, and make the cutting of roads for horses very difficult. There is a tradition among the 'orcjones' of Cuzco that Tupac Inco Yupanqui crossed these mountains with a great army, and that most of the peoples he found there were very difficult to conquer and subdue. On the slopes towards the Southern Sea lived people of fair intelligence, all of whom wore clothes and were subject to the laws and customs of the Incas. But it is well known that on the eastern slopes, towards the other sea, the natives have less knowledge and intelligence. These grow a herb much prized by the Indians of which I shall speak later and which is called coca. And since those mountains are very high the reports are credible that they contain many animals, such as bears, tigers, lions, tapirs, wild boar and jaguars and many other remarkable creatures. And some Spaniards have seen snakes as thick as beams, which though of monstrous size and fierce appearance never attack or kill or hurt anyone even if they are trodden on. I was once talking about these snakes to some Indians in Cuzco, and they told me this story which I will record since they vouched for it: Once in the time of the Inca Yupanqui, who was the son of the Inca Viracocha, certain captains were sent at his command with a large army to explore the Andes and subdue such Indians as they could to the Incas' authority. When they entered the mountains, however, these snakes killed the greater part of the captain's men. The disaster greatly distressed the Inca, and when the news of it came to a certain old witch, she offered to go to the Andes and put the snakes so deeply asleep that they would do no more harm. On receiving the Inca's consent, she went to the scene of the disaster. Here she performed her enchantment, reciting certain spells which transformed the snakes from the fierce and wild creatures they once were into the tame and foolish creatures they now are. This may be a fiction or fable, but it is certainly true that though these snakes are large they do no harm.

The Incas had houses and princely lodgings in the Andes, which were in parts thickly populated. The land is very fertile, yielding maize, yuccas and other root crops, also some excellent fruit. Most of the Spanish inhabitants of Cuzco have made plantations there of oranges and limes, figs and vines, and other plants from Spain. In addition there are great banana palms and sweet and delicious pineapples. Right in the interior of the mountains and forests, there are said to live people so primitive that they have neither huts nor clothes, but go about like animals killing the birds and beasts that are their food, and living in caves and hollow trees scattered about the land. Throughout most of the Andes (it is said, though I have never seen them), there are very large she-monkeys which live in the trees, and which these men, by the temptation of the devil (who is always seeking opportunities for bringing men into great and deadly sin), use as their wives. It is told that some of them are delivered of monsters with the heads and sexual organs of men and the hands and feet of monkeys, and small bodies of monstrous shape all covered with hair. In fact (if they really exist) they must look like the devil, their father. They say also that these creatures have no speech but a fearful groan or howl. I do not affirm this story, nor do I find it incredible. For since many men of reason and understanding, who know of the existence of God, heaven and hell, forsaking their wives, defile themselves with mules, bitches, mares and other animals that it distresses me to mention, this story may well be true. Once in 1549 when I was travelling in Charcas to inspect the provinces and cities of that land – for which purpose I carried letters from President Gasca to all magistrates, asking them to help me learn and discover the most notable facts about the provinces – one night I shared a tent with a man from Malaga called Iñigo Lopez de Nuncibay, and a Spaniard who joined us told us both that he had seen with his own eyes the body of one of these monsters dead on the mountain. And Juan de Varagas of La Paz solemnly informed me that the Indians of Huanuco had told him they had heard the howling of these devils or she-monkeys. So there is at least a strong belief that these wretched men do commit this sin. I have also heard on good authority that Francisco de Almendras, who was a settler in La Plata, found an Indian woman committing the sexual act with a dog and had the woman burnt. In addition, I heard from Lope de Mendieta and Juan Ortiz de Zarate and other settlers in La Plata that they had heard from their Indians how in the province of Aulaga an Indian woman bore three or four monsters by a dog and they lived for a few days. May it please God that, though our wickedness is great and perpetual, we may not commit such gross and ugly sins.

In all parts of the Indies that I have visited, I have noticed that the natives take great delight in chewing roots, stems or herbs. Round the city of Antioquia, for instance, some men used to chew a small coca leaf, and in the province of Arma another herb; in Quimbaya and Ancerma they cut twigs from a young very green tree of medium size, which they always keep between their teeth. In most of the villages that are subject to the towns of Cali and Popoyan they chew this same small coca leaf, and they carry in calabashes some mixture that they make with it and a kind of earth like lime, which they chew perpetually. Throughout Peru they chewed and still chew this coca, which they keep in their mouths from morning till night, and are never without it. When asked why they always have this herb in their mouths – for they never swallow it but merely hold it in their teeth – the Indians say that when they chew it they are never hungry, but always full of strength and vigour. I think there must be some truth in this, though it seems to me a vicious habit suitable only to people like these Indians. This coca is grown in the Andes from Huamanga to La Plata. The tree is small and they cultivate it with great care, watering it liberally so that it may yield this leaf, which is like myrtle and is dried in the sun. It is afterwards packed in long, narrow baskets, which contain a little more than twenty-five pounds each. And this coca used to command such a price in Peru in the years '48, '49, '50 and '51 that one can think of no root or herb or fruit of a tree that is so valuable – except of course spices, which are a different thing. The produce chiefly of Cuzco, but also of La Paz and La Plata, amounted to eighty thousand pesos a year, more or less, and consisted entirely of this coca. When a man received an *encomienda* of Indians he immediately assessed its value by the number of baskets of coca that it yielded. In fact he was assessed in Trujillo by his possession of this herb. Coca was taken for sale to the mines of Potesi, and so much was invested in the planting of trees and gathering of leaves that the price of the herb declined considerably, though it will never cease to be valuable. There are some persons in Spain who are rich from the profits of trading in coca, buying it and selling it again and bartering it with the Indians in the *tiangues* or markets.

5. *The Indians kill many reinforcements sent by the Governor to his brothers in Cuzco*

AMONG the favours for which Francisco Pizarro petitioned his Majesty as a reward for the services he had done by the conquest of Peru was the *encomienda* of twenty thousand Indians in perpetuity for himself and his descendants in the province of Atabillos, with their rents and tributes and jurisdiction and the title of Marquis of that province. His Majesty granted him the title, but in the matter of the Indians answered that he would inquire about the quality of the land, and the damage or prejudice that might result from the grant. He promised, however, to do him every favour that he reasonably could. So from that place in the letter onwards he addressed him as Marquis and ordered that he should be so called, and we shall henceforth refer to him as the Marquis throughout this history.

Now when the Marquis received news of the Indians' rebellion from their own lips, having had no thought of any such danger, he began to send reinforcements to Hernando Pizarro at Cuzco, little by little as he could collect them, ten one day and fifteen the next and so on according to opportunity. But, hearing that these reinforcements were on the way, the Indians posted large numbers of warriors at the narrow and dangerous passes on the road to intercept them. And so all whom the Marquis sent at different times were defeated and killed; which would not have happened if he had taken the precaution of sending them all together. After paying a visit to the cities of Trujillo and San Miguel, the Marquis sent one Diego Pizarro with seventy horsemen to reinforce Cuzco, and they were all killed at a very wild pass fifty leagues from the city, which is called the Parcos hill; and one of his brothers-in-law called Gonzalo de Tapia whom he sent afterwards with eighty horsemen met with the same fate. The Indians also defeated Captain Morgovejo and Captain Gaete with their followers on different days, and hardly a man escaped. Those who were riding behind were not aware that those ahead had been overwhelmed, since the attack took this form: the Indians let the Spaniards enter a very deep and narrow valley, and blocked both the entrance and the way out with great numbers of men. Then they hurled so many stones and boulders down on them from the slopes that they killed almost all of them without coming to close quarters; and from the dead, who amounted to more than three hundred, they took great quantities of jewels and arms and silk clothing.

Seeing that he had received no news of any of these contingents, the Marquis sent Francisco de Godoy of Caceres with forty-five horsemen who came across the only two survivors of Gaete's men and, having heard their news, returned with great speed although the Indians had already occupied the passes through which he had advanced. They followed him for more than twenty leagues, attacking him from in front and behind so that he could only travel by night; and thus he reached the city of Los Reyes, as did also Captain Diego de Aguero with some people who had escaped by the skin of their teeth, for the Indians had tried to kill them in their own villages. Learning that Diego de Aguero was being followed by a great horde of Indian warriors, the Marquis sent one Pedro de Lerma with seventy or more horsemen and many friendly Indians, who went out to fight the Inca's men. The battle lasted almost all day, until the Indians fortified themselves on a crag where the Spaniards completely surrounded them. That day Captain Lerma's teeth were knocked in and many other Spaniards were wounded, but only one horseman was killed. The Christians pressed the Indians so hard that if the Marquis had not ordered a retreat this would have been the last day of the war. For the Indians were hemmed in on that small mountain and had no room to fight.

So when the Spaniards retired, the Indians gave great thanks to the Lord for having rescued them, offering both prayers and sacrifices. Then, raising their camp, they came and pitched it on a high hill close to the city of Los Reyes, on the opposite side of the river, and fought continuously with the Spaniards. The leader of these Indians was a chief called Tizoyapangui and with him was a brother of the Inca, whom the Marquis had sent with Gaete. In this war waged by the Indians against the city of Los Reyes, many Yanacona Indians, who were servants of the Spaniards, went by day to earn wages from the Indians and returned at night to sup and sleep with their masters.

6. The Marquis sends in various directions to beg for help, and Captain Alonso de Alvarado comes to his aid

SEEING such a multitude of Indians attacking Los Reyes, the Marquis felt certain that Hernando Pizarro and all those at Cuzco had been killed, and that this rising had been so general that Don Diego and those who had gone with him to Chile would have been destroyed also. And to prevent the Indians from thinking that they kept the ships there out of fear and in order to escape in them, and also to prevent the Spaniards from relying on the possibility of leaving the land by sea and consequently fighting less courageously, the Marquis dispatched his fleet to Panama, and sent with it, to the viceroy of New Spain and all the Governors in the Indies, entreaties for help and accounts of the dire straits he was in. The words of this message were less courageous than was usual with him, for he listened to the persuasions of certain poor-spirited men among his followers. At the same time he sent orders to his lieutenant in Trujillo to evacuate the town and to embark the women, children and property on a ship that he would send to carry them to Tierra Firme. He and his men were then to come to reinforce him, bringing nothing but their horses and their arms. For he felt certain that the Indians would attack Trujillo also, and since he was in no position to save them, it would be better that its inhabitants should join him and form a single body. He ordered them, however, to come secretly, thinking that if the Indians remained in ignorance they would divide their forces to attack Trujillo. The settlers abandoned the town. But just as they were departing, Captain Alonso de Alvarado reached them with all the men he had taken to explore Chachapoyas. For the Marquis had sent him orders to break off his expedition and come to their aid. So, leaving some of his soldiers to defend Trujillo, he brought the rest to Los Reyes to help the marquis. And when he arrived, the Marquis made him captain-general in place of Pedro de Lerma, who had held the office till then; and this slight was the cause of Lerma's subsequent mutiny.

When the Marquis found himself provided with a powerful force, he decided to deal with the most urgent situation, and sent Captain Alonso de Alvarado with three hundred Spanish foot and horsemen, to raze and conquer the country. Four leagues from the town of Pachacamac, Alvarado fought a hard battle with the Indians, whom he defeated, killing many. He then continued on his way to Cuzco. Further on he suffered great hardships crossing a desert where more than five hundred of his Indian auxiliaries died of thirst; and if the horsemen had not galloped ahead and returned with vessels of water for the foot-soldiers, such was their exhaustion that they would probably all have perished. As he continued his conquest, he was overtaken in the province of Jauja by Gomez de Tordoya of Villanueva de Barcarote, with a further two hundred foot and horsemen whom the Marquis had sent after him. Then with a combined force of five hundred men, Alonso de Alvarado advanced to the bridge of Lumichacha, where the Indians surrounded him; but he defeated them in battle, killing many. Nevertheless they continued to attack him all the way to the bridge of Abancay, where he received news of the imprisonment of Hernando and Gonzalo Pizarro and other events in Cuzco, whereupon he decided to advance no further till he received orders what to do.

Now when Diego de Almagro learnt that Alonso de Alvarado was approaching, he sent Diego de Alvarado with seven or eight horsemen to notify him of his letters-patent. But when they arrived Alonso de Alvarado took them prisoner, saying that he would send to notify the Marquis of these letters since he was not competent to deal with this matter himself. When Don Diego saw that his messengers did not return, he was afraid that Alonso de Alvarado was advancing by another road. So to prevent his entering Cuzco, he retired in great haste from his position three leagues outside the city.

A fortnight later, however, he led his army out against Alonso de Alvarado, having heard that Pedro de Lerma had planned a mutiny and would come over to him with more than eighty men. And when Don Diego came close to Alonso de Alvarado, his outriders captured Pedro Alvarez Holguin, who was reconnoitring the field, in an ambush which they laid for him. On hearing of his capture, Alonso de Alvarado decided to arrest Pedro de Lerma, of whom he had suspicions, but Lerma fled in the night, taking with him the signatures of all those who had agreed to go over with him. On the same night Diego de Almagro came to the bridge where he knew Gomez de Tordoya and a son of Colonel Villalva were waiting for him. He sent a great part of his army over by the ford, however, for he had been informed that the crossing was guarded by Don Pedro de Lerma's fellow-conspirators, who surrendered it to him and encouraged him to pass over without fear. Indeed some of the plotters had been so zealous that during their night guard they had stolen fifty or more lances belonging to Alvarado's men and thrown them in the river. When Alonso de Alvarado decided to attack, therefore, not only were the mutineers missing but many other soldiers of his army failed to arrive because they were looking for their lances. So Don Diego defeated them without the loss of a Spaniard, though Rodrigo Orgoñez had his teeth knocked out by a stone.

Having looted the camp and taken Alonso de Alvarado prisoner, Don Diego returned to Cuzco, where he treated his prisoners with some cruelty. He and his men behaved with great arrogance. They said that not a slate* should remain in all Peru for anyone to stumble over, and that the Marquis and his brothers could go and govern the mangrove-swamps below the equator.

7. The Marquis advances to the aid of his brothers in Cuzco, but on hearing of Alonso de Alvarado's defeat, returns to Los Reyes

AFTER Alonso de Alvarado's victories over the Indians on the road to Cuzco both at Pachacamac and Lumichaca, the Inca and Tizoyopangui thought it best to raise their siege of Los Reyes. Finding himself free and with a large army, the Marquis then set out for Cuzco with more than seven hundred horse and foot soldiers to the aid of his brothers, whom he supposed to be hard pressed by the Indians. For he had heard nothing of Don Diego de Almagro's return from Chile or of the events that had followed. A large part of his army had been sent by Don Alonso de Fuen-Mayor, archbishop and lord president of the island of Santo Domingo, under his brother Diego de Fuen-Mayor, and some had been brought by the lawyer Gaspar de Espinosa from Panama. One Diego de Ayala (whom the Marquis had sent to Nicaragua) had also arrived with some reinforcements.

* A crude pun on Pizarro's name; *pizarra* is a slate.

When the Marquis had led his army some twenty-five leagues from Los Reyes along the road through the plains, news reached him in the province of Nasca of Don Diego's return and all the events that had followed. This naturally distressed him. And since his army was only equipped to fight with Indians, he decided to return to Los Reyes and prepare it for a battle against Spaniards.

The Marquis prepared for battle, but sent the lawyer Espinosa to Cuzco to open negotiations with Don Diego, using the argument that if His Majesty were to hear what had happened and that they were in disagreement, he would send someone to replace them both and enjoy the conquests they had so painfully made. He instructed Espinosa at all costs to secure the release of his two brothers, and if necessary to agree to Don Diego's remaining in Cuzco so long as he did not come any further north until His Majesty had been consulted and had sent his ruling in the matter of the boundaries between their governorships. Espinosa left on this mission; but he could find no basis of arrangement and died without bringing the matter to a conclusion.

Don Diego came down with his army on to the plains leaving Captain Gabriel de Rojas as his lieutenant at Cuzco, in charge of his prisoners Gonzalo Pizarro and Alonso de Alvarado, and taking Hernando Pizarro as a prisoner with him. And so he continued on his way to the province of Chincha, which is twenty leagues from Los Reyes, and there he made a settlement in a place that was certainly within the Governor's territory.

8. The Marquis raises fresh troops, and Alonso de Alvarado and Gonzalo Pizarro escape from prison. Their further adventures

ON reaching Los Reyes, the Marquis immediately had the drums beaten and paid his men. Then he expanded his army under the pretext of protecting himself against Don Diego who, he said, was coming to occupy his government. In a few days he had collected more than seven hundred foot and horsemen, among them many arquebusiers. For in Diego de Fuen-Mayor's company there had come a Captain Pedro de Vergara (who, as we have already said, was entrusted with the exploration of Bracamoros) and he had brought from Flanders, where he had married, a great number of arquebuses and their furniture. For until then there had not been enough in Peru to form a company or even a small unit.

The Marquis appointed Vergara and Nuño de Castro to command the arquebusiers, and Diego de Urbina of Orduna, nephew of the master of the camp Juan de Urbina, to command the pikemen, and Diego de Rojas, Peranzures and Alonso de Mercadillo to command the horsemen, and he made Pedro de Valdivia master of the camp, and Antonio de Villalva, son of Colonel Villalva, chief sergeant.

In the meantime Gonzalo Pizarro and Alonso de Alvarado escaped from their imprisonment in Cuzco, and joined the Marquis with more than seventy men, bringing with them Don Diego's lieutenant Gabriel de Rojas, whom they had captured. The Marquis was greatly delighted by their coming, both because they were now out of danger and because their escape brought general encouragement. He immediately made Gonzalo Pizarro captain-general and Alonso de Alvarado captain of the horsemen.

When Don Diego heard of the prisoners' escape and of the great army that the Marquis had assembled, he decided to come to some agreement with him, and even to make the overtures himself. So he sent Don Alonso Enrique, the factor Diego Nuñez de Mercado and the auditor Juan de Guzman with full powers to propose an interview. And after long negotiations the Marquis left the whole matter in the hands of Fray Francisco de Bobadilla, provincial of the Mercedarian order in those parts, who was to effect a compromise; and Don Diego did the same. Fray Francisco exercised this power and pronounced the following decision: that in the first place Hernando Pizarro should be released and the possession of Cuzco restored to the Marquis who had held it in the first place; that the armies should then be broken up and the companies sent just as they were to explore the country in various directions; and that the whole case should be laid before His Majesty, who would resolve it. And in order that the Marquis and Don Diego might meet and talk, he requested them each to come with twelve horsemen to the village of Mala which lay between the armies. So they set out for their meeting, though Gonzalo Pizarro, not trusting in the truce or Don Diego's word, followed immediately after the Marquis with all his men, and took up his position in secret not far from Mala. He ordered Captain Castro with forty arquebusiers to lie in ambuscade in a canefield beside the road by which Don Diego would come, to see if he brought more than the agreed number of men; in which case they were to fire their weapons and he would come up immediately.

9. The Meeting of the Governors and the release of Hernando Pizarro

ON setting out from Chincha to Mala with his twelve horsemen, Don Diego left his lieutenant Rodrigo Orgoñez in command, with instructions to exercise every precaution and keep his army in readiness to come up quickly if the Marquis were to bring more than the stipulated number of men. As for his treatment of Hernando Pizarro, this must accord with the treatment Don Diego received at the interview.

The two governors embraced warmly when they met. After they had exchanged some conversation, however, without touching on the matter in hand, one of the Marquis' gentlemen who had received news of Gonzalo Pizarro's approach went up to Don Diego and whispered in his ear: 'You would do well to leave here immediately, your lordship. Take this warning from your humble servant.' Upon this Don Diego hastily sent for his horse. On seeing that Don Diego was about to go, some of the Marquis' men urged their chief to seize his rival, which could easily have been done by Nuño de Castro's arquebusiers, who were in ambuscade. But the Marquis would not agree since Don Diego had come under his safe-conduct, and he did not believe he would return without concluding the business he had come for. But as he rode off, Don Diego saw the ambuscade, and believed the warning he had received. On returning to his camp, he complained of the Marquis, saying that they had tried to capture him, and refused the explanations which the Marquis offered.

Nevertheless, at the intercession of Diego de Alvarado, Don Diego de Almagro released Hernando on terms agreed between them: that the Marquis should give him a ship and a safe port for communications with Spain, and that neither should attack the other but await fresh instructions from His Majesty. The release of Hernando Pizarro was strongly opposed by Rodrigo Orgonez, who had seen him gravely ill treated during his imprisonment at Cuzco, and thought that he would seek to take revenge when in power; and his vote remained unchanged, that Hernando should be executed. But Diego de Alvarado's opinion prevailed, and he trusted in the agreement that had been made. When Hernando Pizarro was released, Don Diego sent him to the Marquis in the company of his own son and another gentleman. But the moment he had left, Don Diego repented of his decision; and it is believed that he would have restored him to prison had Hernando not been in such haste to escape from his power, that in a short time he had travelled more than half the road and met some of the Marquis' principal followers who had come out to meet him.

10. The Marquis attacks Don Diego, who retires to Cuzco

AFTER the conclusion of this agreement, the Marquis received His Majesty's ruling and command, brought by Pedro Anzures, that each governor should remain in the land that he had discovered, settled and conquered at the time of this notification, even though it was within the boundaries of the other's government, until such time as His Majesty should give his judgement in the principal matter under dispute.

As soon as he had welcomed his brother, the Marquis sent a message to Don Diego demanding that, in view of this ruling, he should retire from the land and towns that he, Francisco Pizarro, had discovered and settled. Don Diego replied that he was ready to observe the ruling and all its conditions, which were that each should remain in the land and towns exactly as he had held them at the moment of receiving the notification. By this same ruling, therefore, he demanded that the Marquis should leave him in peace and without contention exactly where he was at that date. He further assured the Marquis that he would fulfil any later commands His Majesty might send him in this matter.

The Marquis replied that he had been the first to hold those towns and the city and territory of Cuzco, which he had discovered and settled, and that Don Diego had dispossessed him of them by force. Therefore Don Diego must quit all this territory in accordance with His Majesty's commands; in default of which he, Francisco Pizarro, would throw him out, since the truce and agreement between them had now been superseded by His Majesty's fresh commands. Don Diego refused to retire. So the Marquis attacked him with his whole army and drove him back towards Cuzco. Don Diego then fortified himself in the high *sierra* of Huaytara, cutting all the passes on this very rough road. Hernando Pizarro followed him with a few men and, climbing the *sierra* one night by a secret path, captured the pass with his arquebusiers. Don Diego was forced to flee and, being sick, went ahead, leaving in the rear Rodrigo Orgoñez, who was retiring in good order. But learning one night from two of the Marquis' horsemen whom he captured, that he was being pursued, he hurried his march, although most of his men advised him to turn on the enemy. For everyone knew that men climbing from the plains to the *sierra* were mountain-sick at the beginning and as helpless as on the first days of a sea-voyage. But Rodrigo Orgoñez refused to attack since Don Diego had told him not to, though an attack would probably have been successful. For the Marquis' men were sick and impeded by the heavy snows, and would have suffered great losses. Owing to their poor condition indeed, the Marquis soon withdrew them to the plains. But Don Diego retired to Cuzco, breaking all the bridges because he still believed he was being pursued.

Don Diego spent more than two months in Cuzco collecting an army and munitions and instruments of war, making weapons of copper and silver, casting artillery, and providing himself with all other necessities.

11. Hernando Pizarro advances on Cuzco, and fights the battle of Las Salinas. Don Diego de Almagro is captured

AFTER retreating from the *sierra*, the Marquis collected his whole army on the plains, and found a variety of opinions among his people as to what their next action should be. It was finally concluded that Hernando Pizarro should lead his men to Cuzco and take the city over as the Marquis' lieutenant, and that his brother Gonzalo should go with him as captain-general. The pretext and justification for this action would be to secure justice for the many citizens of Cuzco who were marching with him and complained that Don Diego had forcibly entered and occupied their houses, taking over their *encomiendas* and other property which they held in the city of Cuzco. So Hernando set out, and the Marquis returned to Los Reyes. And when, on a certain evening, after many days' march, Hernando and his men were approaching Cuzco, all the captains wished to go down and sleep that night on the plains. But Hernando Pizarro insisted on pitching his camp in the *sierra*.

At dawn next day, Rodrigo Orgoñez was already in the field with all Don Diego's men, awaiting battle. Francisco de Chavez, Juan Tello and Vasco de Guevara were his captains of horse, and on the *sierra* flank he had some Spaniards and many Indian warriors as auxiliaries; and he left imprisoned in two cells of the fortress of Cuzco all the friends and servants of the Marquis and his brothers who were in the city. They were so many and the place was so small that some of them were stifled.

In the morning, after hearing mass, Gonzalo Pizarro and his men came down to the plain where they drew up their squadrons and advanced towards the city with the intention of taking up their position on a height which commanded the fortress; for they thought that when Don Diego saw the power of their army he would not dare to give battle; and they too wanted at all costs to avoid battle, since they expected heavy casualties.

But Rodrigo Orgoñez was on the main road with all his men and artillery; and he had no such thoughts, since he believed that they would have to advance by this road, all other approaches being blocked by a marsh. On seeing Orgoñez' army in position, Hernando Pizarro ordered Captain Mercadillo to ride ahead with the horsemen and be ready to fight the Indian warriors, if they attacked, or to help in the main battle. And before this began, a fight started up between the Indians on Hernando Pizarro's side and those on Don Diego's. Pizarro's horsemen attempted the marsh, and the leading arquebusiers meanwhile advanced and shot at a squadron of Don Diego's cavalry to such good effect that they forced them to retire. And when the Marquis' master of the camp, Pedro de Valdivia, saw them in retreat he assured his side that the victory was won. Then Don Diego's men fired a cannon that killed five of the Marquis' men. But when Hernando Pizarro and his men had passed the marsh and a near-by stream, they attacked the enemy in good order. Every captain was instructed what to do at the moment of attack, and to encourage his men to the utmost. Seeing that Don Diego's pikemen had their pikes raised, he ordered the arquebusiers to fire high, to such effect that two volleys destroyed more than fifty pikes. At this moment Rodrigo Orgoñez ordered his captains to attack; and when he saw them holding back he charged forward with his band towards the left, where he had seen Hernando Pizarro at the head of his squadrons. Then Orgoñez cried in a loud voice: 'By the Holy Book, follow me who will. I ride to my death.'

On seeing that Orgoñez was exposing his flank, Gonzalo Pizarro and Alonso de Alvarado charged the enemy with such force that they threw more than fifty men to the ground. And when Rodrigo Orgoñez rode up they wounded him with an arquebus shot in the forehead which passed through his vizor. But though wounded, Orgoñez killed two men with his lance and dealt one of Hernando Pizarro's servants a sword-thrust in the mouth, taking him for his master since he was very well attired.

When the two armies were joined they fought fiercely. But finally the Marquis' men forced Don Diego's to turn away. And when Don Diego, on the hill from which he was watching (for being sick he took no part in the battle), saw his men running away, he cried: 'By our Lord, I thought we had come to fight.' And when two gentlemen had forced Rodrigo Orgoñez to surrender, a third to whom he had done some injury cut off his head; and several more who had surrendered were killed in the same way. Hernando Pizarro and his captains were unable to prevent it though they tried extremely hard. But Alonso de Alvarado's men, being ashamed of their defeat at the bridge of Abancay, were anxious to take vengeance in any way they could. They were so savage that when one of them was carrying Captain Ruy Diaz tied on the cruppers of his horse, another rode up and dispatched him with his lance.

On seeing that his army was beaten, Don Diego fled for refuge to the fortress of Cuzco, where Alonso de Alvarado and Gonzalo Pizarro followed him and took him prisoner. When the Indians saw that the battle was decided they deserted him, and went to strip the dead Spaniards. They stripped some who were living also, but too badly wounded to defend themselves. For when the crowd passed in the wake of the victorious army, no one could stop them. All the dead were left naked. And the Spaniards, victors and vanquished alike, came out of the battle in such a state that the Indians could very easily have conquered if they had had the courage to attack them, as they had planned. This battle took place on 26 April 1538.

12. The events that followed the battle of Las Salinas. Don Hernando Pizarro comes to Spain

WHEN the battle was over, Hernando Pizarro worked hard to win the goodwill of Don Diego's surviving captains. But as he failed, he banished many of them from Cuzco. And seeing that it was also impossible to satisfy those who had served him, since each one thought that he deserved at least the whole province, he decided to break up the army and send the soldiers to make fresh discoveries. By this he achieved two results: he rewarded his friends and banished his enemies. So he sent Captain Pedro de Candia with three hundred of his own men and Don Diego's to conquer certain land reputed to be very rich. But as Pedro de Candia could not enter the country owing to the rough terrain, he returned to Collao with his men almost in a state of mutiny. One Mesa, formerly the Marquis' captain of artillery, had said that he would pass through the land of Collao despite Hernando Pizarro. And this he dared to do, thanks to the support he received from Don Diego's people in that company, whose feelings were still unreconciled. Candia therefore sent Mesa as a prisoner to Hernando Pizarro together with the accusation and testimonies against him.

Hernando Pizarro realized that so long as Don Diego was alive the land would never be completely pacified or the people calm. This certainty, and further evidence of conspiracies in various places to release Don Diego from prison and seize the city, convinced him that it would be best to kill him. For Don Diego's death could easily be justified by his guilt in fomenting the recent troubles, of which he could be said to be the cause and fountainhead, since he had entered the city with his army at the beginning and occupied it on his own authority, killing many of those who had resisted him, and had then advanced with an army and flying standards into the province of Chincha (which was undoubtedly part of the Marquis' government). So Don Diego was sentenced to be executed.

On hearing his sentence, Don Diego implored Hernando Pizarro for mercy. He piteously reminded him that he and his brother owed their present high eminence to him, since he had provided their capital. He reminded him also that he had graciously released him from the prison in which he had held him, refusing his captains' urgent persuasions to put him to death. If Hernando had received any ill-treatment in prison, it was not, he said, by his orders and not with his knowledge. He begged Hernando to consider that he was a very old man and that even if he were spared now, time and age would shortly condemn him to death. Hernando Pizarro replied that these were no fit words for a man of his courage, that Don Diego should not show such cowardice but, since his death sentence could not be revoked, accept the will of God and die like a Christian and a gentleman. To this Don Diego replied that Hernando should not be surprised that he feared death, being a man and a sinner, since Christ in His humanity had feared it also. After this, in fulfilment of his sentence, Hernando Pizarro had him beheaded.

Hernando Pizarro then went to Collao to deal with Captain Candia's men and executed Mesa, who had been the leader of the mutiny. And he entrusted these three hundred to Captain Pedro Anzures, with instructions to carry out their original mission. But so bad and marshy was the terrain that they were in danger of dying of hunger.

Meanwhile Hernando Pizarro stayed to conquer the province of Collao, which is a very flat country rich in gold-mines. Maize does not grow there, since it is too cold. The Indians eat a root called the potato which has the shape and something of the taste of truffles. There are also large flocks of the sheep that we have described.

When Hernando Pizarro learnt that his brother the Marquis had come to Cuzco he went to meet him, leaving his brother Gonzalo in his place to continue the conquest. Gonzalo went on to explore the province of Charcas, where he was surrounded and attacked by many Indian warriors, who pressed him so hard that Hernando was forced to return from Cuzco with some horsemen and rescue him. And in order that help should reach him with the greatest speed, the Marquis pretended that he himself was taking part in the expedition, and rode out with it for the first two or three days' march. But when Hernando reached his brother he found that the Indians were already defeated. They spent some days together conquering the country and had many fights with these Indians. Finally they captured Tizo, their captain; and then returned to Cuzco where they were graciously received by the Marquis.

The Marquis gave enough land for subsistence to all those whom the country would contain. The rest he sent on conquering expeditions under Captains Vergara and Porcel; and in another direction he sent Captain Alonso Mercadillo and Captain Juan Perez de Guevara. He sent the master of the camp Pedro de Valdivia to the land of Chile, from which Don Diego had returned.

When these dispositions were concluded, the land settled and the soldiers dispersed, Hernando Pizarro set out for Spain to give an account to His Majesty of all that had happened. Many advised against this course, however, because they did not know how the execution of Don Diego would have been received. At their final interview, Hernando warned the Marquis not to trust Don Diego's men, who were generally known as the 'Chileans', or let them meet together; for if ever he saw six or more of them in a party he could be sure they would be plotting his death.

13. Captain Valdivia's adventures in Chile

WHEN Pedro de Valdivia reached Chile with his army, the Indians received him with a pretence of peace, since they had not gathered their crops, which were not ripe. Once they were brought in, however, the whole land rose in rebellion, and they attacked some Spaniards who had travelled outside the settlement, killing fourteen of them. Valdivia had gone out to their aid. But while he was fighting, some Spaniards decided to revolt against him. On learning of their plot, he hanged them all, including Captain Pedro Sancho de Hoz, who had been acting almost as joint leader. And while Valdivia was out in the country, the city was attacked from another direction by upwards of seven thousand Indian warriors, who pressed hard on the few Spaniards that remained there under Captains Francisco de Villagran and Alonso de Monroy. Amounting to no more than thirty horsemen, they rode out into the fields and fought most valiantly against the Indian bowmen from early morning till night broke off the battle and they retired wounded and exhausted. The Indians too thought it well to retire, owing to the heavy casualties they had received that day. But from this time the whole land was in a state of war for more than eight years, during which Valdivia and his men defended themselves and never left the country. On the contrary Valdivia made his men sow and plough and gather crops to feed them, for they could not use Indian labour.

Thus Valdivia maintained himself till his return to Peru, at the time when the licentiate Gasca was raising an army against Gonzalo Pizarro. He then served and helped Gasca, as will be described hereafter.

BOOK FOUR

GONZALO PIZARRO'S JOURNEY OF DISCOVERY TO THE LAND OF CINNAMON AND THE DEATH OF THE MARQUIS

1. Gonzalo Pizarro prepares for the expedition to the Land of Cinnamon

NEWS had come to Peru that to the east of the territory of Quito some very rich land had been discovered in which there were abundant crops of cinnamon, for which reason it was called the land of Canela or cinnamon. The Marquis decided to send his brother Gonzalo to conquer and settle this land and because the expedition had to start from the province of Quito, and supplies for it had to be gathered and provided there, he handed over the government of Quito to Gonzalo, trusting that His Majesty would confirm him in it. So Gonzalo Pizarro left for Quito with the many men who were to accompany him on this expedition, and on the way was involved in battle with the Indians of the province of Huanuco who attacked him and reduced him to such straits that the Marquis was compelled to send Francisco de Chavez to his aid. Only after this did Gonzalo succeed in reaching Quito.

The Marquis then sent Gomez de Alvarado to conquer and settle the province of Huanuco. For some *caciques* of that province, called the Conchucos, had attacked the city of Trujillo with many warriors, killing all the Spaniards they could and robbing and doing much harm to their Indian neighbours also. They offered the dead and all their booty to an idol called Cataquilla. And they continued their depredations until Miguel de la Serna, a settler of Trujillo, came out of the city with all the men he could muster and, joining Francisco de Chavez, fought the Indians until they were conquered and routed.

2. Gonzalo Pizarro leaves Quito. His adventures on the way to the Land of Cinnamon

WHEN Gonzalo Pizarro had collected the necessary provisions for his journey, he left Quito with five hundred well-equipped Spaniards, a hundred of them horsemen, each with a spare mount, four thousand Indian allies and three thousand head of sheep and hogs. After passing a town called Inga, he reached the land of Quijos, which was the last conquest of Huayna Capac in the north. The Indians of this country came out to fight him, but one night they all disappeared and not one of them could be found again. After they had rested for some days in the Indian villages, there was a great earthquake. The ground shook, there was a rain-storm accompanied with heavy thunder and lightning, the earth opened in many places and more than five hundred houses were engulfed. Then a river which ran close by rose so high that they could not cross it to hunt for food, and so they suffered greatly from hunger.

After leaving these villages, Gonzalo Pizarro crossed some ranges of high cold mountains, where many Indians in his company were frozen to death. And because of the lack of food in that country he did not stop till he came to a province called Sumaco, which lies on the slopes of a high volcano. Since there was much food here the army rested while Gonzalo Pizarro took some of them into the thick forest to find a road. But not finding one, he went to a village called Coca, and from there sent for all his men whom he had left in Sumaco. Throughout the two months that they spent there it rained continuously by night and day, never stopping for long enough to allow them to dry the clothes on their backs. In the province of Sumaco and for fifty leagues around, there was plenty of the cinnamon they had been told of. It is a large tree with leaves like a laurel, and the fruit is a bunch of small seeds shaped something like an acorn. The fruit, leaves, bark and root of the tree all taste and smell and have the substance of cinnamon, but the fruit are the best. In shape they are like the acorns of a cork-tree, but bigger. Although there are many of these woodland trees throughout the land, which seed themselves and bear fruit without cultivation, the Indians have also many on their plantations, which they cultivate and which yield far finer cinnamon than the others. They value it highly and barter it with the neighbouring countries for provisions and clothes and everything else they require for their substance.*

* The accounts of this expedition given by Zarate seem to have been drawn, like those of other historians – Garcilaso de la Vega,

3. The villages and countries through which Gonzalo Pizarro passed on his way to the place where he built a ship

LEAVING the greater part of his men in Sumaco, Gonzalo Pizarro went forward with the fittest and toughest of them to discover a road of which he had been told by the Indians. Sometimes, however, to get him off their lands, they gave him false information* about what lay ahead, as the people of Sumaco had done when they told him of a thickly populated country with plenty of food lying ahead: a false tale, as he discovered, for the land was thinly populated and so barren that he found no source of food till he came to those villages of Coca which lay beside a great river, where he stayed for a

---

Cieza de Leon and Herrera – from survivors. Yet geographically, none of them is very circumstantial. It is not clear, for example, how it was that having taken a large herd of hogs from Quito, the Spaniards should have been starving even before they attempted the passage of the Andes. The place at which they encountered the earthquake probably lay at the foot of the volcano Pichincha, and the location of Sumaco, the Land of Cinnamon, and Coca are known. After this the expedition disappears into the forest, and even the river down which they travelled cannot be identified for certain. Sir Charles Markham, in editing *Expeditions into the Valley of the Amazons* for the Hakluyt Society, 1859, supposes that Gonzalo reached no further than the confluence of the Coca and the Napo. But the distance he claims to have covered would suggest that he got as far as the river Marañon.

*The reason for the frequent misinformation which Gonzalo acquired was very simple. Supposing that the Indians would naturally lie to him, he habitually questioned the chiefs of a village under torture. To save themselves, they told him anything that seemed likely to please him. This accounts for many El Dorado tales collected by Spaniards in remote places. The Indians knew that what the Christians most desired was gold. Other misconceptions of course arose from misunderstandings of language. The porters whom Gonzalo brought from Quito could not speak or understand the languages of the upper Marañon, and communication was largely by signs and gestures.

month and a half waiting for the men he had left at Sumaco. The *cacique* of Coca treated him kindly. And from there the whole expedition went on down river till they came to a waterfall more than 14,000 feet high. The sound of the river falling from this height was audible for more than six leagues. Some stages further on, the river ran into a gorge so narrow that it was not twenty feet from bank to bank, and the height from the cliffs down to the water was equal to that of the falls. The cliffs were perpendicular on either side, and for fifty leagues of the road they could find nowhere to cross, till they came to a crossing defended by Indians. When the arquebusiers had captured it, a wooden bridge was built which they all crossed in safety.

They then took a road through the forest to a land which was called Huema, which was rather bare with many swamps and some rivers. Here there was a great shortage of food, for the natives ate only wild fruit. Finally they reached another country where there was some food and which was moderately well populated. Here the Indians wore cotton, whereas in all the other lands through which they had passed, the inhabitants went naked, either on account of the excessive and continuous heat, or because there was no cloth. They wore only a cotton strip over the penis, tied to a band round their loins. The women wore loincloths also, and no other clothes.

Here Gonzalo Pizarro built a brigantine in which to visit other parts of the river and look for food, also to carry the clothing and baggage and the sick. He was anxious to travel by water because the ground was so swampy that even with machetes and axes they could not make a road. They had great trouble in building the ship because they had to rig up a forge for the ironwork, for which they used the shoes of horses that had died on the journey, having no other iron.* They also set up charcoal furnaces. And at all these tasks, Gonzalo Pizarro made everyone work from the greatest to the least, and he himself was the first to pick up an axe or hammer. In place of

* Garcilaso says that they brought iron from Quito, which seems probable since the shoes of the dead horses would hardly have supplied them with enough nails to build a ship that would take 50 men.

pitch they used a gum distilled from the trees and for tow the Indians' old blankets and the Spaniards' shirts which had rotted in the great rains. Each contributed what he could. And so they finally completed their task and, after launching the brigantine on the river, put all the baggage aboard. They also made some canoes to accompany the brigantine.

4. Francisco de Orellana rebels and seizes the brigantine, and the hardships that followed

WHEN Gonzalo Pizarro had made the brigantine, he thought that all his labours were over and he could explore the whole country in it; and so he continued on his way, the army going by land through the great swamps and quagmires on the river banks and the thick forests and reedbeds. They hacked their way by main force with swords, machetes and axes and when they could not advance on one side of the river they crossed to the other in the brigantine. The order of their march was so strict that those on land and those aboard ship all slept at the same time.

When Gonzalo Pizarro saw that they had travelled more than two hundred leagues downstream and had found nothing to eat except wild fruit and some roots, he ordered one of his captains Francisco de Orellana to go further down the river with fifty men in search of food and, if he found any, load it on the brigantine, leaving the clothes it was carrying at the confluence of two great rivers, which they had been informed lay eighty leagues ahead. On his way, Orellana was to leave two canoes on a certain river, so that Gonzalo's men could cross in them when they came there.

Orellana set out, and soon the current became very swift. He reached the promised river junction in a very short time, without finding any food. Reflecting that the distance he had travelled downstream in three days was greater than he would be able to travel upstream in a year, since the waters were very rapid, he decided to let himself be carried down where chance might guide him, though he knew that the proper course was to stay where he was. So he went on and did not leave the two canoes; which was an act of rebellion or mutiny. Many of his companions requested him not to disobey the general's orders. Fray Gaspar de Carvajal in particular, a Dominican, insisted that this was wrong. But Orellana abused the friar in words and deeds.

So Orellana continued on his way, making some forays on land and fighting the Indians, who defended themselves. Very often great numbers of canoes came out into the river, and they were so tightly packed in the brigantine that they had difficulty in fighting them. So, at a place where he found material, Orellana stopped and built another brigantine. Here the natives came out peacefully to meet him and provided him with food and other necessities. And in a province further on he fought and conquered the Indians; and here he received a report that some days' journey inland was a country inhabited only by women, who fought and defended themselves from their neighbours. He listened to this news but went on his way, finding neither gold nor silver nor any trace of them in the whole land, and following the river current until he came out in the Northern Sea, three hundred and twenty-five leagues from the island of Cubagua. This river is called the Marañon because the first to sail up it was a captain of that name. It rises in Peru on the slopes of the Quito mountains and runs in a straight line (calculated by the height of the sun) for seven hundred leagues. But with the turns and twists that it takes anyone following it would travel more than one thousand eight hundred leagues from its source to the place where it enters the sea. At its mouth it is fifteen leagues wide, and at some places on its course the distance is two or three leagues from bank to bank.

From here Orellana went to Castile, where he informed His Majesty of his discovery, claiming to have made it on his own initiative and at his own cost. He reported the existence in this territory of a very rich land inhabited only by women, and from this fable this country received the name by which it is now generally known: 'the conquest of the Amazons'. Orellana petitioned the king for the governorship, which was granted him. He then collected more than five hundred men, including many gentlemen and persons of credit, and embarked with them at Seville. But owing to bad seamanship and shortage of food his people began to desert him at the Canaries, and a little later the expedition broke up completely. He himself died on the voyage, and his company dispersed among the islands, going in various directions and none of them arriving at the river.

Gonzalo Pizarro complained bitterly of Orellana, both for leaving him in such straits, without food and with no means of crossing the rivers, and because he had taken much gold and silver and many emeralds in the brigantine, all of which Orellana spent in preparing his petition to His Majesty and equipping his expedition.

5. *Gonzalo Pizarro returns to Quito, suffering great hardships on the way*

WHEN Gonzalo reached the place at which Orellana should have left the canoes in which he was to cross the streams that fell into the main river near-by, he did not find them and had great difficulty in getting his men across. He was compelled laboriously to construct rafts and some more canoes. Then when he reached the river junction at which Orellana should have waited for him, he was informed by a Spaniard, whom Orellana had left behind for opposing the continuation of his journey, that Orellana had renounced his authority, and purposed to make discoveries in his own name, not as a lieutenant of Gonzalo Pizarro. This man* also told him that Orellana had persuaded his men to elect him as their new captain.

Finding himself robbed of his ship, which had been his only means of collecting supplies, and with only a few bells and

* This was Hernan Sanchez de Vargas, a young gentleman from Badajoz, who had attempted to raise resistance to Orellana. Orellana had put him ashore at a lonely point on the river, where, according to Garcilaso, 'he could escape neither by water nor land, and so would perish of hunger'. He struggled through, however, to the river junction, and there awaited Gonzalo's arrival.

mirrors left for barter, he – and his men also – lost confidence and decided to return to Quito, more than four hundred leagues away, by bad roads and over mountains and wastes. When they considered the way they had come, they felt that they would never get back but die of hunger in those forests, where more than forty of them actually perished with no hope of rescue. They leant against the trees and begged for food, but were so thin and weak that they died of starvation.

So, commending themselves to God, Gonzalo Pizarro's men returned, departing from the road by which they had come since it led over so many bad places and through such foodless country. They chose another at random, but it was no richer in foodstuffs than the one by which they had come, and they only kept alive by killing and eating their remaining horses and a few greyhounds and dogs of other kinds that they had with them. They also fed on some shoots, which are like the shoots of a vine and taste of garlic. A wild cat or a fowl changed hands at fifty pesos, and a pelican, which has been described earlier as sea-carrion, at ten. Thus Gonzalo Pizarro pushed on towards Quito, where he had sent news of his return a long time before. The people of Quito collected great numbers of pigs and sheep, and some horses and clothes for Pizarro and his captains, and brought them out to meet him on his way. This succour reached him when he was still more than fifty leagues from Quito, and he and his men received it with great joy, especially the food. They were travelling almost naked, for their clothes had rotted long ago with the continuous rains. All they wore was a deerskin before and behind, some old breeches and leggings and caps of this same skin. Their swords were sheathless and eaten with rust. They were all on foot, and their arms and legs were scored with wounds from the thorns and bushes. They were so pale and disfigured that they were scarcely recognizable. They told a story of great hardships, saying, however, that what they had lacked most had been salt, of which they had found no trace for more than two hundred leagues. When they reached the province of Quito and received food and help, they kissed the ground, thanking God for bringing them through all their hardships and perils. And they fell on their provisions with such voracity that they had to be restrained until their stomachs gradually became reaccustomed to the work of digestion. When Gonzalo Pizarro and his captains saw that their rescuers had brought them only enough horses and clothing for themselves, they refused to mount or change their dress, so that all should remain equal, like good soldiers. So one morning in the state we have described they entered the city of Quito, going straight to the church to hear mass and thank God for rescuing them from their distresses. Then each re-equipped himself according to his resources.

This land in which cinnamon grows is below the equator, in the same latitude as the Moluccas, where the cinnamon grows that is generally eaten in Spain and the rest of the Eastern world.

6. The Chile party plot the Marquis' murder

WHEN Hernando Pizarro had captured and executed the adelantado Don Diego de Almagro at Cuzco, he sent to Los Reyes a son of Don Diego's by an Indian woman, who was called like his father Don Diego de Almagro. He was a good lad of fine spirit and had been well educated, both to ride, in both styles, which he did most skilfully and gracefully, and also to read and write, at which he was more proficient than was necessary for a gentleman. His father had put him in charge of Juan de Herrada, who had acted as his tutor, and at his death entrusted him to Herrada's care.

Now when this lad and his tutor came to live in Los Reyes, they collected and boarded at their house some men of their faction who had been wandering the country without means of support, since no one was willing to take in the beaten side. When Juan de Herrada saw Hernando Pizarro depart for Spain and Gonzalo to explore the land of cinnamon, having been released by the Marquis (by whose authority he had been up to that time imprisoned) he and his friends began to collect arms and prepare to avenge the killing of the boy's father and the destruction of his following, whose memory they preserved in their hearts with mingled grief and resentment. So, although the Marquis tried several times to make peace, he could never achieve normal relations with them. In order to deprive the young man of means to support the people who were continually joining him, the Marquis took away the *encomienda* which he held. But this had no effect. These men were such close allies that they shared all their possessions in common, and enrusted everything they gained by gambling or trade to Juan de Herrada, to be shared out for their expenses. Every day they collected more men and arms.

The Marquis was informed of all this by many different people. But he was so confident and easy in his mind and conscience that he answered: 'Let the poor fellows alone. They have enough to bear in their poverty, shame and defeat.' So, trusting in the Marquis' confidence, kindness and patience, the defeated faction began to become insolent. On occasions the leaders would pass him without raising their caps or acknowledging him. And one morning, three ropes were seen hanging on the pillory, where they had been placed in the night, one facing the Marquis' house, one his lieutenant's and the third his secretary's. The Marquis ignored all this, saying in their defence: 'It is because they are beaten and shamed that they do these things.' Taking advantage of his forbearance, they assembled without fear, some of the faction who had been exiled coming from as far as two hundred leagues away; and they plotted together to kill the Marquis and raise a revolt in the land; which they eventually did. But they decided to wait until a decision had been received from Spain. For Captain Diego de Alvarado had gone there to accuse Hernando Pizarro of his past actions, whereupon Hernando had been arrested, and his trial was now proceeding. They had learnt, moreover, that His Majesty had appointed the lawyer Vaca de Castro to take information about the recent disorders. He was not, however, acting as strictly and harshly as they would have liked. They planned therefore to do what some of them subsequently did, though they decided to wait till they knew Vaca de Castro's intentions before acting.

The plan was not accepted by all members of the faction, in which there were many gentlemen who, though they resented the Adelantado's execution, wished to avenge it only by judicial means, without opposing His Majesty or doing him a disservice. The majority of the faction assembled in Los Reyes. They were Juan de Saavedra, Don Alonso de Montemayor, the accountant Juan de Guzman, the treasurer Manuel de Espinar, the victualler Diego Nuñez de Mercade, Don Cristobal Ponce de Leon, Juan de Herrada, Pero Lopez de Ayala and a few others. They elected Don Alonso de Montemayor to go and welcome Vaca de Castro on behalf of them all, for Don Alonso was a man of importance and great intelligence. Having taken his credentials and other documents, he departed to find Vaca de Castro at the beginning of April 1541, and travelled till they met; and it was not until Don Alonso had performed his mission that the Marquis was killed (as will shortly be told). Afterwards Don Alonso Montemayor and his companions stayed with Vaca de Castro, following in his company till he defeated the young Don Diego de Almagro in the battle in the valley of Chupas. Here Don Alonso and other partisans of the late Adelantado followed the royal standard, setting aside the sympathy they felt for his cause to follow His Majesty's representative, for in this matter Vaca de Castro was acting in the king's name.

7. *The Marquis is informed of the plot to kill him*

THE plot to kill the Marquis was so well known in Los Reyes that many informed him of it. But he replied that the heads of the plotters would answer for his and, when they advised him to take a bodyguard, that he did not wish it to be thought that he was protecting himself from the judge sent by His Majesty. Then one day Juan de Herrada complained to the Marquis of certain rumours: men were saying that he intended to kill him and his friends. The Marquis swore that he had never had such a thought. Juan de Herrada replied that this was hard to believe since he had been seen buying lances and other weapons. The Marquis assured him that they had not been bought for use against him and his friends. He picked some oranges, which were much valued as the first of the crop, and gave them to

Juan de Herrada, asking him at the same time to go and see if he was short of anything, and he, the Marquis, would provide it. Juan de Herrada kissed his hand in acknowledgement and departed, leaving the Marquis assured and confident. He then returned to his house, where he planned with his principal supporters that the Marquis should be killed the following Sunday, since they had not killed him on St John's Day, as originally agreed. On the Saturday, however, one of them revealed the plot in confession to the priest of the great church, who went that night to tell the Marquis' secretary Antonio Picado, and ask for an interview with the Marquis. The secretary took him to the house of the Marquis' brother Francisco Martin, where the Marquis was supping with his sons. The Marquis got up from the table, the priest told him what was afoot and he was for a moment disturbed. But a little later he told his secretary that he did not believe the story since only a few days ago Juan de Herrada had come and spoken to him most humbly. He said that the man who had given the priest this warning must want to beg some favour of him, and had invented the story to put him under an obligation. Nevertheless, he sent for his lieutenant Doctor Juan Velazquez. But the doctor was ill and could not come. So the Marquis went to his house that night accompanied only by his secretary and two or three others, and lighted by a single torch. Finding his lieutenant in bed, he informed him of events, and Velazquez assured him: 'You need have no fear, my lord. So long as this wand is in my hand, no one in the whole country will dare to rebel.' He does not seem to have spoken falsely, for afterwards, when the Marquis was being attacked and he was running away, he put the wand in his mouth while jumping out of the window into the garden.

8. The Killing of the Marquis Francisco Pizarro

DESPITE these assurances the Marquis was so worried that he decided not to hear mass in church that Sunday but, in order to preserve the maximum security, to have it said in his own house. On coming out of church Doctor Juan Velazquez and Captain Francisco de Chaves – then the chief man in the land under the Marquis – went with many others to the Marquis' house. Then, having paid their visit, the others went home, leaving the Doctor and Francisco de Chaves to dine with the Marquis. When the meal was over – which would have been between twelve and one in the afternoon – having discovered that everyone in the city was quietly at home and the Marquis' servants had gone to dinner, Juan de Herrada and some eleven or twelve others gathered at his house, which was about three hundred yards from the Marquis', and separated by the whole breadth of the square and some part of the street. They then came out, drawing their swords and shouting as they crossed the square: 'Death to the tyrant! Death to the traitor who killed the judge sent by His Majesty!' The reason for this noisy and public demonstration was, as they afterwards explained, that they wanted to persuade the rest of the city that they had many supporters. For if they had not they would hardly have dared to do the deed so openly. They reasoned also that however fast help came, it would not arrive in time to stop them. They would either have achieved their purpose or died in the attempt.

So they came to the Marquis' house and, leaving one of their number at the door with his sword drawn (and bloody from a sheep they found in the forecourt), went on, shouting, 'The tyrant is dead! The tyrant is dead!' Some neighbours who were about to interfere went home thinking that this must be true. And so Juan de Herrada climbed the stairs with his men. Warned by some Indians who were standing at the gate, the Marquis ordered Francisco de Chaves to close and guard the hall door while he went in to arm himself. But Francisco de Chaves was so bewildered that he went out on to the staircase, shutting none of the doors. One of the conspirators gave him a thrust and he, feeling a wound, put his hand to his sword and cried: 'What! Your friends too?' Then all the rest attacked and stabbed him. Leaving him dead, they rushed on to the Marquis' parlour. A dozen or more Spaniards who were in the room fled, jumping out of the windows into the garden; among them Doctor Juan Velazquez, who put his wand in his mouth, as we have said, to free his hands as he let himself down from the window. The Marquis was arming himself in his chamber with his brother Francisco Martin, two other gentlemen and two grown-up pages, Juan de Vargas, son of Gomez de Tordoya, and Escandon. Seeing the enemy so near when he had not yet finished doing up the straps of his cuirass, the Marquis ran to the door with a sword and shield. Here he and his friends defended themselves so valiantly that for a long time they kept the enemy from breaking in. 'At them, brother,' the Marquis shouted. 'Kill them, the traitors!'

The conspirators fought so hard that they killed Francisco Martin, but one of the pages took his place. When they saw that the defence was so strong that help might come and they, caught between the two forces, might easily be killed, the attackers decided to force the issue by advancing one of their number who was the most stoutly armed. And to make it more difficult for the Marquis to kill him, they seized their opportunity to push through the door. Then they all fell on the Marquis with such fury that he was too exhausted to brandish his sword. And so they finished him off with a thrust through the throat. As he fell, he cried for a confessor. But his breath failed him. Making a cross on the floor, he kissed it and so gave up the ghost. The Marquis' two pages died with him, and of the Chile faction four were killed and several wounded.

When the news spread through the city, more than two hundred declared for Don Diego; for though they had been advised they had not dared to declare themselves till they saw how things turned out. They then ran through the city, taking and confiscating the arms of all those who had supported the Marquis. And when the killers came out with bloody swords, Juan de Herrada had Don Diego lifted into the saddle and paraded through the city, crying that there was no other governor in all Peru, not even the king himself. And when they had sacked the houses of the Marquis and his brother and Antonio Picado, Herrada compelled the city council to accept Don Diego as governor, by right of the grant made by His Majesty at the time of the discovery, that Don Diego de Almagro should have the governorship of New Toledo, and after him his son or whoever he should name; and they killed some citizens whom they knew to be clients and servants of the Marquis. It was pitiful to hear the wailing of the wives of the dead and despoiled. Some wretches carried or dragged the Marquis to the church. But no one dared to bury him until Juan de Barbaran of Trujillo (who had been the Marquis' client) and his wife buried him and his brother as decently as they could, having first asked leave of Don Diego. And they did it so hurriedly that they hardly had time to clothe him in the cloak of the order of Santiago in the manner of the knights of that order, for they were warned that the Chile faction were coming in great haste to cut off the Marquis' head and put it on the gibbet. And so Juan de Barbaran buried him, performing the funeral ceremonies on the spot and providing the cost and candles from his own store. And leaving the Marquis in the grave, they brought his children into safety, who were wandering about, hiding where they could since the Chile faction were in possession of the city.

Thus one sees the way of the world and the varieties of fortune: that in so short a time a gentleman who had discovered and governed great lands and kingdoms, and possessed such huge riches, and conferred rents and estates equal to those conferred by the mightiest princes in the world (in their time) should come to die without confession, leaving his soul uncomposed and his estate and succession in disorder; that he should be killed by a dozen men in the middle of the day, in a city where all his neighbours were his clients and debtors and soldiers, and had eaten richly of his food, yet none of them came to his aid; that he should have been buried as ignominiously as we have related, and that of all the wealth and riches he had possessed, he should come in a moment to lack even enough to purchase the candles for his funeral; and that all this should befall him despite the various warnings he had received and the many other reasons he had for suspicion. His death took place on 26 June 1541.

9. *The habits and qualities of the Marquis Don Francisco Pizarro and of the Adelantado Don Diego de Almagro*

SINCE the whole discovery and history of Peru originates with the two captains, the Marquis Don Francisco Pizarro and the Adelantado Don Diego de Almagro, who have so far been the subject of our story, it is now proper to describe and contrast their qualities and ways of life, after the manner of Plutarch when he describes the deeds of two captains who are in some way similar.

All that can be known about their descent has already been said. For the rest they were both bold and brave men, capable of sustaining great hardships. Both were generous, and delighted to give pleasure to others even at their own cost. They were very similar in their inclinations and particularly in their domestic life. Neither of them married, though both lived to be old men, the Marquis, who was the younger, dying at the age of 65. Both were attached to the profession of war, though the Adelantado enjoyed the pursuit of gain when there was no occasion for fighting. Both began the conquest of Peru at an advanced age, and both underwent hardships, as we have told. But the Marquis was more often in danger than the Adelantado, and the risks he took were far greater. He undertook the greater part of the discovery, while the Adelantado stayed in Panama sending him the necessary supplies. Both had high courage which inspired them to lofty designs, but at the same time they were very human and on friendly terms with their men. They were also liberal in fact, though in appearance the Adelantado had the advantage since he loved to announce his gifts with sound of trumpet, whereas the Marquis, on the contrary, was annoyed when his liberalities were known and endeavoured to conceal them, being more concerned to supply the needs of the recipient than to gain honour by the gift. He once learnt by chance that the horse of one of his soldiers had died. Before going down to the ball-court of his house where he expected to find this man, he put an ingot of gold weighing five hundred pesos under his coat, intending to hand it to him. But not finding him there he took part in a game that was just being arranged, and played without taking off his coat, so that no one should see the ingot. He was unable to bring it out for over three hours, until the soldier arrived to whom he was going to give it. Then he quietly called him into a room apart and said as he gave it to him that he would rather have given him three such ingots than suffer the discomfort he had been put to by his delay. Many other instances of such actions could be adduced, since surprisingly the Marquis never gave anything except in person and generally contrived that no one should know. For this reason the Adelantado was generally considered the more open-handed, for much though he gave he always contrived that it should appear more. But in this virtue of generosity, the two men can justly be considered equal. For (as the Marquis himself said) by reason of their joint ownership of the expedition's wealth neither gave anything of which the other did not supply half. So the partner who knowingly allowed the gift gave as much as the actual giver. This is sufficiently proved by the fact that though in their lives both were the richest of men, in money and rents, and could give or keep more than any uncrowned prince for ages past, yet both died so poor that not only is there no record of any property or estates that they left, but scarcely enough was found in their possession to cover the costs of their burial. Similar accounts are given of Cato and Sulla and other Roman captains who were buried at the public expense.

Both were very fond of benefiting their servants and soldiers by enriching them and promoting them and saving them from danger. But the Marquis was much the superior in this. Once when they happened to be crossing the Barranca river, one of the Yanacona Indians in his service was swept away by the swift current. The Marquis plunged in, swam after him and pulled him out by the hair, exposing himself to great risk from the furious waters. This was more than anyone in his whole army had the courage to do, though many of his soldiers were both brave and young. When some captains reproached him for his foolhardiness, he replied that they did not know what it was to care for a servant.

Although the Marquis governed more peacefully and for a longer time, Don Diego was much the more ambitious and anxious for command and authority. Both were lovers of antiquity, so attached to what was old that they rarely gave up the fashions of their youth, particularly the Marquis, who commonly wore a high-waisted black cloth coat falling to his ankles, white deerskin shoes, a white hat and a sword with an old-fashioned hilt. And when, on certain feast-days, he was persuaded by his servants to wear the sable cloak that the Marquis del Valle had sent him from New Spain, he would take it off after returning from mass, and remain in his doublet, generally wearing a towel round his neck so that he could wipe the sweat off his face, for in peace-time he spent most of the day at bowls or pelota.

Both captains had great physical endurance and thought nothing of hunger. The Marquis showed this especially in his addiction to these games in which few young men could tire him out. He was much more given to games of all kinds than the Adelantado; so much so that sometimes he would play bowls all day and did not care with whom he played. Even if it was a sailor or a miller, he would not allow him to hand him the bowl or pay him other courtesies befitting his dignity. Seldom could business make him leave the game, especially when he was losing. Only if there were some fresh Indian disturbance, for he was very quick on such occasions, would he put on his cuirass and run through the city with lance and shield, making straight for where the trouble was without waiting for his men, who caught up with him later, running at full speed.

Both captains showed such skill and courage in the Indian wars that neither would have hesitated to attack a hundred of the enemy unaided. They had very good judgement and understanding in all matters both of war and government, considering especially that they were not only uneducated but unable to read or even sign their names, which was a great defect in them. For with the exception of this fault which prejudiced them in the important business they had to do, their tastes and qualities were entirely those of noblemen, though the ancients always considered illiteracy a sign of low breeding. The Marquis so trusted his servants and friends that on all the orders he dictated, both in matters of government and when conferring *encomiendas* of Indians, he signed by drawing two lines, between which his secretary Antonio Picado wrote the name Francisco Pizarro. They could offer the excuse with which Ovid defended Romulus for being a bad astrologer that he knew more about arms than letters, though he had great difficulty in conquering his neighbours.

Both of them were so easy and affable with their fellow-citizens that they would go from house to house visiting their neighbours and dining with the first who invited them. They were equally abstinent and temperate, both in food and drink and in sexual matters, particularly regarding Spanish women, for they thought that they could not sleep with them without hurting their neighbours whose wives and daughters they were. And even with Indian women of Peru, the Adelantado was extremely restrained; he was not known to have had any child or relations with any woman. The Marquis was somewhat less so; he had an Indian lady, a sister of Atahuallpa, as his mistress, by whom he left a son Don Gonzalo, who died at the age of 14, and a daughter called Doña Francisca. And by another Indian woman of Cuzco he had a son Don Francisco. But the Adelantado had only that son who, as has been said, killed the Marquis, by an Indian woman of Panama.

Both received favours from His Majesty. Don Francisco de Pizarro, as we have said, received the title of Marquis and governor of New Castile, and was made a knight of Santiago. And Don Diego de Almagro received the government of New Toledo and was made adelantado. The Marquis, especially, greatly honoured and respected Their Majesties' name; so much so that he abstained from doing many things that were in his power, on the plea that he did not wish His Majesty to say that he was extending his territory. And very often when present at the meltings, he would rise from his seat and pick up the small pieces of gold and silver that fell from the knife with which they separated the royal fifth, saying that even the mouth should be used to collect royal treasury if there were no other means. Finally they were alike also in their ends and the nature of their death. The Marquis' brother killed the Adelantado, and the Adelantado's son killed the Marquis.

The Marquis was very diligent in improving, working and cultivating the land. He built some fine houses in the city of Los Reyes; and in the river there he left two mill-dams. He devoted all his spare time to these constructions, himself employing the craftsmen who built them. He was at great pains to build the great church in the city of Los Reyes also, and the monasteries of Santo Domingo and the Merced to which he made grants of Indians for the upkeep and repair of their fabric.

10. Don Diego de Almagro raises an army and kills some gentlemen. Alonso de Alvarado raises a standard for His Majesty

HAVING secured the city and taken their wands from the councillors to confer them with his own hand, Don Diego de Almagro arrested the Marquis' lieutenant Doctor Velazquez and Antonio Picado his secretary, and appointed Juan Tello of Seville and Francisco de Chaves* and one Sotelo captains, and on the rumour of these appointments, all the wasters and vagabonds who were roaming the land came to beg for authority to rob and live at their pleasure. To find pay for his officers, Don Diego took the royal fifth and the estates of the dead and the savings of those who had left the city. But soon dissensions began to arise among his followers. Impelled by envy, some of the most important plotted to kill Juan de Herrada. For, though Diego de Almagro was nominally governor and captain-general, it was Herrada who governed and did everything. When the plot became known, some of the plotters, including Francisco de Chaves, were executed. And Antonio de Orihuela of Salamanca was also beheaded for saying, on arriving from Spain, that Herrada and his men were

* Clearly a second man of this name.

tyrants. Don Diego sent messengers to all the cities in the land demanding that the councils should accept him as governor. The majority complied out of fear. But when his messengers reached Chachapoyas, where Alonso de Alvarado was in command, they were arrested. Alonso rose in rebellion and fortified the place. Relying on its natural strength and his army of a hundred men, he raised a banner for His Majesty, and neither the threats nor promises in Don Diego's letters made him change his mind. In answer to these letters he said that he would not accept Don Diego as governor except at His Majesty's express command. He hoped on the other hand, with the help of God and the gentlemen of his company, to avenge the Marquis' death and the insults offered to His Majesty at any time in the past.

Don Diego immediately sent Captain Garcia de Alvarado with many horse and foot soldiers against him. He instructed him to go first to the city of San Miguel and take all the arms and horses of the citizens, and on his way back to visit Trujillo and do the same. Thus armed, he was then to attack Don Alonso.

Garcia de Alvarado set out, travelling by sea to the port of Santa which is fifteen leagues from Trujillo. Here he met Captain Alonso Cabrera, who had fled from the city of Huanuco with all his men to join the citizens of Trujillo against Don Diego. He captured Cabrera and some of his men and, on reaching San Miguel, beheaded him and his companions Vozmediano and Villegas.

11. Cuzco rises for His Majesty. Pedro Alvarez Holguin is made captain. His actions

WHEN Don Diego's messengers reached Cuzco with his orders, Diego de Silva, son of Feliciano de Silva of Ciudad Rodrigo, and Francisco de Carvajal, afterwards Gonzalo Pizarro's master-of-the-camp, were magistrates. They and the members of the council decided not to accept Don Diego, though they dared not refuse openly till they saw whether he had the men and arms to overcome their defences. So they replied with a request that Don Diego should show fuller authority, in which case they would receive him. And since Gomez de Tordoya, an important member of the council, had not been at the meeting, being away hunting, they sent to inform him of what had transpired. Their messengers met him near the city and, on hearing their news, he wrung the neck of a very precious hawk that was on his wrist. 'This is a time for fighting, not hawking,' he exclaimed. He entered the city by night and secretly consulted with the council as to the course to be pursued. Then, on the same night, he rode out of the city again, and went to join Captain Castro, and together they sent messengers to Pedro Anzures, who was lieutenant in Charcas, and immediately raised a banner for His Majesty. Gomez de Tordoya then set out to follow Captain Pedro Alvarez Holguin, who had gone with more than a hundred horsemen on an expedition against the Indians. On catching up with him, he told him what had happened and begged him to take command of their just and honourable enterprise. And as further persuasion, he offered to serve under him and be the first to obey him. Pedro Alvarez accepted and raised a banner for His Majesty. And from there they summoned the citizens of Arequipa, who came in a body to Cuzco, where many had now declared for Don Diego; and when they learnt that these two captains were coming, more than fifty fled to join him. But Captain Castro and Hernando Bachicao went out to pursue them with some arquebusiers and, attacking them in the night, captured them and returned to Cuzco.

Following the example of all these captains from other places, the council of Cuzco accepted, nominated and swore allegiance to Pedro Alvarez Holguin as captain and chief magistrate of Peru, until His Majesty should decide otherwise. They then declared war against Don Diego, and the citizens of Cuzco undertook to refund all that Pedro Alvarez should take out of the royal treasury to support his soldiers if His Majesty should not approve of his expenditure. And for the prosecution of the war, all the citizens there present of Cuzco, Charcas and Arequipa offered their persons and possessions. In a short time more than three hundred and fifty men assembled: a hundred and fifty horsemen, a hundred arquebusiers and a hundred pikemen.

Having heard that Don Diego had upwards of eight hundred soldiers, Pedro Alvarez dared not wait in Cuzco, but went into the *sierra* to join Alonso de Alvarado, whom he now knew to be on His Majesty's side, and also to collect on the way those friends and servants of the Marquis who were hiding in the hills. He marched with his men always in battle array, so as to be ready to fight Don Diego, should he intercept him. On riding out of Cuzco, he left sufficient men to defend the city. He had appointed Gomez de Tordoya master-of-the-camp and Garcilaso de la Vega* and Pedro de Anzures captains of the horsemen. He entrusted the infantry to Captain Castro and made Martin de Robres bearer of the royal standard.

12. Don Diego goes in search of Pedro Alvarez and, not finding him, enters Cuzco

ON learning of events in Cuzco, and that Pedro Alvarez had left the city with such soldiers as he had, Don Diego immediately realized that he must be going into the *sierra* to join Alonso de Alvarado, since he had not enough men to make it credible that he was coming against Don Diego himself. So Don Diego decided to intercept him and cut off his advance. But he could not start as soon as he wished, since he had to wait for Garcia de Alvarado, whom he had summoned by messengers, and who came to join him without fulfilling the purpose of his expedition, which was to attack Alonso de Alvarado. Garcia would have descended on Alonso, however, while passing through Trujillo, if he had not been prevented by the people of Levanto, which is in Chachapoyas.

When Garcia de Alvarado reached the city of Los Reyes, Don Diego immediately set out against Pedro Alvarez with three hundred horsemen, a hundred arquebusiers and a hun-

* Father of the historian Garcilaso de la Vega 'The Inca', whose mother was a Peruvian noblewoman.

dred and fifty pikemen, and before his departure he banished the Marquis' sons from the country and beheaded Antonio Picado, having first severely tortured him to make him tell where the Marquis had hidden his treasure. He then rode out of the city; and when he had gone only two leagues, secret orders arrived from the lawyer Vaca de Castro, sent from the province of Quito and directed to Fray Tomas de San Martin, provincial of the Dominican order, and Francisco de Barrio Nuevo, asking them to undertake the government of the city until he arrived. The city council assembled in secret in the convent of Santo Domingo and obediently acknowledged Vaca de Castro as governor, and Hieronimo de Aliaga, chief governmental secretary, as his lieutenant, for it was Aliaga who had brought the orders. As soon as these proceedings were completed, the magistrates and many other citizens fled to Trujillo, but not so secretly that Don Diego did not learn of their flight that night. He wished to return and sack the city, but was afraid that Pedro Alvarez would escape him if he did so, and also that his men would discover that a new governor had arrived. He therefore continued on his way. But when it became known in Don Diego's camp that there was a new governor in the land, many fled, chief among them the provincial of the Dominicans, and Diego de Aguero, Juan de Saavedra, Gomez de Alvarado and the victualler Illan Suarez de Carvajal. And since Juan de Herrada then fell ill of the sickness by which he died, Don Diego was compelled to halt his march. Therefore Pedro Alvarez escaped him down the valley of Jauja where Don Diego decided to intercept him. Don Diego continued to follow him, however.

When the two armies were close together Pedro Alvarez saw that he had not enough men to defend himself against Don Diego's greater numbers. So he devised a stratagem and deceived him in this manner. He sent twenty horsemen to make a night attack on Don Diego's vanguard and capture as many men as possible. Three prisoners were brought in. Pedro Alvarez hanged two and promised the third not only to release him but to give him a thousand gold pesos if he would return to Don Diego's army and warn some of his friends that Pedro Alvarez was going to attack the camp next night on the right flank. He extracted a solemn oath from the soldier not to reveal the ruse and pretended to put great trust in him. Greedy for the thousand pesos, the young man departed immediately and made the journey safely, since he was a soldier of Don Diego's. On learning that the other two men had been hanged and this soldier released for no known purpose, Don Diego suspected a ruse, and on his suspicions had the man tortured, whereupon he confessed all that had happened. Believing in the promised attack, Don Diego posted the greater part of his army on the traverse which the soldier had said Pedro Alvarez would attack. But Pedro Alvarez had so little intention of doing so that he struck camp as soon as the soldier was dispatched and, the night being dark, continued on his way with the utmost speed. His enemies continued to expect him, however, until they realized that they had been tricked.

Don Diego resumed his rapid pursuit, and when Pedro Alvarez saw that he was close on his heels, he sent a messenger to Alonso de Alvarado, asking him for aid. Alvarado then advanced to reinforce Pedro Alvarez with all his men and some of the men of Trujillo, and after some days' march joined forces with him. And when Don Diego (who was now very far away) learnt that the two armies had united, he gave up the pursuit and went with his men to Cuzco.

Pedro de Alvarez and Alonso de Alvarado sent a messenger up the Quito road, to inform Vaca de Castro of recent events, and advise him to make great haste since, to judge by these good beginnings, they would soon deliver the land to him. Juan de Herrada died at Jauja, and Don Diego sent some part of his army across the plains to collect his men who were in Arequipa. When his captains reached the city, they pillaged everything in the place and dug up the entire convent of Santo Domingo, because they were told that many of the inhabitants had buried their possessions there.

13. *Vaca de Castro arrives at the Camp of Pedro de Alvarez and Alonso de Alvarado and is received as governor. His further dispositions*

VACA DE CASTRO had a bad voyage from Panama to Peru. After losing an anchor, he finally arrived at the port of Buenaventura, went overland to the province of Benalcazar, and from there entered Peru. He had severe difficulties on the road on account of the great distances and shortage of food, and also because he was himself very sick and unaccustomed to such hardships. Nevertheless, after learning at Popayan of the Marquis' murder and the events that had followed, he pursued his march without a pause in order to remedy things by his presence. It must be stated that although the principal purpose of Vaca de Castro's visit was to investigate the matter of Don Diego de Almagro's death and the events that had followed it, but not to suspend the Marquis from office, he carried in addition a secret warrant entitling him to take over the government should the Marquis happen to die during his visit or while he was on his way, and to exercise it until His Majesty's further pleasure. By virtue of this warrant he was recognized as governor when he reached the joint camp of Alvarez and Alvarado together with a number of men who had come down to welcome and escort him on his arrival. One of the chief of these was Captain Lorenzo de Aldana, the Marquis' governor of Quito. Vaca de Castro sent Captain Pedro de Puelles ahead to begin collecting arms and supplies, and dispatched Gomez de Rojas of Cuellar with his full authority to enter and take over Cuzco, which he did with such skill and dispatch that he reached the place before Don Diego, and presented his credentials, which were accepted.

When Vaca de Castro was passing the frontiers of Bracamoros, Captain Pedro de Vergara, who was engaged in the conquest of that province, came out to meet him and, in order to accompany him, took away the inhabitants of the town he had just settled and fortified against Don Diego. On reaching

Trujillo, Vaca de Castro met Gomez de Tordoya who had left the camp of the two captains after quarrelling with Pedro Alvarez. With him were Garcilaso de la Vega and some other gentlemen.

When Vaca de Castro left Trujillo for Pedro Alvarez' camp, he had more than two hundred well-equipped soldiers with him; and on reaching the camp he was pleasantly received by Pedro Alvarez and Alonso de Alvarado. When he presented the royal authority they handed him the standards, and he returned them to their holders except for the royal standard, which he kept for himself. He made Pedro Alvarez Holguin master-of-the-camp and sent him with the whole army to Jauja to wait there while he went down to the city of Los Reyes to gather all the men and arms and munitions that he could obtain, and impose order on the city. He commanded Captain Diego de Rojas to ride twenty leagues ahead of Pedro Alvarez with thirty horsemen to reconnoitre the country, and he sent Captain Diego de Mora to Trujillo as his lieutenant-governor. Indeed he made these and all other arrangements necessary for the enterprise with as much skill and dispatch as if he had been a trained and lifelong soldier.

14. Don Diego kills Garcia de Alvarado at Cuzco and brings his men out against Vaca de Castro

HAVING failed to catch up with Pedro Alvarez, Don Diego went to Cuzco, which he found already in the possession of Cristobal de Sotelo, whom he had sent in advance and who had appointed magistrates on his behalf, dismissing those appointed by Vaca de Castro. When Don Diego arrived, he began to manufacture artillery and powder. For there is plenty of metal in Peru suitable for cannon and some craftsmen from the Levante* with a good knowledge of casting. Powder manufacture was also an easy matter since there are great quantities of saltpetre in those parts. Having repaired all the armour in

* The district of Valencia.

the country he made new armour for those men in his army who had none from alloy of silver and copper which makes very good corselets. So the worst provided man in his army had at least a coat of mail, a corselet or cuirass and a helmet of this alloy, which the Indians skilfully copied from original pieces from Milan. Thus he was able to equip two hundred arquebusiers and, with his new resources, some light horsemen also, although up till then horsemen in Peru had always fought in full armour, and light cavalry were seldom or never used.

When things had reached this stage a quarrel broke out between Captains Garcia de Alvarado and Cristobal de Sotelo in which Sotelo was killed. This quarrel had a very bad effect on the army, for both men had many friends and the whole camp was now divided. Indeed if Don Diego had not calmed them by a friendly speech, the two factions would have fought to the death. Knowing that Don Diego had been greatly attached to Sotelo and would try to avenge him, Garcia de Alvarado behaved very cautiously from that moment, both for his own safety and because he was planning to kill Don Diego. This he attempted to do. One day he invited Don Diego to dinner, intending to kill him during the meal. But after accepting the invitation, Don Diego became suspicious and pretended to be ill. Thereupon Garcia de Alvarado, who had made all necessary preparations, decided to go with his friends and beg Don Diego to come to the feast. On the way he casually told one Martin Carillo why he was going, and Carillo tried to dissuade him, saying that in his opinion Don Diego knew his reasons. Another soldier said much the same. Nevertheless Garcia de Alvarado persisted.

Don Diego was lying on his bed. But he had concealed several armed men in the room. On entering, Garcia de Alvarado addressed him: 'Be pleased to get up, your honour. This sickness will soon pass. So come and enjoy yourself. Even if you only eat a little, at least come and sit at the head of our table.' Don Diego consented. He got up and, since he was lying in his doublet, called for his cloak. But under his doublet was his breastplate, and his sword and dagger were within reach. The party began to leave the room, Garcia de Alvarado walking in front of Don Diego. But when he reached the door Juan

Balsa, who was on guard, suddenly closed it and, seizing Garcia de Alvarado with both arms, cried: 'You are a prisoner.' And Don Diego, putting his hand to his sword, exclaimed as he stabbed him: 'Not a prisoner but a corpse.' Then Alonso de Saavedra and Diego Mendez, the brother of Rodrigo Orgoñez, and others emerged from their hiding places and dealt him so many wounds that he fell dead. When news of his death reached the city there was an uproar. But Don Diego came out into the main square and calmed the people, whereupon some friends of Garcia de Alvarado fled.

Don Diego then led his army out of the city to attack Vaca de Castro. Knowing that he had joined up with Pedro Alvarez and Alonso de Alvarado, Don Diego took the road to Jauja in search of him. Throughout the whole campaign Atahuallpa's brother Paolo, whom Don Diego's father the Adelantado had made Inca, served under him; and his help was of great importance for he marched ahead of the army and, although he had not many Indians with him, owing to his presence all the provinces in the country supplied provisions and Indians to carry the baggage and all other necessities.

15. Vaca de Castro marches from Los Reyes to Jauja. Events at Jauja

ON arriving at the city of Los Reyes, Vaca de Castro had many arquebuses made by the good band of craftsmen whom he found there and provided himself with all necessities. He borrowed more than seventy thousand gold pesos from the citizens and merchants, for Don Diego had taken and spent all the royal treasure. Leaving Francisco de Barrio-Nuevo as his lieutenant in Los Reyes and Juan Perez de Guevara as captain of the ships, Vaca de Castro set out for Jauja with all the men he could take, leaving orders in the city that if Don Diego were to descend on it by another road, as rumour said he would, all the citizens and their wives and possessions should be taken aboard the ships and remain there until he returned in pursuit of Don Diego. When he reached Jauja, Pedro Alvarez was waiting for him with all his men and a store of guns and pikes and much powder that had been made there. Vaca de Castro divided the horsemen he had brought among the companies of Pedro Alvarez, Pedro Anzures and Garcilaso de la Vega, who were captains of horse; and he divided his foot soldiers between Pedro de Vergara and Nuño de Castro, who were captains of infantry; and he made two new companies, one of horse which he entrusted to Gomez de Alvarado, and another of arquebusiers which he put under the command of the bachelor Juan Velez de Guevara, who was not only a scholar but a very good soldier and a man of such ingenuity that he had himself learnt to make the arquebuses with which the men of his company were equipped though he continued to concern himself with the law. Indeed both then and later, at the time of Gonzalo Pizarro's rebellion, when he was appointed magistrate, he would go about until noon in a neat lawyer's gown receiving petitions and deciding suits, and from noon onwards would dress as a soldier in red hose and doublet magnificently embroidered with gold, and plumes and a leather jacket. In the afternoon he would go out with an arquebus on his shoulder for shooting practice with his men.

Vaca de Castro made the following dispositions for his army, which contained seven hundred men in all, including three hundred and seventy horsemen and a hundred and seventy arquebusiers. He made Francisco de Carvajal, afterwards master-of-the-camp to Gonzalo Pizarro, chief sergeant of the whole camp; and Carvajal acted as commander of the army, since he had gained great experience of war in the forty years and more he had been a soldier and second-in-command to a captain in Italy.

Messengers now reached Vaca de Castro from Gonzalo Pizarro, who had returned from his expedition to the land of cinnamon and offered to come to his aid with all the survivors of his party. Vaca de Castro wrote to thank him, but ordered him not to bring his army, which must remain at Quito, since having come to establish peace in the land, Vaca de Castro still had hopes of coming to an agreement with Don Diego. He thought that this message would have the effect of curbing Gonzalo Pizarro's presumption. For he was afraid that Gonzalo's desire to avenge his brother might prejudice his own position with Don Diego, who would not put himself in his power if he knew Gonzalo Pizarro to be in the camp, where he would necessarily exercise great influence on account of his many friends. Others say he was afraid that if Gonzalo came he would be elected general since everyone then regarded him so highly, and Vaca de Castro was anxious that the objectives of the war should be justice rather than vengeance. In addition, he sent instructions to those in charge of the Marquis' children that they should stay where they were in the cities of San Miguel and Trujillo until further orders and not come to Los Reyes. His excuse for these orders was that they were safer and more peaceful there than they would be in Los Reyes.

16. Vaca de Castro advances with his army from Jauja to Huamanga, and what happened to Don Diego

AFTER making his dispositions at Jauja, Vaca de Castro took the road to Huamanga, having received news that Don Diego was coming at great speed to establish himself in that place and occupy the river crossing. The situation would have been difficult if the enemy had been the first to occupy Huamanga. For the place is surrounded by very deep valleys or clefts which make it extremely strong. Captain Diego de Rojas, however, who was riding ahead to reconnoitre, had already entered the place with his men and, having also heard that Don Diego was approaching, had built a tower to defend himself till Vaca de Castro's arrival. For this reason Vaca de Castro set out in great haste, sending Captain Castro ahead with the arquebusiers to take possession of a difficult place called the Parco hill, which is near Huamanga.

One evening, when he had arrived within two leagues of Huamanga, Vaca de Castro received news that Don Diego would enter the town that night. This greatly upset him for all his men had not yet arrived, nor would the rest have arrived so quickly if Alonso de Alvarado had not returned to fetch them. Though some of the rearguard had marched five leagues that day, fully armed and with all their equipment, and had suffered great hardships on the road, which was rough and very steep, they all joined together and immediately set out in very good order. Passing through the town, they remained all night under arms on the other side, and received no news of the enemy until next morning they were informed by scouts who had ridden more than six leagues forward that Don Diego was nine leagues away. On learning this Vaca de Castro wrote to him by Don Francisco de Idiaquez, brother to Alonso de Idiaquez and His Majesty's secretary, who had come from Don Diego's camp, requesting him in His Majesty's name to come and put himself beneath the royal standard. If he did so, and also dissolved his army, all the past would be forgiven. Otherwise Vaca de Castro would proceed against him with all just rigour as a traitor and disloyal subject of his prince.

While these messengers were on their way, Vaca de Castro sent a servant, who know the country very well, to visit Don Diego's camp in Indian disguise and deliver letters to many gentlemen in it. Secretly though he travelled, however, his tracks were discovered on a snowfield, and he was pursued and captured. Complaining bitterly of Vaca de Castro's duplicity in discussing terms and at the same time trying to raise a mutiny in his army, Don Diego had the man hanged.

In the presence of Vaca de Castro's messengers, Don Diego reviewed his army and ordered his captains and soldiers to give battle. He promised that whoever killed a settler should have his Indians, his possessions and his wife. He then answered Vaca de Castro by the same Idiaquez and Diego de Mercado, to the effect that he would not obey him under any conditions so long as he kept company with his enemies, Pedro Alvarez Holguin and Alonso de Alvarado and those of their party. He further refused to disband his army until he saw His Majesty's pardon signed with his royal hand and not with that of the Cardinal of Seville, Fray Garcia de Loayse, whom he did not recognize as governor, having no knowledge that he had any power to act for His Majesty in any matter concerning the Indies. He said, furthermore, that Vaca de Castro was much deceived if he supposed or had been led to believe that any men would desert Don Diego's army for his. On the contrary he, Don Diego, would give battle and defend the land against all comers, as Vaca de Castro would learn by experience should he hold his ground. For he, Don Diego, was now coming to look for him.

17. Vaca de Castro brings out his army to give battle

ON receipt of Don Diego's answer, and in view of his obstinacy, Vaca de Castro led his army out on to a plain that is called Chupas, a little way from Huamanga, which was too rough a terrain for fighting; and there in Chupas he waited three days under continuous rain, for it was the middle of the winter. The soldiers remained ready under arms for all that time, since the enemy was very near, and Vaca de Castro was resolved to fight, since he could see no alternative.

On the next day, which was Saturday, at the hour of mass, the scouts called the army to arms, the enemy being very near. Indeed they had slept the night only two short leagues away and, having left the road, were marching against the left flank of Vaca de Castro's army across some low hills, in order to avoid the marshes which lay immediately in front. Their intention was to take the town of Huamanga before giving battle, since they felt quite certain of victory on account of their great force of artillery. When they came within hailing distance of the scouts, and within arquebus range also, Vaca de Castro sent Captain Castro with fifty arquebusiers to skirmish with them while the main forces climbed a hill, a perilous manoeuvre since, should Don Diego turn in that direction, his artillery would inflict great losses on Vaca de Castro's whole infantry force, which was exposed. To avoid all delay and bring the army up the slope with the greatest possible speed the chief sergeant Francisco de Carvajal ordered that each company should make the ascent separately and reform only when they reached the crest, for if the ascent had been slow the casualties would have been heavy. His order was carried out, and before they reached the crest Captain Castro's arquebusiers started an action against Don Diego's rearguard, which did not break off its march, however, until it reached its positions and was ready to give battle.

18. Vaca de Castro advances his squadrons against Don Diego to give battle

WHEN Vaca de Castro saw his whole army up the slope, which was no more than a low hill, he ordered the chief sergeant to draw up his squadrons, and, when this was done, addressed them saying: 'Consider, gentlemen, who you are, whence you come and for whom you are fighting. The strength of this kingdom is in your hands and depends on your courage. If you are beaten neither you nor I will be spared. But if you conquer, in addition to doing your duty as loyal servants of your king, you will be masters of the wealth and concessions of the enemy. Those of you who have none will receive some from me in His Majesty's name. It is for this that the king desires this land, to give it to those who serve him loyally, I well see that there is no need to exhort gentlemen of your nobility and courage. By your faces I know that you are men of valour. So, instead of offering you an example I will take an example from you and ride ahead to break the first lance.'

All the soldiers answered with great spirit that they would do as he said, and would rather be cut to pieces than defeated. For each one took this cause as his own. The captains besought Vaca de Castro most insistently not to lead the vanguard, saying that they would on no account agree to it. They persuaded him to remain in the rear with thirty horsemen, so that he could bring help wherever it was most needed; and this he did. But seeing that there was only an hour and a half left before nightfall, he wanted to postpone the battle till next day. Captain Alonso de Alvarado, however, said that unless they fought that night they would lose the battle. For the soldiers' resolution was now high, but if he waited they might have second thoughts.

Vaca de Castro took Alvarado's advice, though he was still afraid of fighting in the dark and said he wished he had Joshua's power to stay the sun in its course. At this moment Don Diego's artillery began to shoot; and since the army could not advance straight down the hill to attack without sustaining heavy casualties – for they would present a ready target – the chief sergeant and Alonso de Alvarado sought a safer approach towards the left where it dropped to a valley along which they could come at the enemy out of range of his artillery, whose fire would pass over their heads.

So the squadrons came down in good order. On the right was Alonso de Alvarado who with his company guarded the royal standard, which was carried by Cristobal de Barrientos of Ciudad Rodrigo, a citizen of Trujillo; and on the left went the four captains Pedro Alvarez Holguin, Gomez de Alvarado, Garcilaso de la Vega and Pedro Anzures, all leading their companies, which followed their standards in good order, and each riding in the first file. Between the two forces of cavalry came Captains Pedro de Vergara and Juan Velez de Guevara with the infantry; and Nuño de Castro went out in front with his arquebusiers to start a skirmish and retire in due course on the squadrons. Meanwhile Vaca de Castro remained in the rear with his thirty horsemen, at some distance from the main army, so that he could see where his help was most needed in the battle.

19. *The battle of Chupas*

AS Vaca de Castro's army advanced, they were continuously fired on by Don Diego's artillery, though all the shot passed over their heads. This aroused Don Diego's suspicions. Fearing that Captain Candia, the chief gunner, had been bribed and was deliberately firing high, he rode up to him and killed him with his own hand. Then he himself fired a shot which fell among the squadron and killed some men

When Captain Carvajal saw this, he realized that the artillery they carried could not be brought up in time. So they decided to leave it behind in order to advance faster. At that hour Don Diego and his captains – Juan Balsa, Juan Tello, Diego Mendez, Malaver, Diego de Hoces, Martin de Bilbao, Juan de Olea and the rest – had their horsemen in two squadrons with the infantry between, and the artillery in front, trained in the direction from which Vaca de Castro would have to attack. But considering it cowardly to remain halted the squadrons and artillery moved forward to meet him. This was done against the advice of Don Diego's chief sergeant, Pedro Suarez, who, as a man experienced in war, considered that they should stay in position. On seeing the artillery moved, indeed, he gave the battle up for lost. In its original position it had a large field of fire and would have inflicted great casualties on the enemy as they crossed it. But when it was moved forward its range became restricted and it had less opportunity of playing on the enemy. Nevertheless the gunners advanced and took up their position near the point where Vaca de Castro would appear over the hill. The artillery, however, could not catch his men till they came very near, since it was placed too low to cover the ground between. On seeing that his advice was not taken, Pedro Suarez put spurs to his horse and rode over to join Vaca de Castro.

Paulo, the Inca's brother, then attacked Vaca de Castro's left flank with many Indian warriors, pelting them with stones and darts. But when the leading arquebusiers killed some of them, the rest immediately fled. After this Martin Corte, captain of Don Diego's arquebusiers, advanced on that flank with his company, and a brush took place between them and Captain Castro's men. The squadrons advanced step by step to the sound of the drums till they appeared on the brow of the hill, where they were stopped by the artillery, which fired so rapidly that it gave them no chance to attack. Although it was very close, the shots passed over their heads. But had they advanced another twenty paces it would have struck them point-blank. Vaca de Castro's infantry, however, suffered heavy losses, for it was further up the hill and exposed to the guns. One ball took a whole file, ploughing its way right through the squadron. The captains, however, were at great pains to fill the breach, and threatened the soldiers with their bare swords till the ranks were closed.

The chief sergeant, Francisco de Carvajal, prevented the captains from charging until the artillery fire had died down. Climbing a little up the slope, Don Diego's leading horsemen killed Pedro Alvarez Holguin and Gomez de Tordoya with two shots, and killed and wounded others. Wounded by an arquebus, Captain Pedro de Vergara began to shout to the cavalry, calling on them to charge before all the infantry were shot down at short range. Then the trumpets sounded for the attack, and Vaca de Castro's cavalry squadrons charged Don Diego's, who came out bravely to receive them. The two parties met with such an impact that almost all their lances broke and there were many fallen and dead on both sides. Throwing down their lances, they mingled in battle, wounding one another most cruelly with their swords and clubs and axes. Some even fought with hatchets, which they wielded in both hands, striking so hard that where they struck no armour could resist them. So they fought until they were forced to rest by lack of breath.

Vaca de Castro's infantry captains attacked Don Diego's, defying the artillery. Captain Carvajal rode ahead to encourage them, shouting 'Don't be afraid of the guns. They haven't hit me and I'm as fat as two of you together.' And fearing they might think it was trust in his armour that made him so bold, he suddenly took off the mail coat and helmet he was wearing and threw them to the ground. Remaining in his linen doublet, he charged against the artillery with a partisan, and they all followed him. So they captured the guns, killing the gunners. Then they turned them against the rest of the enemy, fighting so valiantly that a major share of the victory was attributable to them.

By this time the night was so dark that the companies could scarcely recognize one another except by their war-cries. The horsemen returned to the fight, and victory was already declaring itself in Vaca de Castro's favour when he attacked with his thirty horsemen on the left, where two companies stood firm for Don Diego, still crying that victory was theirs, even though all Don Diego's other companies were retiring in defeat. When

Vaca de Castro charged them the fight broke out afresh. Some of the thirty were wounded and overthrown, and Captain Jimenez, a certain Montalvo of Medina del Campo and some other gentlemen were killed. But Vaca de Castro's men fought so hard that Don Diego and his soldiers turned their backs and fled, pursued by Vaca de Castro's men who mingled with them, killing and wounding still more. When Captain Bilbao and Cristobal de Sosa, on Don Diego's side, saw their men in flight they were so ashamed that they flung themselves desperately on the enemy, dealing wounds on all sides, and each shouting his name: 'I am Bilbao (or Sosa) who killed the Marquis,' and thus they fought on until they were hacked to pieces. Many of Don Diego's men escaped in the darkness after taking their badges from some of the slain. Vaca de Castro's men wore red bands and Don Diego's white.

So the victory was patently Vaca de Castro's, although before they came to close fighting many more of his men had been killed, so many indeed that Don Diego thought he had won. All the Spaniards who fled up the valley were killed by Indians; and a hundred and fifty of Don Diego's horsemen who fled to Huamanga, two leagues away, were disarmed and captured by the few settlers who had remained in the town. Don Diego and Diego Mendez fled to Cuzco, where they were arrested by Rodrigo de Salazar of Toledo, who was Don Diego's own lieutenant, and Antonio Ruiz de Guevara, one of the city magistrates. Thus ended the rule and governorship of Don Diego, who one day was lord of Peru and the next was arrested by a magistrate whom he had appointed on his own authority. The battle of Chupas took place on 16 September 1542.

20. *Vaca de Castro thanks his army for the victory*

FOR a great part of the night the army could not be reformed because the men were busy looting the tents of Don Diego's soldiers, and killing some of them who had concealed themselves or were wounded. But when they were all collected, for fear that Don Diego's men might reform their ranks all the infantry and cavalry were put on the alert. Vaca de Castro spent the greater part of the night praising his army in general and thanking each soldier in particular for having fought so well. Many captains and soldiers greatly distinguished themselves in this battle, especially Don Diego, who in pursuit of this enterprise, which seemed to him so just, since he was avenging his father's murder, did more than could have been expected from his years, for he was only twenty-two; and not only Don Diego but some others in his army fought valiantly. Many of Vaca de Castro's men distinguished themselves also. For they had believed so strongly in the Marquis that they would bravely have faced any peril to avenge his murder. More than three hundred died on both sides, including many captains and distinguished men, chief among them Pedro Alvarez Holguin and Gomez de Tordoya who, to call attention to their deeds in that battle, wore over their armour white velvet cloaks richly embroidered with gold, by which they were recognized and shot down by the arquebusiers, as has been told. Alonso de Alvarado also distinguished himself, and Captain Carvajal, who fearlessly charged the artillery, where the bullets of the arquebusiers defending it were so thick that it was incredible he was not hit by at least one. By despising death he seemed to avoid it, as frequently happens in moments of danger. For danger pursues those who most fear it, as happened in this battle, where a young man who was too frightened to fight went and hid behind a crag. But a fragment of the crag was blown off by a cannon ball and, breaking his skull, killed him.

(Here follows a list of the principal officers on Vaca de Castro's side, and a further list of those of the Chile faction who joined him when they realized that he had the king's authority. These latter were rewarded with estates to live on when Vaca de Castro divided the territory.)

21. Vaca de Castro's treatment of Don Diego's party

ON the night of the victory there was a great frost, and many of the wounded died of cold. Since the baggage had not yet arrived, there were only tents for Gomez de Tordoya, who was still alive, and Pedro Anzures, who was wounded. Next morning Vaca de Castro gave orders for the treatment of the four hundred wounded and had the dead buried. The bodies of Pedro Alvarez and Gomez de Tordoya were solemnly interred in the town of Huamanga. That same day Vaca de Castro had those of the prisoners who had taken part in the Marquis' murder beheaded, and on arriving next day at Huamanga, found that Diego de Rojas had executed Juan Tello and other captains. Vaca de Castro entrusted the trial of the rest to the lawyer de la Gama, who hanged and beheaded forty of the most guilty, exiled some others and pardoned all the rest. About sixty persons were executed in all. All the settlers were then given leave to return home, and Vaca de Castro went to Cuzco, where he instituted a fresh prosecution of Don Diego, whom he beheaded a few days later. Diego Mendez and two other prisoners escaped from jail and fled to the Inca in the Andes mountains, the approach to which is so wild that they are considered impregnable. The Inca welcomed them. He was extremely grieved by Don Diego's death, since he had been very fond of him. When he learnt of the fighting, he had sent him all the coats of mail, corselets, breastplates and other arms that he had taken from the Christians he had defeated and killed. These were the men whom the Marquis had sent to the aid of Gonzalo and Juan Pizarro in Cuzco (as has been related in an earlier chapter). The Inca had kept secret agents in the camp who had advised him of the outcome of the battle.

22. *Vaca de Castro sends expeditions of discovery to various parts of the country*

AFTER the defeat of Don Diego and the pacification of the country, Vaca de Castro thought that it would be impossible to disperse and reward his soldiers except by sending them to conquer and explore different parts of the country. So he ordered Captain Vergara to return with the men he had brought to his territory of Bracamoros, and sent Captain Diego de Rojas and Felipe Gutierrez with upwards of three hundred men to explore the land towards the east, that is to say to the Rio de la Plata, which they afterwards settled; and he sent reinforcements to Captain Pedro de Valdivia in Chile under one Monroy, and Captain Juan Perez de Guevara to conquer the land of Mullobamba, which he had discovered. This is a land containing more mountains than plains; and from the foothills of these mountains rise the two great rivers that drain towards the Northern Sea. One is the Marañon, of which we have already spoken; the other the Rio de la Plata. The inhabitants of this land are Caribs who eat human flesh; and the climate is so hot that they go about naked except for the cloths that they wind round their bodies.

Here Captain Juan Perez received news of another large country on the other side of the last mountain chains towards the north in which there are rich gold-mines and camels and fowls like those in New Spain,* and sheep rather smaller than those of Peru. And all their cornlands are irrigated, because it seldom rains in the land. But there is a lake whose shores are thickly populated, and in all the rivers there are fish of the shape and size of large dogs, who bite and eat the Indians who go into the water or pass near it – for they also come out on the banks. This land is bounded by the river Marañon on the north and by the land of Brazil – which is owned by the Portuguese – on the east and the Rio de la Plata on the south;

* Turkeys.

and it is said that those Amazon women of whom Orellana heard live there also.

After sending his captains off on these explorations, Vaca de Castro stayed in Cuzco for upwards of a year and a half apportioning the Indians who were masterless and putting the land in order. He drew up ordinances which were most useful and beneficial to the Indians.

At that time there were discovered in the region of Cuzco the richest gold-mines that have ever been seen in our times. The best of them are on a river called the Carabaya, and they are so productive that an Indian may bring in fifty pesos in one day. The whole country was quiet; and the Indians were protected and relieved of the great burdens inflicted on them in the recent wars. Then Gonzalo Pizarro came to Cuzco, since he had not received permission to do so before. And after spending a few days there he went to Charcas to attend to his affairs, where he remained until the arrival of the viceroy Blasco Nuñez Vela.

The conclusion of the story narrated by Agustín de Zárate covers the rebellion and eventual defeat of Gonzalo Pizarro, the last of the brothers surviving in Peru. After Francisco's murder Hernando did not return. For twenty years he was confined in the fortress of Medina del Campo for his part in the killing of Diego de Almagro. Never formally accused or sentenced, he was, however, continually persecuted by his former aide Diego de Alvarado who had gone to Spain to defend the claims of Don Diego de Almagro the younger. When he was eventually released, Hernando was an old man, and most of his fortune had been either confiscated or used up in litigation. He died at the age of 100.

I give books five to seven of Zárate's work only in part.

BOOK FIVE

BLASCO NUÑEZ VELA'S MISSION

1. His Majesty's Ordinances for the Government of the Indies. Blasco Nuñez Vela is sent as Viceroy of Peru to implement them

NOW and for some time previously certain men of religion, who believed themselves to be moved by pious zeal, had been sending information to His Majesty and the lords of the Royal Council concerning the great cruelties and injustices commonly practised on the Indians by the Spaniards: the ill-treatment and killing of persons, the taking of goods, the imposition of excessive tribute and the sending of many to the mines and pearl-fisheries, where they all died. Indeed the native population had been decreasing at such a rate that soon none would have been left in New Spain or Peru or the other countries where they still survived. In Santo Domingo, Cuba, Puerto Rico, Jamaica and other islands there was already no memory of any natives at all. To convince His Majesty, these men of religion narrated some cruelties that had been practised on the Indians, and added others of which there is no confirmation. One of the chief evils was the excessive loads which the Indians were made to carry; and the principal sinners in this respect were the governors and their lieutenants, His Majesty's officials, and the bishops and monasteries and other favoured and privileged persons, who were confident that they could not be prosecuted. The chief layer of this information was a Dominican friar, Bartolomé de las Casas, whom His Majesty appointed Bishop of Chiapa.

On hearing these complaints, His Majesty decided to remedy them, in order to relieve his royal conscience. So he summoned his Council of the Indies, and many other learned and religious men, who looked into the case and discussed it most diligently. Certain ordinances were then promulgated which seemed likely to remove the abuses that Fray Bartolomé had set out. It was decreed that no Indian should be sent to the mines or the pearl-fisheries, or carry burdens except in those districts where it was unavoidable, and then they should be paid for their labour. Tributes payable to the Spaniards should be regulated; all Indians who were left masterless at the death of their present owners should revert to the Crown; the grants and assignments of Indians (*encomiendas*) owned by all bishops, monasteries and hospitals in the Indies, also by former governors or their deputies, and by present officials of His Majesty, should be confiscated and might not be retained even though these officials should offer to resign their posts. In the province of Peru in particular, all those who had been implicated in the disputes and hostilities between Don Francisco Pizarro and Don Diego de Almagro should have their Indians taken from them; and all Indians so taken in one manner or another, also their tributes, should be assigned to His Majesty. From this final ordinance it is clear that no one in Peru could retain his Indians, since, as can be gathered from this history, there was no Spaniard great or small who had not been as passionately partisan in these disputes as if his life and wealth had depended on them. Indeed the quarrel had even spread to the Indians themselves, among whom there were frequently great battles, arguments and private contentions, according as their sympathies were with Don Diego's men, whom they called the Chile party, or the Marquis', whom they called the men of Pachacamac.

Another of the ordinances, designed for the good government of the provinces, was that the province of Peru, the chief and richest in the Indies, should be placed under a new audiencia, consisting of four judges and a president with the title of Viceroy or Captain-general, as the importance of Peruvian affairs required. Hitherto Peru had been subject to the Audiencia of Panama, where there were only two judges and long delays in the dispatch of business owing to the great distance between Peru and Panama, and the fact that the voyage was impossible in either direction for a great part of the year. It was for this reason that most of the wrongs so far recorded had not been remedied, and those which should arise in the future could not be dealt with in Panama.

These ordinances were made and published at Madrid in the year 1542, and copies were sent to various parts of the Indies, where they were received with great indignation by the conquerors, especially in Peru, where the effect was greatest. Every settler would lose his entire wealth, and have to look for a new means of providing for himself. The settlers said that His Majesty had been misinformed concerning the factions. If they had supported one party or the other, it had been because they had considered its leaders as governors with a right to command them in His Majesty's name. This was no crime for which they should be despoiled of their possessions; and moreover, at the time when they had discovered the province of Peru at their own cost, it had been agreed that they should be given Indians to support them, who were to be inherited by their eldest sons at their death, or by their wives if they died without issue; in confirmation of which His Majesty had sent them orders only a few days before, that they should marry under pain of losing their Indians, and in obedience most of them had indeed married. It was unjust, they protested, that now when they were old and tired and married, and wanted a little peace and quiet, they should have their possessions taken away, especially as they were too old and had not the health to seek new lands and discoveries.

The settlers came to Cuzco from all parts of the country to lay their complaints before Vaca de Castro, and he replied that he had no doubt His Majesty would right this wrong when fully informed of the facts. To this end he advised that procurators should be elected by all the cities and meet to choose some of their number to go before His Majesty and the royal council and protest against these ordinances in the name of the whole country. To facilitate their assembly, he offered to go to the city of Los Reyes, which was more convenient both for the cities of the plain and those of the mountains. Thus in order to play his part, he was willing to share the hardships of travel also. And so he left Cuzco for Los Reyes, taking with him procurators from all the cities in the Cuzco district, also other gentlemen who formed his escort.

[*At the same time as Vaca de Castro was temporizing with the old settlers, the Emperor was sending a new viceroy, Blasco Nuñez Vela, and new judges to administer the new laws. A rather imperious old gentleman, coming straight from an administrative post at court, Blasco Nuñez was free from prejudices in regard to Peru. His first act on reaching the New World, however, was to lay an embargo on a shipload of Peruvian silver lying in port, on the grounds that it was the product of slave labour. He also liberated three hundred Peruvian slaves who had been brought to Panama, and ordered that they should be sent home. On meeting with protests at Los Reyes he replied that he had come 'not to tamper with the laws but to execute them'.*

In Blasco Nuñez' company came Agustín de Zárate, the author of this history, who was secretary of the royal council. He came to audit the accounts of the province on behalf of the royal treasury. For 'accounts had not been demanded of the treasurers and other officials of the royal treasury since the discovery of the province'. Zárate admired the new viceroy's ruthless execution of the ordinances in each town through which he passed. At San Miguel and Trujillo citizens came to request that action should at least be postponed until they had an opportunity of lodging an appeal before the judges in Los Reyes. Blasco Nuñez was travelling in advance of his judges. But he refused to accept their plea.

As soon as he landed Blasco Nuñez sent to relieve Vaca de Castro of his authority. The Emperor had sent him a fulsome letter of thanks and summoned him home, not recognizing the great efforts he had made to pacify the country. To the last, Vaca de Castro tried to persuade the rebellious settlers to receive the new viceroy with suitable honours and hope that in time he and his judges would secure the repeal of the unjust ordinances. The settlers who had looked on Vaca de Castro as a potential leader then turned against him; he was coldly treated on his way from Cuzco to Los Reyes, and though he secured Blasco Nuñez' peaceful reception at the latter city, where a number of men from Cuzco were trying to organize resistance, the new viceroy did not trust him either, but put him under arrest, alleging that he had abetted the Cuzco faction.

The men of Cuzco seized all the artillery that Vaca de Castro had stored at Humanga, on the pretext that they were still in danger from the armies of the Manco Inca, who was roaming the mountains. Disillusioned with Vaca de Castro, they invited Gonzalo Pizarro to be their chief. He had refused a previous invitation, and was living on his estates at Charcas. This time he decided to go to Cuzco with about twenty men.]

4. Gonzalo Pizarro enters Cuzco and is chosen Procurator-general of the land

WHILE Gonzalo Pizarro was collecting money from his estates, letters came to him from all parts, both from city councils and private persons, persuading him that it was his duty to complain of the ordinances and obtain their repeal, both because he was most affected by them and because he had a natural right to be governor of the province. Some offered him their persons and goods. Others wrote that the Viceroy had said he was going to cut off his head. So in various ways they succeeded in arousing his indignation and bringing him to Cuzco to resist the Viceroy's entrance. Because of these persuasions and the desire he had always had to be governor of Peru, Gonzalo collected a hundred and fifty thousand castlins from his estates and Hernando Pizarro's, and came to Cuzco, bringing twenty men with him. All the citizens came out to receive him and welcomed him with great delight. Every day men came to Cuzco, fleeing from the Viceroy and his actions, and each one brought some additional fuel for the citizens' anger. In the council chamber of Cuzco there were many meetings, both of the council itself and of all the citizens to discuss what should be done about the Viceroy's coming. Some said they must receive him and that, as for the ordinances, they must send a procurator to His Majesty to obtain their repeal; others said that if they once received him, to judge by the way he was executing the ordinances, he would take away their Indians; and once they had been taken it would be very difficult to get them back. In the end it was decided that Gonzalo should be chosen procurator of Cuzco, with Diego Centeno, who was there to represent the town of La Plata, as his deputy, and that Gonzalo should go to Los Reyes with the title of Procurator-general to plead against the ordinances in the royal court.

At first there were differences of opinion as to whether he should take soldiers with him; it was finally decided that he should, and there were various excuses for this: first that the Viceroy had already called out soldiers at Los Reyes with the intention of coming to punish them for seizing the artillery; secondly that the Viceroy was a harsh and rigorous man and was executing the ordinances without regard to the complaints against them that had been lodged with him, and without waiting for the royal court which was equally responsible for their execution; also that the Viceroy had many times said that he had commands from His Majesty to execute Gonzalo Pizarro for the past disorders and the death of Don Diego. And others who viewed the business more objectively excused the raising of an army by the fact that on his way to Los Reyes Gonzalo must pass through territory where the Inca was in armed insurrection and must take soldiers to protect himself from him; and others put the matter even more directly, saying that he was taking soldiers to protect him against the Viceroy, who was a stubborn man and did not observe the rules of justice. Indeed there was no certainty of obtaining justice from him, and they cited witnesses to all these facts. There were even lawyers who stated and argued that there was no contempt of law in this, and they had a right to do it, since force can and should resist force, and a judge who acts arbitrarily may be arbitrarily resisted. And so it was agreed that Gonzalo Pizarro should raise a standard and recruit men; and many of the citizens of Cuzco offered him their persons and goods. So for the journey of protest Gonzalo received the title of Procurator-general of the country, and for defence against the Inca he was named Captain-general. In addition certain edicts were passed that are used to lend colour to such business, and he began to collect men, paying them out of the royal treasury and from the goods of the dead and other deposits, which he took by way of a loan.

[*Los Reyes was in confusion. Though some citizens of Cuzco came over to Nuñez Vela, the prevailing drift was in the other direction. All the settlers feared for their wealth and estates. The Viceroy was at odds with the citizens of Los Reyes and also with the judges of the Audiencia, who disagreed with the ordinances and resented his arrogance. An ill-timed murder perpetrated by Nuñez and his attendants made his situation desperate. He decided to re-*

treat to Trujillo, leaving Los Reyes stripped of its citizens and evacuating its women, children and wealth by sea. He was prevented from carrying out his plan by the judges of the Audiencia, who arrested him and decided to send him back to Spain in the company of a lawyer who would explain his deposition.

Meanwhile Gonzalo was approaching Los Reyes, and had reached Jauja, a hundred and fifty miles away. News had reached him of the murder of Manco Inca, the last titular ruler of Peru, whose presence in the mountains above Cuzco had provided Gonzalo with the excuse for himself raising an army. With him had been some adherents of the Almagro faction, one of whom had killed him in a quarrel over a game of bowls. The Indians had then slaughtered the murderer and all his Spanish comrades.

The judges of the Audiencia sent an embassy to Gonzalo announcing Nuñez Vela's deposition and the suspension of the ordinances. The embassy consisted of Agustín de Zárate himself and Antonio de Ribera, a citizen of Los Reyes.]

13. The judges send an embassy to Gonzalo Pizarro, requesting him to disband his army. The results of the embassy

THE messengers received their credentials and left for the valley of Jauja, where Gonzalo Pizarro's army was then encamped. He had already been advised of the embassy, and was afraid that if news of its coming were to reach his men's ears, a mutiny would break out. For they were most anxious to enter Los Reyes as an army, and to sack the city if an opportunity offered. So he sent his captain Hieronimo de Villegas along the road by which the messengers were coming with thirty mounted arquebusiers. He allowed Antonio de Ribera to go to the camp, but arrested Agustín de Zárate and took the dispatches he was carrying. He then sent him back along the road as far as the province of Pariacaca, where he kept him prisoner for ten days, during which time his men tried to frighten him into abandoning his mission. Agustín de Zárate was held here until Gonzalo Pizarro arrived with his army and summoned him to explain the reasons for his coming. Zárate had been advised that he would be in danger of his life if he were openly to proclaim the provisions of the judges' message. After listening to them in private, Gonzalo Pizarro led him into a tent where all his captains were assembled, and ordered him to tell them all that he had told him. And Zárate, realizing his purpose, gave them an honest account of the situation, using the discretion provided by his credentials and speaking of their duty to His Majesty and the good of the country. But the only reply he received was that it would be for the good of the country if Gonzalo Pizarro were made governor, and that everything else could be attended to afterwards. They threatened that if Gonzalo were not made governor, they would sack Los Reyes. Agustín de Zárate returned with this answer to the judges, though he had several times refused to carry it.

[*Gonzalo Pizarro then marched on Los Reyes, and when he reached the suburbs sent a lieutenant to arrest those citizens of Cuzco who had deserted him to join Nuñez Vela, and publicly hanged them outside the city. The judges of the Audiencia, in fear of their lives, then invited him to enter Los Reyes, which he did in battle array on 28 October, 1544, to the fervent applause of the inhabitants. He there took the oath as Governor and Captain-general of Peru 'until His Majesty's pleasure shall be known', and moved into his brother's palace where Francisco had been murdered a little more than three years before.*]

14. Character of Gonzalo Pizarro

WHEN Gonzalo Pizarro began to assume the dictatorship he was forty years old, tall and well-proportioned; his complexion was dark, his beard black and very long. He was a lover of warfare and very patient of hardship. He was a very good rider in both styles and a good shot with the arquebus; and considering his poor education, expressed himself well, though in very coarse language. He was very bad at keeping a secret; and indiscretion often led him into trouble in the course of his wars. He was a very poor giver, which was also prejudicial to him, and immoderate in pursuit of women both Indian and Spanish.

[Gonzalo Pizarro now began to arrest his enemies, some of whom he condemned to death but eventually spared. Many were driven into exile. He had at first some hope of gaining favour with the crown but was persuaded that the Emperor would surely be against him, since Nuñez Vela had dutifully sent the royal fifth and he had withheld it. Meanwhile Vaca de Castro, whom the Viceroy had detained, escaped to Spain where he was again held for some time as a prisoner on the unjust suspicion that he had made an illegal fortune in Peru. He was afterwards released and restored to the Royal Council.

Nuñez Vela was also released by the escort which was taking him by ship to Panama. Once at liberty, he directed the captain to land him at Tumbez, to try his fortune again. He was after all still Viceroy. Having proclaimed Gonzalo a traitor, he collected some followers from the cities of the north, and for many months Gonzalo pursued him and his army through the northern wastes and deserts. But Nuñez Vela did not trust even the men who had joined him, and executed several on the march. Finally he faced battle with Gonzalo and after a vain attempt to catch him by a trick, was overwhelmed and killed at the battle of Quito. The soldier who had dismounted him was the lawyer Carvajal, whose brother he had killed in Los Reyes. Carvajal was with difficulty dissuaded from himself beheading the Viceroy. The task was given to a Negro slave.

Gonzalo was now master of Peru, and by virtue of his fleet controlled the Pacific as far as Panama. Nombre de Dios was also his. He did not, however, renounce his obedience to the Emperor. Though counselled by his lieutenant Francisco de Carvajal to make himself king of Peru and marry an Inca princess, he continued to consider himself merely governor. Though he had a bodyguard of eighty and lived in some luxury, he was readily approachable. He was also impartial in his treatment of Spaniards and Indians. The Inca Garcilaso as a boy frequented his court. He was popular among the settlers for he safeguarded them in their tenure of land and wealth; and rewarded many of his friends with new lands. Despite his active defiance of the Emperor, he continued to hope that by sending a mission to Spain he would secure an amnesty for the past and a confirmation of his authority as his brother's successor in the government of Peru. Meanwhile the land prospered. At Potesi a vein of silver was discovered that was far richer than any so far discovered in Charcas. Indeed all the earlier mines were soon closed. The Potesi mine was discovered by his lieutenant Carvajal, who had gone into La Plata to suppress a revolt by one of Pizarro's captains.]

BOOK SIX

THE COMING OF PEDRO DE LA GASCA TO PERU. HIS CAMPAIGN AGAINST GONZALO PIZARRO

4. Discovery of the mines of Potesi. Captain Francisco de Carvajal takes possession

FORTUNE was so kind to Captain Carvajal that there was no resistance to him in those parts. But a new event occurred to raise him to an even higher peak of prosperity. When out one day with some Yanacona Indians belonging to Juan de Villarcel of La Plata, he found a very high hill eighteen leagues from the city which showed signs of containing silver. When they began to assay the ore they took from it, it proved more or less pure silver wherever they tested. The smallest yield was eighty marks to a hundredweight. No richer mines have ever been found or heard of. When news of the discovery came to La Plata, all law was at an end. The citizens began to divide the land for mining and stake their claims, each taking as much as he could. So many Yanacona Indians had come there to work that in a short time the site was occupied by six thousand Indians, who proved such skilled miners that by agreement each one gave his master two marks of silver a week, which they extracted so easily that they kept much more than they gave. The quality of the ore is so fine that it cannot be melted with bellows or treated with ash as in other mines. It is melted in *guiaras*, which are small ovens heated with charcoal and sheep's dung. The force of air is enough in itself. The mines took their name of Potesi from the hill which Carvajal discovered.

The Indians worked so easily and profitably that, thanks to the prevailing agreement, one of them had as much as three or four thousand pesos of his own, and once they came to the mines they could not be sent away. Moreover, there were none of the dangers that arose in the working of the other mines from the operation of the bellows, the smoke of the charcoal and the melting of the vein itself.

The mines then began to be provided with all necessary stores, though there could never be enough because of the number of people who flocked there. Owing to the shortage a *hanega* [1·6 bushels] of maize was worth more than twenty castlins, and wheat was as dear. A basket of coca was worth thirty pesos, and it became much dearer later on. Because of the great wealth found at Potesi the other mines in the district were deserted, the Porco mine in particular, in which Hernando Pizarro had a share and from which he had got great riches. The miners who had gone to dredge for gold in the Carabaya and other rivers left everything and came to Potesi where they gained an incomparably greater profit. Experts in silver mining see signs that the yield of the mine is inexhaustible.

Thanks to this good fortune Carvajal began to amass money; and he was so skilful at this that by taking over all the Indians of dead settlers and of his enemies who had fled, and by bringing in more than ten thousand loads of food on the backs of animals belonging to His Majesty's Indians and those of other districts, in a short time he amassed more than seven hundred thousand pesos. He gave no share of this to any of the soldiers who had followed him; and his refusal drove them to such fury that a little more than a month after his arrival in La Plata about thirty of them plotted to kill him. But owing to some difficulties they postponed their attempt until a later date, and by some unknown means Carvajal got wind of it. Whereupon he hanged and quartered the ringleaders and ten or a dozen more and banished some others. The men were so frightened by these savage sentences that no one dared to plot his assassination again. For on discovering not even a plot but the faint suspicion of one, Carvajal immediately pronounced sentence of death. So brother no longer trusted brother and, understandably, many important persons in the kingdom blamed His Majesty's servants for not having executed Carvajal if only in order to save their persons from this rigorous and perilous servitude. There was no rebellion against him of which he was not informed, and the four or five plots that he discovered cost more than fifty men their lives. The people were so terrorized by the great danger to the ringleaders and by the large rewards that he offered to informers that they thought it best to temporize with the tyrant until a favourable opportunity or situation should occur. So peace was restored, and frequent news of events in Charcas was sent to Gonzalo Pizarro, together with large quantities of silver both from Carvajal's estate and the royal fifth which he took, and from the yield of the Indians belonging to the men he had executed, which he took to himself as a contribution towards the upkeep of his army.

[*After defeating the Viceroy, Gonzalo Pizarro dispatched expeditions in various directions, reinforced the expedition to Chile and himself moved his residence from Quito to the city of Los Reyes. He was suspicious of Carvajal but expected no open opposition and still thought that His Majesty would make a favourable agreement with him. He pretended to be receiving favourable messages from Court, but no one believed him. His reception at Los Reyes was magnificent and he now began to behave as if he were really Viceroy. There was a beginning of popular discontent.*

The Emperor, who was in Germany dealing with the heresies of Luther and others, received news from both parties of events in Peru, and appointed the lawyer Pedro de la Gasca, a modest and skilful cleric and a member of the Council of the Inquisition, as chief of the royal Audiencia of Peru, with plenary powers to deal with the pacification and government of the country. Arriving at Panama, the new President began to collect friends, chief among them the marshal Alonso de Alvarado who, as one of the original conquistadors and an old friend of the Marquis and his brothers, exerted great influence.

Gasca brought a letter from His Majesty to Gonzalo Pizarro forgiving past actions but requiring him henceforth to obey the new President. Gasca sent with it a longer letter in which he proclaimed his intention of revoking the ordinances, and pointed out that Gonzalo had no longer any cause for disobedience. Both Hinojoso, the governor of Panama, who was a loyal friend to Gonzalo, and other supporters asked Gasca if he had authority to confirm Gonzalo in the governorship. Gasca did not give a straight answer. He cunningly pointed out to Gonzalo that those who had aided him against Nuñez Vela had done so to preserve their own property, and that this motive no longer held since the ordinances were to be revoked and all were to be pardoned.

Opinions were divided in Los Reyes. Though the majority were for temporizing at least for so long as it would take to send a delegation to Spain to put Gonzalo's case before the Emperor, some were in favour of assassinating Gasca. But many more were pre-

paring to desert Gonzalo. He did not know whom to trust. Even when choosing such important clerics as the archbishop of Los Reyes and the provincial of the Dominican order to form his delegation, he was uncertain whether they would not declare against him when they reached Spain. If they were his secret enemies, however, it might be better for him to remove at least the latter from the country. On all accounts they were the most reputable representatives he could send, since they had taken no active part in the civil disturbances.

Gonzalo decided to dispatch Lorenzo Aldana, whom he considered more trustworthy, ahead of them to explore the situation at Panama, and send back immediate information, which should arrive by Christmas (1546); that is to say in something like ten weeks. He established relays of posts to bring him Aldana's letters the moment his ship came into port. But even before reaching Panama, Aldana was wavering. On his arrival he understood for the first time the force of Gasca's case; all that Pizarro had fought for was now granted. Hinojosa, the commander of Pizarro's fleet at Panama, was holding out against Gasca until he should hear His Majesty's answer to Gonzalo's letter. Aldana, however, proved more pliable. He argued that in view of Gasca's mission there could be no doubt of the royal decision. Hinojosa was persuaded, and both men put themselves and Pizarro's ships at the President's disposition. Gasca in return confirmed them and all their officers in their posts, and sent Aldana with four ships to cruise off the coast and pick up any of His Majesty's party whose lives might be in danger from Gonzalo Pizarro.

On receiving copies of the royal letter and Gasca's letter accompanying it, Gonzalo was left in no doubt of his position. He had no alternative but to fight or surrender his usurped governorship. Of his two counsellors, Carvajal was for accepting the royal pardon, but the lawyer Cepeda, once the adviser of Blasco Nuñez and afterwards chief of the Audiencia which deposed him, counselled resistance. There was no hope for him now except under Gonzalo. Even if the grace extended to him his career as a judge was ruined.]

10. *Gonzalo Pizarro receives the royal message and learns of the surrender of his fleet*

PEDRO HERNANDEZ PANIAGUA, who had been entrusted with the President's letters to Gonzalo, reached Peru at the time when Gonzalo was expecting news from Panama of the outcome of Lorenzo de Aldana's mission. This was in the middle of January 1547. On landing at Tumbez, Paniagua went straight to San Miguel, where he was arrested by one Villalobos, Gonzalo's lieutenant there, who took his dispatches and sent them at great speed to Los Reyes in the hands of Gonzalo's lieutenant at Trujillo, Diego de Mora.

On learning of Paniagua's arrival, Gonzalo sent a trusted officer to bring Gasca's messenger to him, but to take care that he spoke with no one on the road. On reaching Los Reyes, Paniagua presented his credentials and letters in the presence of all Gonzalo's captains. Gonzalo commanded him to give any message that had been entrusted to him in addition to the letters, and promised that he should come to no harm whatever he might say. But Gonzalo warned him not to speak to anyone in public or private about the President or his affairs, for on the slightest evidence Gonzalo would have him executed.

Paniagua then boldly proclaimed his message, and when he had done so was asked to retire. Several voices were raised for killing him, on the excuse that he had revealed his mission to certain people whom he trusted. Gonzalo Pizarro did not show either the President's or His Majesty's letter to any of his captains. All his sympathizers said that the President must not be allowed to enter Peru, and some spoke openly in his presence against His Majesty, employing most disrespectful language. Gonzalo showed his delight at this.

Gonzalo wrote promptly to Carvajal asking him to bring from La Plata to Los Reyes as quickly as he could all the gold and silver, arquebuses and other arms that he had. Gonzalo's reason was not that these supplies might be needed for defence or any warlike purpose – since no news had or could have arrived of the surrender of his fleet or other events in Panama – but to satisfy the complaints made against Carvajal all over the country regarding his continual murders and robberies. Some said that Gonzalo intended to execute him, others that he intended only to recover the hundred and fifty or so pesos that he had stolen during the conquest of Charcas.

All this time there was little discussion of affairs at Los Reyes. For no one trusted his neighbour or dared to speak of the situation, since the slightest excuse might cost him his life. Gonzalo himself was so suspicious that, during the illness of the lawyer Zárate* (whose opinion he knew to have been against him in many matters) he sent him some powders, ostensibly to restore him to health, which actually caused his death; and this despite the fact that Pizarro's own daughter was married to Zárate's brother. It was certainly supposed that these powders had caused Zárate's death, and some of Gonzalo's servants confirmed the rumour. However this may be, Gonzalo showed pleasure on hearing of his death.

Pedro Hernandez Paniagua now began to negotiate his return with the help of the lawyer Carvajal. The other captains were against it. But delay would have been very dangerous to Paniagua especially if he were still to be at Los Reyes when news came of the surrender of the fleet. No rumour of this had yet reached Los Reyes, but a very bad impression prevailed on account of the long delay in the arrival of news from Panama. On his suspicion alone, Gonzalo wrote to Pedro de Puelles, his officer in Quito and all his other captains, warning them to maintain precautions and keep their men on a war footing.

At this point Captain Carvajal arrived from Charcas with a hundred and fifty soldiers, three hundred arquebuses and upwards of three hundred thousand pesos. On the day he entered Los Reyes he was given a most solemn reception. Gonzalo Pizarro and all the inhabitants without exception came out to meet him, and there was much music and festivity. But at the same time news arrived from Puerto Viejo that the four ships had been observed off shore and that on sighting land they had

* Not Agustín the historian.

taken a fresh tack to sea, neither putting in nor taking aboard provisions in the usual way. This was considered a bad sign, that they had come to fight.

[*Gonzalo awaited confirmation of this news of Aldana's four ships from his lieutenant at Trujillo, Diego de Mora. But he and the men of Trujillo had changed sides, and Mora was now in Cajamarca organizing resistance to Gonzalo. Gonzalo then nominated a new lieutenant for Trujillo and divided the land and Indians of the deserters among his own followers. But the new lieutenant deserted also. Gonzalo now began to organize the defence of Los Reyes which he had so far neglected, taxing the merchants and peaceful population to provide arms and horses for those soldiers who had none. He appointed Carvajal, whom he could not now dispense with, master of the camp. The banner of his army bore his own initials intertwined with the royal crown above them.*]

11. Gonzalo Pizarro prepares resistance and states his case

GONZALO PIZARRO sent messengers in all directions summoning men and instructing his captains as to their equipment and dispatch. His orders were, in short, that no arms or horses or other munitions should be left in any province that might be of use to men joining the President. He justified his case to them all with the most specious arguments he could find. He said that he had sent Lorenzo de Aldana, on his own behalf and that of everyone in the kingdom, to inform His Majesty of all that had happened, and that Aldana had then joined the President and was coming against him in his own ships, which he had seized, and which had cost more than eighty thousand castlins. Gonzalo claimed that His Majesty had sent the President to secure the peace and quiet of the kingdom, but that on his own authority he had collected an army and was coming with all the force he could muster to punish those who had been most zealous in the recent business; and that since everyone had been concerned in it, everyone must see that he was as much involved now as Gonzalo himself. Everyone was involved because the pardon which the President was said to bring for all those who took his side was a trick; even if it existed it only forgave the past, which did not cover the battle of Quito and killing of the Viceroy, which had taken place after the President left Spain. So until His Majesty was informed of everything and sent fresh instructions, he was determined to resist the President's entry to the country, especially since he had been informed by many people who had written to him from Spain that His Majesty had not sent the President to depose him as governor but to preside over the royal Audiencia. Gonzalo claimed to be quite certain of this by reason of a letter he had received from Francisco Maldonado, whom he had sent to Spain, and also from the President's own words in the letter he had sent him by Pedro Hernandez Paniagua. He said that the President's own captains had subsequently tricked him into an armed invasion of the country, which would greatly annoy His Majesty when he heard of it. By this and other arguments Gonzalo sought to establish that the President had committed a great crime in detaining his messengers and that he was therefore justified in making war on him.

[*Gonzalo attempted to strengthen his case by instituting proceedings against Gasca and his captains before the lawyers in Los Reyes, and demanding the death penalty for Hinojosa, Aldana and others. One lawyer objected that this would prevent these deserters from returning to their allegiance to Pizarro and that furthermore since Gasca was a cleric, any sentence against him might lead to the excommunication of the signators. As a result the matter was dropped. Aldana was at pains to circulate the details of the President's proclamation among Pizarro's followers. Although allegiance was demanded under pain of death from the soldiers and citizens of Los Reyes, one by one they began to drift away towards Trujillo. Among the deserters was the Licentiate Carvajal, whose brother had been put to death by Blasco Nuñez and who had revenged himself by causing the Viceroy to be beheaded at the battle of Quito. If he could trust in the proffered pardon, all the rest of Pizarro's followers could do so too. Consequently his example proved disastrous. Meanwhile resistance began to grow around*

Cuzco also. Diego Centeno, who had spent more than a year hiding in a cave, emerged on hearing of the President's coming and began to collect his former followers. Though he had only forty men, he decided to assault the city, confident that the enemy would have no heart to fight even for their own homes and possessions. By a clever ruse he seized the city, and collecting more followers, closed the passes to the south against Gonzalo. Centeno publicly beheaded Gonzalo's lieutenant, and divided among his followers a hundred thousand pesos of Gonzalo's which he had captured.*

Desertion followed desertion, and the army that Mora was assembling at Cajamarca increased. Gonzalo decided to move south so that if he were beaten he could leave Peru for new lands in Chile or on the Rio de la Plata, and start a fresh career of conquest. Even the summary execution of defecting soldiers and the division of their possessions among the rest was ineffective; he made a further speech of justification to his followers, assuring them that they had no alternative but to fight, and demanding their fidelity, at the same time threatening them with death if they refused it. He had decided to send his army south against Centeno when Lorenzo Aldana's ships arrived off the port of Los Reyes. The President's party continued to circulate copies of the pardon and withdrawal of the ordinances among Pizarro's soldiers, who were encamped half-way between Los Reyes and the sea. The rate of desertion was so high that he decided to make for Arequipa, one of the few towns still safely in his hands. He arrived there with only two hundred men, on the first stage of his proposed journey to Chile. Those left in Los Reyes then declared for the Emperor, Lorenzo de Aldana landed, and Gonzalo's one remaining army, which had marched south to attack Cuzco, turned back with only a third of its strength to rejoin Gonzalo at Arequipa. The rest of the country had risen against him, and his only loyal lieutenant, Pedro de Puelles, was murdered by his own officers at Quito.]

* One of Gonzalo's captains whose revolt had been cruelly repressed by Carvajal in the province of Charcas, shortly before the discovery of Potosi.

BOOK SEVEN

THE PRESIDENT COMES TO PERU. THE DEFEAT OF GONZALO PIZARRO AND THE PACIFICATION OF THE COUNTRY

1

[The President sailed from Panama in April 1547 with five hundred men, and his fleet reached Tumbez in June. He made a general rendezvous for those who were rallying to him at the town of Jauja, and set off to cross the mountains. Gonzalo Pizarro had found Arequipa deserted, but learnt there that Centeno had blocked his escape route to Chile. With the men of Cuzco, Charcas and Arequipa he had taken up his position at Collao, near lake Titicaca, with a force amounting to a thousand men. Gonzalo wrote to Centeno, reminding him of their common past and asking him to come to his support. Centeno's response was to refuse. He advised Gonzalo to take advantage of His Majesty's pardon while there was still time, and even offered to intercede for the rebellious Governor. Gonzalo publicly burnt Centeno's letters unread and decided to set out for Charcas.]

2. *Gonzalo faces the opposition of Diego Centeno and Alonso de Mendoza*

SOME said that Gonzalo Pizarro was willing to forgo a battle if Centeno would let him pass. Others say that he was determined to fight in any case. He made straight for the place where Diego Centeno and Alonso de Mendoza had taken up their positions; and Captain Carvajal, who was leading the advance-guard, hanged more than twenty men whom he met on the march, among them a mass-priest called Pantaleon for having carried letters from Diego Centeno. He hanged him with a breviary round his neck and an ink-bottle at his throat. And they rode on till Thursday, 19 October 1547, when the scouts of both parties met and talked, and returned with news to their commanders. Gonzalo Pizarro then sent one of his chaplains to ask Centeno once more to let him pass and not compel him to give battle. He reminded Centeno of the heavy casualties that a battle would cause. The bishop of Cuzco, who was in Diego Centeno's camp, had this chaplain arrested and brought to his tent. Centeno ordered his men to sleep that night fully armed. He himself had been very sick of a fever for a month and had been bled six times. Indeed no one expected him to live, and on account of his illness he slept that night in his tent.

It was decided that night in Gonzalo Pizarro's camp that Juan de Acosta should take twenty men and, riding secretly by a roundabout route, fall on Centeno's tents. For they had heard that Diego Centeno was ill in his bed. This manoeuvre was executed so speedily that they captured the sentinels before being detected. When they reached the tents some Negroes saw them and called out the guard. Juan de Acosta then ordered the arquebuses to be fired, which put the whole camp in such alarm that many of the horsemen rushed to the tents and some of Valdivia's men threw down their pikes and fled. In the end Juan de Acosta made his escape without losing a single man and regained camp. Next morning the scouts of both parties advanced and the two armies showed themselves. Diego Centeno had almost a thousand men; two hundred horsemen and a hundred and fifty arquebusiers and the rest armed with pikes. [*A number of his officers are named.*] Gonzalo Pizarro had three hundred very good arquebusiers and eighty horsemen; the rest of his five hundred men were pikemen. [*A further list of officers is omitted.*]

3. The battle between Gonzalo Pizarro and Diego Centeno, generally called the battle of Huarima

So the two armies joined battle in good order, Gonzalo advancing with a great music of trumpets and fifes. When the armies were six hundred paces apart, Captain Carvajal ordered his men to halt. Diego Centeno's men advanced another hundred yards before halting also. Then forty of Gonzalo's best arquebusiers came out from his army, and two more bands each of forty arquebusiers drew aside. Gonzalo Pizarro took up his position between the infantry and the cavalry.

Thirty of the best arquebusiers then drew apart from Diego Centeno's army, and the two parties began to skirmish. When Captain Carvajal saw Diego Centeno's men halt, he tried to disconcert them. He ordered his men to advance ten yards further in very extended order. On seeing this some of Centeno's men said that the enemy were gaining honour in this way and all began to march forward. Gonzalo Pizarro's army then halted.

On seeing Captain Carvajal advancing, Centeno ordered a few arquebusiers to fire in order to provoke a quick volley from the enemy. They fired, and his infantry then began to advance with lowered pikes. The arquebusiers fired again to no effect, for they were three hundred yards away. Carvajal did not allow any of his arquebusiers to fire until the enemy were a little more than a hundred yards away. Then he ordered the artillery to be discharged and the arquebusiers, who were many and skilful, killed more than a hundred and fifty, including two captains, with their first volley. The squadron then began to waver, and at the second volley broke up entirely and started to flee in disorder. Captain Retamoso, who was lying wounded on the ground, called to them in vain. On seeing the rout of the infantry, the horsemen attacked, doing great damage and killing Gonzalo Pizarro's horse. He was thrown to the ground but not otherwise hurt. Pedro de los Rios and Pedro Ullea, who were determined to attack Gonzalo's infantry, made a ring round the army in order to take his squadron on the flank. But they struck one of the lines of arquebusiers and sustained heavy casualties, Pedro de los Rios and some of his men being killed by the first round. When those who were still standing saw that not only were the infantry defeated but the cavalry more or less beaten also, they all fled as best they could.

Gonzalo Pizarro's men advanced in good order to Centeno's tents, killing everyone they met on the way. Many of Centeno's men who were in flight came on Gonzalo Pizarro's camp, which they found so deserted that they were able to take the horses and mules that the infantry had left there. Stealing all the silver and gold they could find, they rode safely away and continued their flight.

When Diego Centeno's cavalry charged, Captain Hernando

Bachicao, seeing his men falling, imagined that the victory was Centeno's and fled to his side; but not so secretly that Captain Carvajal did not observe and intercept him. Carvajal hanged him, calling him cousin, which indeed he was, and mocking him in other ways as he did so. At the time of the battle Diego Centeno was some distance away, being carried in a hammock by six Indians and so ill that he was almost unconscious. In the defeat he escaped with the help of his friends, who took great care to save him. Thus this bloody encounter ended. More than three hundred and fifty died on Diego Centeno's side, and thirty more were executed by Captain Carvajal after his victory, among them one priest, Don Gonzalo, a Mercedarian, and some other men of importance. About a hundred men were killed on Gonzalo Pizarro's side.

Captain Carvajal followed the fugitives for some stages down the Cuzco road, hoping to catch the bishop of Cuzco in particular, against whom he had a great grudge both because he had taken Diego Centeno's side and because he had played a personal part in the battle. He could not catch up with him, however, but he hanged many whom he caught on the road, including a brother of the bishop's and a Dominican friar who was with him. So he turned back, and Gonzalo Pizarro divided the land among his soldiers, saying that it was all for them. He had the wounded brought in and treated, and some of the dead were buried. Then he sent Dionisio de Bobadilla with a few men to the town of La Plata and the mines, to bring all the gold and silver they could find, and Diego de Carvajal, who was nicknamed the Gallant, went to Arequipa to do the same. And Juan de la Torre went to Cuzco, where the acting mayor Vazquez de Tapia and the lawyer Martel were executed. Torre also ordered that all those who had been soldiers of Centeno should come and enlist under his banner, on pain of death. He forgave them all the past except those who had particularly distinguished themselves in His Majesty's service. He sent Pedro de Bustincia with some soldiers to compel the *caciques* of Andaguailas and the neighbouring districts to supply the army with food. A few days later, Gonzalo Pizarro came to Cuzco with more than four hundred men and began to equip himself with all that he needed. He and his men had taken great courage from their victory of Huarina. They were proud that with unequal numbers they had gained such an advantage and killed so many of the enemy.

4. The President collects his army in the valley of Jauja

NOT wishing to enter the city of Los Reyes, the President followed the road across the mountains to the valley of Jauja, taking with him the men he had brought from Tierra Firme, and those that Captains Diego de Mora, Gomez de Alvarado, Juan de Saavedra and Porcel and the rest had collected at Cajamarca. He sent orders to Captain Salazar, who was in Quito, to advance with his men and join him. The President also instructed Captain Lorenzo de Aldana to follow after him with the men of his fleet and the citizens of Los Reyes. So he reached the valley of Jauja with almost a hundred men, and was the first to get there. The district being, as has been said before, amply provided, he then began to collect the supplies and munitions he needed. On the day of his arrival he was joined by Carvajal the lawyer, Gabriel de Rojas, Hernan Mejia de Guzmán and Juan Alonso de Palomino, each with his men. They had left Lorenzo de Aldana with his company in command of Los Reyes, since it was necessary on all accounts to keep the city and its harbour safe. So in a short time more than fifteen hundred men were gathered in the valley of Jauja. The President was most assiduous in erecting forges and collecting smiths to make new arquebuses and repair the old ones, also to make lances and all kinds of arms. He was as skilful in these matters as if he had been used to them all his life. He was at pains to inspect the camp and oversee all that was being done there, also to see that the sick and wounded were well looked after. Indeed it seemed impossible that one man could attend to so much, and in a short time he won the affection of the whole army.

While the President was at Jauja, news reached him of Diego Centeno's defeat, which grieved him deeply. In public, however, he put up a most courageous pretence of taking it lightly. The general expectation of the army had been completely contradicted by events. The President had frequently been advised not to raise an army since Diego Centeno's alone would be enough to defeat Gonzalo Pizarro. On learning that this was not so, the President immediately sent Captains Lope Martin and Mercadillo with fifty men to the town of Huamanga thirty leagues ahead to occupy the roads and get news of the enemy, and at the same time collect the fugitives who would arrive from Cuzco. This move was successful in another way also. Hearing that Pedro de Bustincia was at Andaguailas, Lope Martin advanced with fifteen arquebusiers and surprised him by night, capturing and hanging some of those who were with him. He also called together the *caciques* of the district, and took measures to announce the President's coming in all places. The President began to organize his army at Jauja, and sent Marshal Alonso de Alvarado to the city of Los Reyes to bring the men who were there and some pieces of artillery from the fleet, also clothing and money for the soldiers. All this was done very rapidly; and the army was drawn up in this way: Pedro Alonso de Hinojosa remained commander as he had been at the time when he handed over the ships at Panama, Marshal Alonso de Alvarado was made master of the camp; the lawyer Benito de Carvajal lieutenant-general, and Pedro de Villavicencio major-general. Twenty captains [*named by Zárate*] were appointed to companies of horse and foot. The President had with him the archbishop of Los Reyes and the bishops of Cuzco and Quito, the provincial of the Dominicans, Fray Tomas de San Martin and the provincial of the Mercedarians, also many other monks, priests and friars. In his final review he counted seven hundred arquebusiers, five hundred pikemen and four hundred horsemen. But in their march from Jauja to Xaquixaguana they were joined by so many more men that their numbers reached nineteen hundred.

The army struck camp at Jauja on 29 December 1547, and advanced in good order along the Cuzco road, looking for the safest place to cross the Avancay river.

5. Pedro de Valdivia and other Captains join the President's army

WHEN the President had left the valley of Jauja, Captain Pedro de Valdivia, governor of the province of Chile, joined his camp. He had come by sea to the harbour of Los Reyes, bringing with him the men with whom he had completed the conquest of Chile, also plenty of clothing and supplies. He learnt the state of affairs on disembarking. He then equipped himself and his company, for they had a great deal of money with them, and went to find the President, whose army they joined. This was very fortunate. For although the President had experienced captains and soldiers in his army, no one in the country was as skilled and practised in war as Pedro de Valdivia. Till then there had been no strategist equal to Francisco de Carvajal, who had planned and organized so many victories for Gonzalo Pizarro, especially his defeat of Diego Centeno at Huarina, which everyone attributed to Francisco de Carvajal's military skill alone. So there had been some alarm in the President's camp, which was much encouraged by Valdivia's arrival. Captain Diego Centeno also arrived at this moment with thirty or more horsemen who had escaped with him from the defeat at Huarina. And so they continued their march, suffering great shortages of food, till they reached Andaguairas, where the President stayed for a large part of the winter. All that time there was much heavy rain. Indeed it never stopped by day or night, and all the tents rotted since there was no opportunity of drying them. The maize they ate was soft with the damp, and many fell sick of dysentery. Some indeed died of it. The President was very solicitous for the nursing of the sick, which he entrusted to Fray Francisco de la Rocha of the Trinitarian order. There were more than four hundred sick, and they were as well provided with doctors and medicaments as if they had been in a healthy, populous and well supplied place. Thanks to this care almost all recovered. The army was still at Andaguairas when Valdivia and Centeno joined it, and their coming was celebrated with great feasts and jousts and tilting at the ring. After this Valdivia, with Alvarado and Hinojosa, began to concern himself with the conduct of the war. At the coming of spring, when the rains were ending, the army left Andaguairas and took up its position at the bridge of Avancay, twenty leagues from Cuzco, and it halted there until bridges were constructed over the Apurimac river, which is twelve leagues from that city. The enemy had broken all the bridges over this river, and the President's forces appeared to have no way of reaching the other side except by making a detour of more than seventy leagues. The best course was seemingly to try and build bridges. To deceive the enemy and leave them in doubt where they should go to prevent the repair work, the President had bridge-repairing materials taken to three different points, one on the royal road, one in the valley of Cotabamba, twelve leagues higher up, and the third near some villages belonging to Don Pedro Portocarrero, much higher up still, where Don Pedro himself was guarding the crossing with a few men. At this place on the river they made some of those twisted cables with which, as has been said, bridges are built in Peru, so that they could be suspended on the beams and supports as soon as the battle was joined.

But for these precautions, Gonzalo and his men would have prevented the repair of the bridges. Not knowing where to go, however, they became confused and did not keep a guard anywhere, only scouts who were instructed to report as soon as the building work began so that Gonzalo's men could then go and prevent it. But the crossing place was kept so secret that no one in the camp knew it except the President and the members of his war council.

Once the materials were ready the army marched down the road to Cotabamba, which was the point where the river was to be crossed. But there were such bad places and snow-covered mountains on this road that some of the captains objected to the plan, holding that it would be safer to cross fifty leagues further up. Lope Martin, however, who was guarding Cotabamba, considered it the safer crossing. In the course of argument the President sent for the opinion of Valdivia and three other captains, all of whom agreed that this was the least dangerous place. Once their opinions arrived, the army pressed forward faster. On coming near to the bank, Lorenzo Martin with a detachment of Spaniards and Indians, began to throw the cables across, and three of them were secure before Gonzalo Pizarro's scouts arrived and, meeting no resistance, cut two of them. News of this greatly depressed the President and his army, for they now knew for certain that Gonzalo and his men would defend the crossing.

Taking with him the Archbishop, his commander-in-chief, Alonso de Alvarado, Valdivia and some infantry captains, the President advanced with great speed to the bridge. He gave orders that some infantry captains should make a crossing on rafts, which would be dangerous both on account of the violent current and the enemy, whom they believed to be guarding the other bank. One of the first to cross was the lawyer Polo Hondegardo, and after him various foot and horsemen began to get across. Such efforts were put into this operation that more than four hundred men crossed on that day, swimming their horses over with armour and arquebuses strapped to their backs. But more than sixty horses perished. Their reins were broken by the swift current and they were dashed against the rocks with no chance to swim, for the current was too strong. When the army began to get across, Gonzalo Pizarro's scouts went to report it; and he sent Captain Juan de Acosta with some two hundred mounted arquebusiers with orders to kill everyone who had crossed the river except those who had recently arrived from Spain. Observing the state of things, the few who had already crossed took up their position on a declivity, and mounted the Indians and Negroes whom they had brought with them – for almost all the horses were now across – so that they should be less hampered next day. They equipped them with lances and they made a fine squadron, the heading files being all headed by Spaniards. So when Juan de Acostas sent to reconnoitre, he concluded that the numbers were heavily against him. He dared not attack therefore, but returned for more men. Meanwhile the President got his whole army across the bridge, which was now completely rebuilt. This was a result of Gonzalo Pizarro's gross carelessness in not taking up a position beside the river from which he could prevent a crossing. A mere hundred men at each crossing place would have been enough to defend it.

6. The President's actions between the river crossing and the battle

HAVING got the whole of his army across on the following day, without a single casualty, the President sent Juan de Sandoval to locate the enemy and Sandoval came back with the news that he had ridden three leagues and failed to discover either Gonzalo Pizarro or his army. The President then commanded General Hinojosa and Pedro Valdivia with some squadrons to occupy the top of the pass, an ascent of a league and a half, since if Gonzalo Pizarro were to get there first he could do them great harm before they reached the top; and so they climbed the pass.

In the meantime Juan de Acosta had sent news of events to Gonzalo, and asked him for three hundred arquebusiers, who would be enough to defeat those who had already crossed the river before the rest could get over. And while Juan de Acosta was turning back one Juan Nuñez de Prado of Badajoz deserted his army, and brought news to the President of events in general and the reinforcements that Juan de Acosta was expecting. Supposing that Gonzalo Pizarro would attack with his whole army, the President stayed on guard all night with the nine hundred foot and horsemen that he now had at the top of the pass. When next day Juan de Acosta's reinforcements arrived, the President's scouts came to inform him, and he sent his Marshal back to the river to bring up the artillery, and to muster and bring also the rest of the army. Pizarro's standards appeared before the Marshal could return. So the President, with only nine hundred men, drew them up in battle order prepared to fight now if necessary. But he abandoned this intention when he saw that the enemy were not staying for battle, and that no more than three hundred arquebusiers had come to reinforce Juan de Acosta. Acosta retired when he saw his adversaries' strength, which he reported to Gonzalo Pizarro.

The President remained at the top of the pass for two or three days while the rest of his army and the artillery were brought up the steep road. During this time a cleric arrived from Gonzalo Pizarro with the request that the President should disband his army and cease hostilities till the arrival of new commands from the Emperor. The bishop of Cuzco arrested this cleric. Somewhat earlier Gonzalo had sent another cleric to win General Hinojosa and Alonso de Alvarado over to his side. His coming had been less public, and he had been unwilling to return. In fact he had already arranged his brother's escape.

The President wrote from there to Gonzalo Pizarro, as he had done at various places on the road, urging him to resume obedience to His Majesty and sending him a copy of the pardon. Generally the runners who carried dispatches and letters for Gonzalo would hand them over to his runners to be delivered to him.

When Gonzalo Pizarro learnt that the President had brought his army across the river and reached the top of the pass, he came out of Cuzco with nine hundred foot and horse, his five hundred and fifty arquebusiers and six pieces of artillery, and pitched his camp at Xaquixaguana, five leagues from Cuzco, on the plain below the road by which the President's army must descend from the mountain. His position was extremely strong, since it could only be attacked frontally through a narrow defile. On the one side it had the river and marsh, on the other the mountain, and a deep rocky cleft behind. Some two or three days before the battle, between a hundred and two hundred men came out of Gonzalo's camp and skirmished with about equal numbers who advanced from the President's army.

The President advanced till he found a safe place to stop. He had now come so close that Pizarro's men below could clearly distinguish their enemies marching across the height to take up their positions, or in their positions when they had taken them up. Gonzalo Pizarro was afraid that his men would lose heart when they saw that the enemy had a great advantage. He therefore ordered them to draw up behind a hill at the rear of his camp on the excuse that if the President were to see the fine quality and equipment of Pizarro's army he would be unwilling to attack. When the President had come down the pass, however, and pitched his camp on the plain, within sight of the enemy, Gonzalo led his whole army out squadron by squadron, having first placed his bands of arquebusiers in battle order. He then began to fire his artillery and arquebuses within eye and earshot of the President. That day scouts and runners from each camp met in a mist, which had suddenly descended.

On seeing that the enemy were ready to give or accept battle, the President would have preferred to postpone the attack, for he believed that many of his opponents would come over to him if they had time. But the position of his army forbade him. They were short of food, there was an extremely sharp frost and no wood for fires. In fact the cold was unbearable, and there was also a shortage of water. Gonzalo Pizarro's army, on the other hand, suffered none of these disadvantages. They had the river as a bastion and plentiful supplies from Cuzco, and their position was quite warm. For although the two armies were very close together, the President's was, as we have said, on the mountain, and Pizarro's on the plain. Such contrasts of climate are most pronounced in Peru. Some men on a mountain may be suffering unbearable cold, with the snow falling round them, while others on the plain, only two leagues away, are seeking shelter from the excessive heat.

This being the situation, Gonzalo Pizarro and his master of the camp decided to send three parties up the mountain that night, to make a surprise attack on the President's camp. But he subsequently abandoned the plan because a soldier called Nava deserted, and they thought he would report it to the President, as he did. This man Nava and Juan Nuñez de Prado advised the President to postpone the battle as long as possible because those men in Gonzalo's army who had been serving under Centeno at the time of his defeat were anxious to come over to him at the first favourable opportunity.

The President's army remained under arms all night. The tents were struck, and they suffered such cold that they could not hold their lances in their hands as they awaited the dawn, which broke very quickly. They then began to blow their trumpets and strike their drums, for a great number of Gonzalo's arquebusiers were making their way over a hill to attack their camp. Captains Hernan Mejia and Juan Alonso Palomino came out with three hundred arquebusiers to meet them, together with Pedro de Valdivia and Marchal Alonso de Alvarado, and they struck the enemy so quickly and hard that they drove him back. While this skirmish was going on, the President came down under cover of this hill with all the rest of his army in the direction of Cuzco; and to deceive the enemy he made a feint of sending thirty arquebusiers and some horsemen under Captain Pardaver down from the hill on which the skirmish had been fought.

On reaching the top of the hill Pedro de Valdivia and the Marshal summoned Captain Gabriel de Rojas to bring up his artillery. Rojas placed his guns in position and began to fire, promising his men fifteen hundred gold pesos for every shot they placed in Pizarro's squadron. And he paid one man afterwards for hitting Gonzalo's tent, which was very conspicuous, and killing a page who was inside. After this shot Gonzalo had all the tents struck since they acted as targets for the enemy. All this time Gonzalo Pizarro's artillery were firing also, and he kept his squadrons in good order. He himself and the lawyer Cepeda were captains of horse; Carvajal, the master of the camp, Juan de la Torre, Diego Guillen, Juan Vélez de Guevara and Francisco de Maldonado led the infantry, and Sebastian de Vergara and Pedro de Soria were the captains of artillery. And all his Indian followers, who were numerous, were detached from the main army and posted on the slope of the hill.

7. The battle of Xaquixaguana

WHILE the artillery were firing the last of the royal army came down on to the plain, the soldiers descending in disorder with all possible speed. The horsemen came down at a run, leading their horses on the rein. For not only was the ground extremely rough, but they were also in danger from the artillery, which might have mown down the squadrons as they descended, since they had no cover. As soon as they reached the plain, however, they reformed under their standards. There were two squadrons of horse and two of infantry. The horsemen who formed the left flank were commanded by Captain Juan de Saavedra and Diego de Mora, and Rodrigo de Salazar and Francisco Hernandez Aldana. With the squadron on the right went the royal standard, carried by Benito Suarez de Carvajal, and guarding it were Captains Don Pedro de Cabrera, Alonso Mercadillo and Gomez de Alvarado. Between these two squadrons of horse came the infantry, marching a little ahead under twelve captains, and in addition, on the right wing, riding somewhat ahead as an advance guard, Captain Centeno, who was most eager to avenge his defeat at Huarina.

Pedro Alonso de Hinojosa, as general, made the dispositions. The President and the archbishop of Los Reyes led the advance on the mountain flank, by which Marshal Alonso de Alvarado and Pedro de Valdivia had descended with their artillery. Here the three hundred arquebusiers were divided into two files under Hernan Mejia and Juan Alonso Palomino, as soon as they reached the plain. Hernan Mejia led his company to the right, in the direction of the river, and with him went Captain Pardaver. Palomino took his company to the left, on the mountain side. And as the artillery was being brought down, the lawyer Cepeda, former judge of the royal Audiencia, also Garcilaso de la Vega, Alonso de Piedrahita and many other captains and soldiers came over from Gonzalo Pizarro's side to the President's. Pedro Martin de Cicilia and a number of soldiers rode out from Gonzalo's army to pursue them, and wounded some of them. A lance struck Cepeda's horse, and he was himself so gravely wounded that he would have been in danger if he had not been well tended on the President's instructions.

All this time Gonzalo Pizarro remained in his camp, believing that the enemy would surely come and deliver themselves into his hands as they had done at Huarina. General Hinojosa advanced his army step by step till he had established himself in a low position within arquebus shot of the enemy, but out of range of their artillery. For though Gonzalo's gunners had considerably lowered their sights, their shot passed overhead.

Meanwhile the arquebusiers of both armies were firing most persistently, and both the Marshal and Pedro de Valdivia rode ahead to encourage their companies. The President and the Archbishop, who were with the advance-guard, wearied the artillerymen with injunctions to fire faster and alter their range as often as necessary. Diego Centeno and Alonso de Mendoza saw that on their flank many of Gonzalo's men were deserting and that Gonzalo had sent a force to pursue them. Some of the fugitives seemed to be in great danger, and Centeno and Mendoza were anxious to descend to the river and help them. But the fugitives themselves implored Hinojosa not to attack or advance his squadrons, for Gonzalo could be defeated without any risk, since his men would come over to them. And it chanced that at that moment one of Gonzalo's companies consisting of thirty arquebusiers was so near the opposing army that they crossed safely over to His Majesty's side. And the troops sent to pursue them began to break up, some fleeing towards Cuzco and others joining the President. Certain of their captains had no courage either to flee or to fight. When he saw this, Gonzalo Pizarro said: 'Since all are going to the king, I will do so also.' And Captain Juan de Acosta is said to have replied: 'Sir, let us attack them and die like Romans.'

And Gonzalo Pizarro is said to have answered: 'Better to die like Christians.'

Catching sight of Major-general Villavicenzio, who was not far from him, he called out that he surrendered and handed him a rapier that he carried in his rest, for he had broken his lance on his own men who were in flight. So he was taken before the President, to whom he addressed a speech which the President considered insulting.* He therefore entrusted Gonzalo to Diego Centeno, to be kept under guard. Now all the

* The historian Gomara relates that when Centeno brought Pizarro before him, the President asked if he still thought he had done right in raising the land against His Majesty. Pizarro replied:

'Sir, I and my brothers gained it at our own expense, and in wishing to be governor, as His Majesty promised, I did not think I was doing wrong.'

Gasca then cried angrily: 'Take him away! Take him away!' He was then put in the custody of Diego Centeno, at Centeno's request.

captains were prisoners and the master-of-the-camp, Carvajal, had fled, intending to hide that night in some reed beds. But his horse carried him into a marsh, where his own soldiers took him and led him a prisoner to the President.

8. The President pursues Gonzalo Pizarro's army. His trial of Pizarro and his men

WHEN, from the hill on which he was standing, the President saw some of the enemy's rearguard fleeing to Cuzco, he called to his horsemen to attack, for the enemy were in flight. None of them broke rank however until the signal was given to charge, for they were very well disciplined. When they saw that all the enemy were routed and fleeing, they followed after them, wounding, killing or capturing all whom they overtook. Gonzalo Pizarro, Carvajal, Juan de Acosta ... All were prisoners and Captain Soria was killed.

The soldiers then captured and sacked Gonzalo's camp, where they found much gold and silver, also horses, mules and other beasts of burden. There was so much treasure lying there that they captured some five or six thousand gold pesos. One soldier, coming on a loaded beast, cut the reins and seized the animal. But when some others came up who were more cunning, they untied the load and found that it was all silver and gold wrapped in Indian cloths for disguise.

The army stayed on the battlefield that day for they were very tired, since they had not laid down their arms for several days. The President sent Hernan Mejia and Martin de Robles with their men to Cuzco to prevent the many soldiers who had gone there from sacking the city and committing murders. For at this moment everyone was trying to use the victory as an opportunity for taking vengeance on his private enemies. These captains also had instructions to arrest the fugitives from Pizarro's army.

On the following day the President committed the punishment of the prisoners to Cianca, the royal judge, and Alonso de Alvarado, as his own master-of-the-camp. Proceeding against

Pizarro on his confession alone, since his actions were notorious, they sentenced him to be beheaded, and ordered that his head should be displayed in a frame which was made for the purpose and hung on the royal pillory of the city of Los Reyes. It was covered with an iron mesh and above it was placed the notice: 'This is the head of the traitor Gonzalo Pizarro who rebelled in this country against His Majesty, and fought against the royal standard in the valley of Xaquixaguana.' The sentence also provided that all Gonzalo's goods should be confiscated and his houses in Cuzco demolished and sown with salt, a notice with the same inscription being placed on the site. This was done on the same day.

Gonzalo Pizarro died like a Christian. He was honourably treated by his custodian Diego Centeno both during his imprisonment and at the time of his execution. Centeno allowed no one to insult him. At the moment of his execution* he gave the very rich and valuable clothes that he was wearing to the headsman. These were a military cloak of yellow velvet, almost entirely covered with gold embroidery, and a hat to match. But in order that he should not be stripped before he was taken for burial, Centeno paid the executioner the value of the clothing, and the next day Gonzalo was given a most honourable funeral at Cuzco. His head was taken to Los Reyes, where it was displayed according to the sentence.

On the same day his master-of-the-camp Carvajal was quartered, and eight or nine of his captains were hanged, and at such times as the rest of his officers were captured, they were executed also.

* Garcilaso de la Vega attributes to Gonzalo the following speech from the scaffold:

'Gentlemen, you well know that I and my brothers won this empire. Many of you have concessions of Indians granted to you by my brother; many others have estates granted to you by me. Many of you also have money that I have lent you; many others have received money from me not as a loan but a gift. I die so poor that even the clothes I am wearing belong to the executioner who will cut off my head; I have no money with which to take care of my soul. I beg you gentlemen, therefore, both those who owe me money and those who do not, as an alms and out of charity to have as many masses as possible said for my soul.'

Gonzalo concluded by making his profession as a Christian.

Then the President went to Cuzco with all his army, and he sent Captain Alonso de Mendoza with an army to the province of Charcas to arrest certain men whom Gonzalo Pizarro had sent there for money, and others who had fled there. Realizing that most of them must have gone there on account of the mines of Potesi, which are in that province, since they are the richest place on earth, he sent the lawyer Polo Hendegardo there as governor and captain-general, to punish those of the fugitives who were guilty both of following Gonzalo Pizarro and of not having come to serve the President when they could. And with him he sent Captain Gabriel de Rojas to superintend the collection of the royal fifth and tributes, and to carry out the governor's sentences. In a very short time Polo collected and sent one million, two hundred thousand castlins, the duty falling to him since Gabriel de Rojas died shortly after his arrival.

Meanwhile the President remained in Cuzco, carrying out fresh executions every day. According to the guilt of the prisoners, some were hanged and quartered, others whipped and sent to the galleys, and other necessary actions were taken for the safety and pacification of the country. By right of the powers conferred on him by His Majesty's commission, the President pardoned all those who had been with him in the valley of Xaquixaguana, accompanying the royal standard, of all wrongs committed during Pizarro's rebellion of which they might be accused. This applied to criminal matters only; in the matter of possessions or civil actions, the rights rested with the parties, according to the letter of the commission. The battle of Xaquixaguana was fought on the first Monday after Easter, 9 April 1548.

9. The President divides the country after his victory

AFTER the victory and the overthrow of Pizarro's tyranny, and the punishment of the guilty, another great problem of much importance for the peace of the country presented itself: how to disperse all the soldiers that were now mustered, so as to prevent the repetition of these disorders. For this much, wisdom and caution were necessary. Since there were more than two thousand five hundred soldiers, and a hundred and fifty divisions of land, it was clear that all petitioners could not be satisfied, and that almost all would remain discontented. After they had arranged the form of the dispersal, for it was a very dangerous matter and could not be delayed, it was agreed that the President and the Archbishop should leave Cuzco for the province of Apurimac, twelve leagues away, to make the division of land. In order to do this more freely and avoid the importunities of the claimants, the President took only his secretary with him.

The matter was concluded in this way. The President gave a banquet to his captains and most important followers, and then, according to the deserts and services of each, increased the share of some and gave new portions to others. The estates that had fallen vacant and were there divided were worth more than a million gold pesos, since as can be gathered from this narrative, all the chief estates in the land were vacant. For Pizarro had killed either by legal pretext or in battle all those who had received grants of land from His Majesty, and the President had executed many of those who had received them from Pizarro, who had however kept all the chief estates in his own charge to cover the expenses of the war.

On those to whom he granted estates, the President imposed taxes of between three and four thousand ducats in money, more or less according to the capital value. This sum was to be divided among the soldiers, to whom he had nothing else to give, so that they might provide themselves with arms and horses and other equipment. He then sent them off in various directions to explore and discover.

In spite of all these provisions, the President thought it more convenient and less dangerous to depart for the city of Los Reyes, and for the Archbishop to return to his see of Cuzco to proclaim the division of estates and distribute the money according to the awards decided. These things were done. But there were great complaints from the soldiers, each of whom protested that he was more deserving of an *encomienda* than the man who received it. The grants and promises made by the

Archbishop and the other captains did not suffice to prevent mutinies and other disturbances among the soldiers, who plotted to arrest the Archbishop and other principal persons, and to send the lawyer Cianca as their ambassador to the President, to request the revocation of this division of estates and the making of a fresh one that would remedy their grievances. They threatened to revolt if this were not done. Fortunately for the good order which had begun to prevail, this plot came to the notice of Cianca himself, who had been left behind as chief justice. He arrested and punished the leaders of the mutiny, and after this the land remained at peace.

[*Having thus pacified the country and collected large sums of money due to the Crown, President Gasca prepared to return to Spain. Many of the dissident soldiers had departed for a career of further conquest in Chile, under the leadership of Pedro de Valdivia, over whom the President asserted his authority by compelling him to hand over some former supporters of Gonzalo Pizarro who had taken refuge under his banner. The courts were now established at Lima. But Gasca still feared for the safety of the vast treasure he had collected and was anxious to transport it to Spain even before the appointment of a new viceroy and governor. He embarked therefore, and from the ship made a further apportionment of lands that had fallen vacant since the first division. For in the interval Diego Centeno, Gabriel de Rojas, and the lawyer Carvajal had all died. Again the claimants were so many that most could not be satisfied, and the President decided to depart without listening to their complaints. He ordered that his decree should not be published until he had been a week at sea, and sailed with a number of important officials in December 1549. Meanwhile a group of ruffians, including discontented adventurers from Peru and remnants of Gonzalo Pizarro's army, had just broken into Panama, and was plotting to seize the President and his treasure when he landed. After murdering the bishop of Guatemala, they were, however, defeated by the citizens of Panama; and the President, who had received due warning and was prepared to fight, re-embarked in safety to land at Seville bringing the royal treasure intact almost exactly four years after his original departure. A messenger was immediately dispatched to the Emperor, who was in Flanders and expressed delight and surprise at the success of the President's mission.*

Gasca, who was at Valladolid, was rewarded with the bishopric of Palencia, which had just fallen vacant. The Emperor then sent for him and his companions, since he wished to have a full account of events in Peru, and to receive some five hundred thousand escudos which Gasca had brought. Shortly before this he appointed Antonio de Mendoza, who had been viceroy of New Spain, viceroy of Peru. The country was at peace and for almost two hundred and fifty years Peru remained a viceroyalty of Spain.

Agustín de Zárate, who had returned from Peru during Gonzalo Pizarro's domination, had preserved his notes of the country's situation and its history, though forbidden by Francisco de Carvajal, under threat of violence, to begin his history while still in Peru. In 1555, he published at Antwerp his History of the Discovery and Conquest of Peru, *which forms the bulk and backbone of this narrative.*]

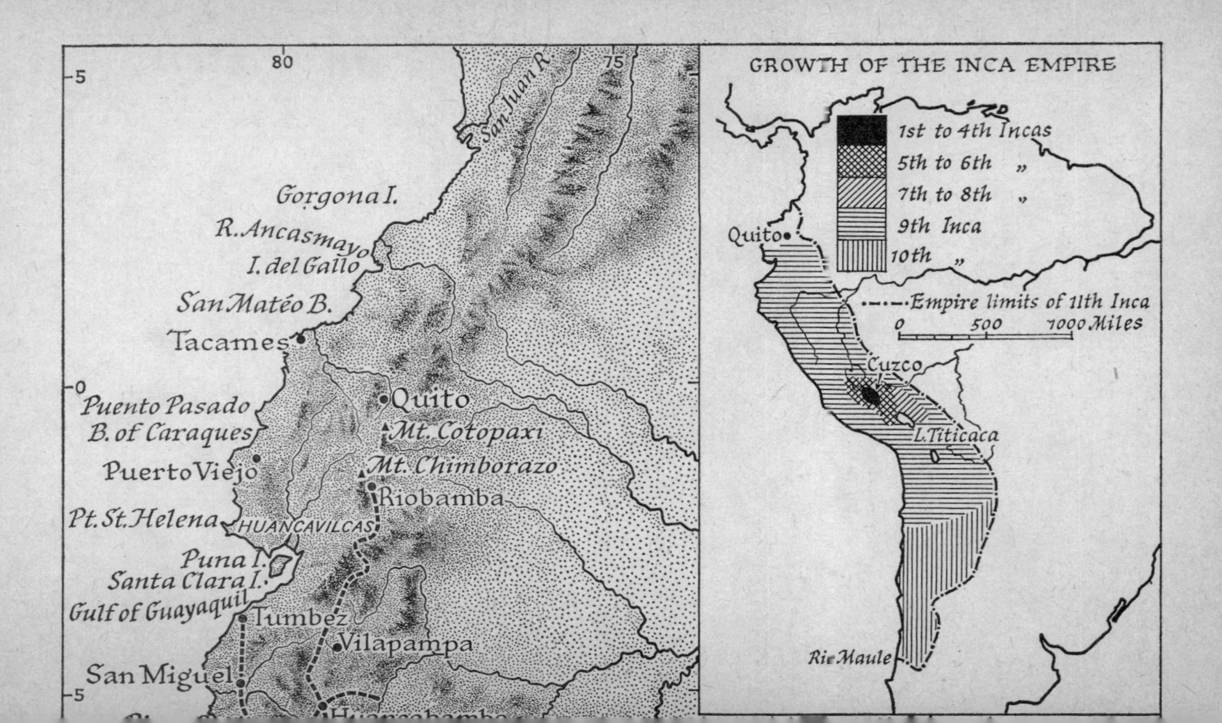

80
75
5
0
5
San Juan R.
Gorgona I.
R. Ancasmayo
I. del Gallo
San Matéo B.
Tacames
Puento Pasado
B. of Caraques
Puerto Viejo
Pt. St. Helena
HUANCAVILCAS
Puna I.
Santa Clara I.
Gulf of Guayaquil
Tumbez
San Miguel
Quito
Mt. Cotopaxi
Mt. Chimborazo
Riobamba
Vilapampa
GROWTH OF THE INCA EMPIRE
1st to 4th Incas
5th to 6th "
7th to 8th "
9th Inca
10th "
Empire limits of 11th Inca
0 500 1000 Miles
Quito
Cuzco
L. Titicaca
Ri. Maule

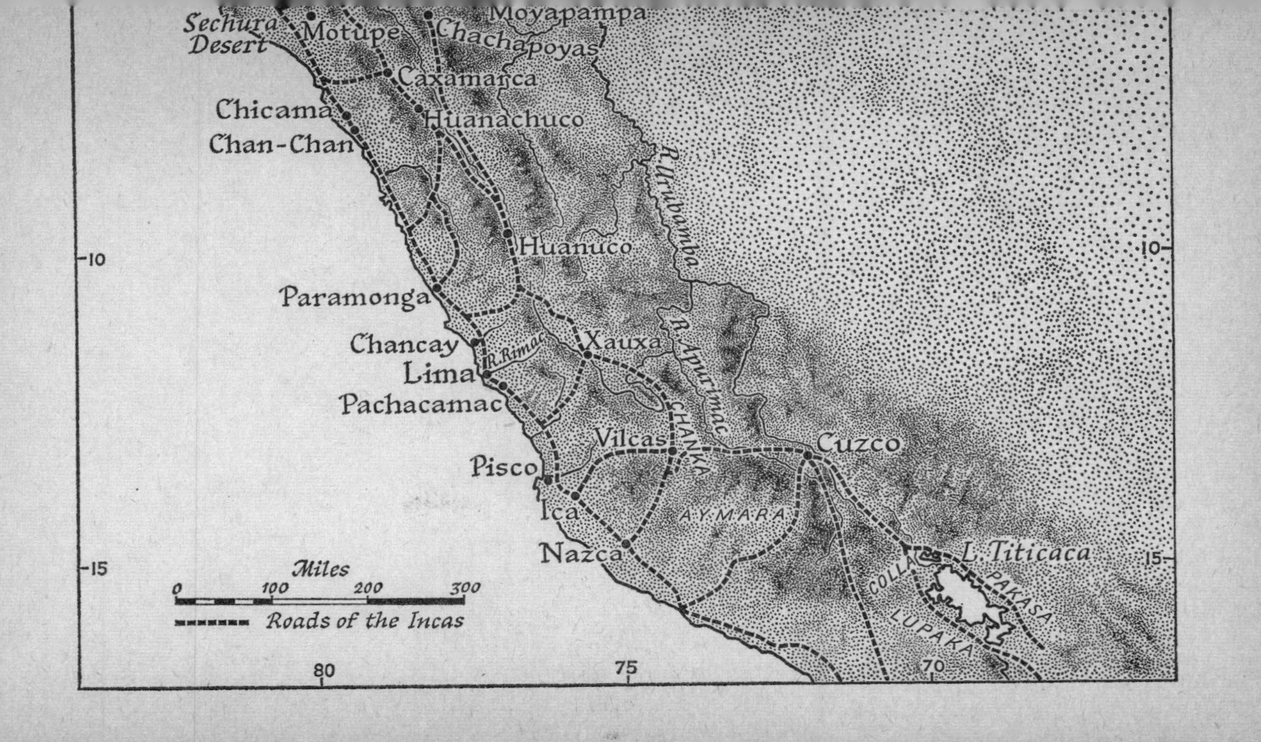
Sechura Desert
Motupe
Moyapampa
Chachapoyas
Caxamarca
Chicama
Chan-Chan
Huanachuco
R. Urubamba
Huanuco
Paramonga
Chancay
R. Rimac
Lima
Xauxa
R. Apurimac
Pachacamac
CHANKA
Vilcas
Cuzco
Pisco
Ica
AYMARA
Nazca
L. Titicaca
COLLA
PAKASA
LUPAKA
Miles
0
100
200
300
Roads of the Incas
10
15
80
75
70

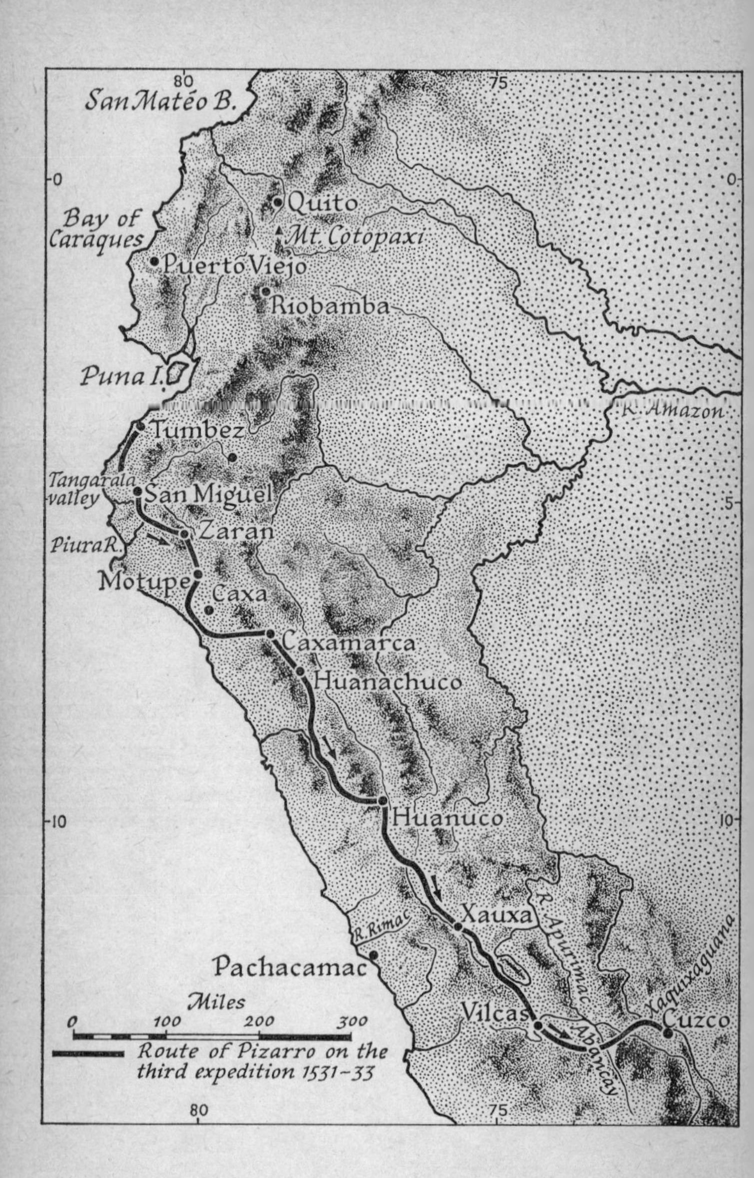

San Matéo B.
Bay of Caraques
Quito
Mt. Cotopaxi
Puerto Viejo
Riobamba
Puna I.
Tumbez
R. Amazon
Tangarala valley
San Miguel
Zaran
Piura R.
Motupe
Caxa
Caxamarca
Huanachuco
Huanuco
Xauxa
R. Apurimac
R. Rimac
Pachacamac
Xaquixaguana
Vilcas
Cuzco
Abancay
Miles
0
100
200
300
Route of Pizarro on the third expedition 1531–33
80
75
0
5
10

MORE ABOUT PENGUINS

Penguin Book News, an attractively illustrated magazine which appears every month, contains details of all the new books issued by Penguins as they are published. Every four months it is supplemented by *Penguins in Print*, which is a complete list of all books published by Penguins which are still available. (There are well over two thousand of these.)

A specimen copy of *Penguin Book News* can be sent to you free on request, and you can become a regular subscriber at 3s for one year (with the complete lists). Just write to Dept EP, Penguin Books Ltd., Harmondsworth, Middlesex, enclosing a cheque or postal order, and your name will be added to the mailing list.

Some other books in Penguin Classics are described on the following pages.

Note: *Penguin Books News* and *Penguins in Print* are not available in the U.S.A. or Canada.

ROUSSEAU

THE SOCIAL CONTRACT

Translated by Maurice Cranston

'Man was born free, and he is everywhere in chains.' These are the famous opening words of a treatise which, from the French Revolutionary Terror to the Dictatorship of the Proletariat, has been interpreted as a blueprint for totalitarianism. But in *The Social Contract* Rousseau (1712–78) was at pains to stress the connexion between liberty and law, freedom and justice. Arguing that the ruler is the people's agent, not its master, he claimed that laws derived from the people's General Will. Yet in preaching subservience to the impersonal state he came close to defining freedom as the recognition of necessity.

THE PENGUIN CLASSICS

The Most Recent Volumes

TERENCE
Phormio and Other Plays *Betty Radice*

JUVENAL
The Sixteen Satires *Peter Green*

CASTIGLIONE
The Book of the Courtier *George Bull*

THE GOLDEN CASKET
Chinese Novellas of Two Millennia *Christopher Levenson*

RACINE
Andromache and Other Plays *John Cairncross*

PASCAL
The Provincial Letters *A. J. Krailsheimer*

*ANTHOLOGY OF CHINESE LITERATURE
Edited by Cyril Birch

†ANTHOLOGY OF JAPANESE LITERATURE
Edited by Donald Keene

LONGUS
Daphnis and Chloe *Paul Turner*

** Not for sale in the U.S.A. or Canada*
† Not for sale in the U.S.A.